# Popular Religion and Modernization
# in Latin America

# Popular Religion and Modernization in Latin America

## A Different Logic

### CRISTIÁN PARKER

Translated by Robert R. Barr

ORBIS BOOKS

Maryknoll, New York 10545

Originally published as *Otra lógica en América Latina: Religión popular y modernización capitalista,* copyright © 1993 by Cristián Parker and Fondo de Cultura Económica S.A. de C.V., Av. Picacho Ajusco 227, Colonia Bosques del Pedregal, 14200 Mexico, D.F. and Fondo de Cultura Económica Chile S.A., Paseo Bulnes 152, Santiago, Chile.

English translation copyright © 1996 by Orbis Books

Published by Orbis Books, Maryknoll, NY 10545-0308
Manufactured in the United States of America

**Library of Congress Cataloging-in-Publication Data**

Parker, Cristián.
    [Otra lógica en América Latina. English]
    Popular religion and modernization in Latin America : a different logic / Cristián Parker : translated by Robert R. Barr.
        p.   cm.
    Includes bibliographical references and index.
    ISBN 1-57075-067-X
    1. Christianity—Latin America.   2. Latin America—Religious life and customs.   3. Catholic Church—Latin America.   4. Latin America—Church history.   I. Title.
BR600.P375   1996
278—dc20                                                          96-11398
                                                                        CIP

# Contents

**PART THREE**
**LIFE**

**PART FOUR**
**PLURALIZATION**

*Chapter 7*
**The Widening Spectrum**        **141**

**PART FIVE**
**RESPONSE**

*Chapter 8*
**Popular Religion and Politics**        **163**

*Chapter 9*
**Opium, or Popular Religious Resistance to a Modernizing**
**Capitalism?**        **191**

## PART SIX
## ALTERNATIVE

# Acknowledgments

A work like the present one necessarily has many direct and indirect collaborators.

First I should like to express my gratitude to Raúl Savioz and Martín Cayuqueo, and through them to all of my friends in the barrios, working class neighborhoods, and rural areas who have taught me so much about their lives, their longings, and their faith.

My sincere thanks go to my professors of sociology at the Catholic University of Chile, as well as to those with whom I completed my training, at Instituto Latinoamericano de Doctrina y Estudios Sociales (ILADES) and at the Catholic University of Louvain, especially my teachers Luis Scherz, Pedro Morandé, Giselle Munizaga, Hernán Godoy, Raúl Vergara, and François Houtart—to the last of whom I owe my academic training in my field of specialization, the sociology of religion. Many friends have shared with me the excitement and effort of studying, from a sympathetic viewpoint, the culture of the "poor," as they are called in church language. Some of these friends have helped me and my work directly. Others have pointed out to me a number of interesting approaches, in terms of knowledge and theory, when it comes to this set of themes. I must not omit Renato Poblete, Aldo Büntig, Christián Lalive d'Epinay, Diego Irarrázaval, Otto Maduro, Francisco López, Philip Setunga, Imelda Vega-Centeno, and Maximiliano Salinas.

I could never have embarked upon a scientific study of popular religion without the support of the then Auxiliary Bishop of Santiago, His Excellency, Enrique Alvear. He symbolizes for me all of the pastoral ministers, priests, and laity who, sealed by the power of the gospel, have committed themselves, in these years, to the difficult, conflictive, and exciting "preferential option for the poor" on our Latin American continent.

Many friends have borne me up in a thousand ways in this undertaking: André Gailly, Philip de Brie, Mr. and Mrs. Morren, Marlyse Strasser, Héctor Valdés, Kenneth Aman, and many others. My thanks to Centro de Estudios de la Realidad Contemporánea

(CERC)—currently at Universidad Academia de Humanismo Cristano —which received me upon my return to Chile after my doctoral studies. I must also gratefully acknowledge the support of a number of religious congregations, such as the Fathers of the Sacred Hearts, the Maryknoll Fathers, and the Jesuit Fathers.

A select group of friends who share a longing for a new and different life for our countries—among whom I should like to mention Ronaldo Muñoz, Francisca Morales, Wenceslao Barra, Gonzalo Arroyo, Josefina Lira, my colleagues of Universidad Academia de Humanismo Cristiano, and so many others—must come in for explicit mention, especially the members of my Tuesday Christian community, Luís Hernán and Guadalupe, Andrés and Ana María, Osvaldo and María Elena, Fernanda and Ulrico.

I should like to thank in a special way those who have collaborated directly in the preparation, revision, and publication of this work: Fernando Morris, Julio Ruiz, Pablo Salvat, Ricardo Salas, Patricia Villanueva, and especially Angélica Crooker. The publisher and the publishing house, without whom the results of all of this effort of years would not have appeared, also deserve a special expression of gratitude.

I should like to thank, as well, my family, my parents and siblings, and especially Isabel Serrano, my wife, who for years has displayed such a hefty dose of patience and tender consideration, and has filled my life with the warmth of our children in our journey toward personal and family fulfillment.

Finally, thanks to all of those persons—women, youth, adults, anonymous subjects living in a situation of poverty—who, from the depths of their distress, declare their faith in God and a different kind of world. And to those who, without their religion, as a singer of the people once put it to me, "would lose trust in the future, and would suffer."

# Preface

Certain behaviors and beliefs of the lowly people—the "unculti-vated," wretched folk of the teeming modern city—bring us up short. We in Latin America are accustomed to regard the simple people with prejudice, and to condemn their "ignorance," their "laziness," and their "vices and bad habits"—projected upon them by an official culture that would prefer to see more discipline. Of course, not everything we see in "our Latin American people" must be an object of contempt; and so the criteria of official judgment are refined, and we gaze with compassionate eyes upon the "ingenious spontaneity" of these "simple folk," whose lives are so full of "folklore." In both cases, the human being—that subject of culture that is every member of the people—lies buried beneath the thick makeup of a deeply elitist official cul-ture that casts a regard of superiority on the thousand forms of cre-ativity that are manifested in various sociocultural contexts. As for popular faith, the churches have historically reacted in similar fash-ion, condemning Latin American popular piety as "pagan." Fortu-nately, times have changed, and so has our view of sociocultural and religious processes.

Still, a cultural distance between "us," those of "cultivated origin," and "them," who are the "folk of the people," cannot be denied. A number of years ago I happened to experience this distance person-ally. As a student in an upper-class Catholic boarding school, I was busying myself with "social works" among a peripheral population of Santiago de Chile. One evening a group of workers assailed me with the question "What are you really here for?" I now recognize that the reason this question kept echoing in my mind afterwards was that it had connotations I had failed to understand at the moment. Something perfectly obvious and reasonable to me was all but im-possible for "them" to understand. The subjects of the urban world of the people had failed to recognize my motivations and values. And on my own side, although trained in the spirit of service and socially motivated by the Medellín Bishops Conference (1968), I failed to understand their way of reasoning, which led them to mistrust an apparently so necessary work of "social assistance."

And so I began to discern, even beyond the manifest diversity of the existential situations and social interests prevailing between myself and the people with whom I was working, the difference in our frameworks of cultural reference. Popular culture and official culture intersect, surely. But they do so in discontinuity, and at many points they fail to interpenetrate otherwise than tenuously and superficially. There was something "different" about these new friends of mine, with their life steeped in the "popular culture." There was something different in the way they saw things.

Today, twenty years after the experience I relate, and after thirteen years of my own immersion in the life experiences and systematic studies of popular religion and culture—now armed with a whole theoretical and methodological apparatus, and having accomplished an "epistemological breach" with a common sense sociology—I can say that I have a somewhat better understanding of popular culture's "different logic." But the reader should be advised: I am not convinced that reality is so "objective" and transparent as to be able to be reflected in all of its wealth and true magnitude by the sociological eye, as the empiricistic myth posits. I am also aware that this book is a scientific essay seeking to understand, in overview, a level of sociocultural manifestation that reflects the depths of the fabric of human existence only by way of approximation—and that therefore, while it is the vehicle of all of the virtues of that approach, it will carry also its defects and lacunae, as well.

It is an ambitious project, to be sure, to undertake to speak of Latin American reality as a whole, especially when the scientist doing the project has been unable to carry out field research in most of the countries of the region. We are confident, however, that the scientific knowledge that we have collected and various types of generalizations that we can make regarding this so vast and rich reality are valid, especially as they are based upon a large number of empirical studies. What we have said does not authorize us, then, to regard our theme as exhausted. But if I can make some contribution to a critical review of our prejudices as "enlightened" persons and stimulate a different, new way of looking at millions of our sisters and brothers who suffer, survive, produce, believe, and celebrate life (and long for a change in that life, too) in the popular barrios and localities of the Latin American continent, the principal end of this work will have been accomplished.

## PART ONE

# GENESIS

She said to him: "Juanito, smallest of my children, where are you going?"

He answered: "Lady, and my little daughter, I must go to your house, in Mexico Tlatilolco, to follow the divine things that our priests, delegates of Our Lord, give and teach us."

Then she spoke to him and discovered to him her holy will. She said to him: "Know and understand, you the smallest of my children, that I am the ever-virgin Holy Mary, Mother of the true God by whom is life, of the Creator at whose side are all things, [of the] Lord of heaven and earth. It is my earnest desire that a temple be built to me here, that therein I may show and give all of my love, compassion, assistance, and defense. For I am your tender and merciful mother— yours, and [the mother] of all of you together, you who dwell in this land, and of the others who love me, who call on me and trust in me. That in that temple I may hear their cries, and heal all their miseries, pains, and sorrows."

Nican Mopohua
(On the apparition of the Virgin of Guadalupe, 1649)

# Chapter 1

# Five Hundred Years: A Genesis

Five hundred years after the origin of what we know today as Latin America, history assails us, obliging us to review a past we had thought so familiar. We know the story of Columbus and his companions, we know the avatars Cortés, Pizarro, Alvarez Cabral, Balboa, Almagro, and so many others. We have known all of these from our earliest years in school. Discoverers, conquistadors, and colonizers came—we have been told—in search of new routes to the Indies, and bore on their standards the sign of the Cross. Indeed, it was the Christianization of the heathen that justified Columbus's adventure.

But what official history has less to say about is that the Cross poses problems. As evangelizing sign and symbol of a civilization meaning to spread its influence to pagan lands, the Cross, in tension and contradiction, accompanies from the beginning the mercantile undertaking and the sword. Official history does not cite the fact that the arrival of the first Europeans in America was actually a product of the adventurous spirit of the Renaissance, and of the expansion of mercantile capitalism, rather than of a burning religious concern to spread the faith to the heathen. Nevertheless, from the first moment of Europeans' "encounter" with the inhabitants of the continent, we are struck by something that would soon become a problem: a mutual cultural "otherness," observable in a difference in language, customs, arts, techniques, and especially, as we know so well, a pre-Columbian religious cultural tradition so foreign to Western Christianity's symbolic universe (and vice versa).

Why look at the past, when our subject is popular religion and its interaction with the modernizations of the present? It is not our intent to write a history of Latin American popular religions.

The topic that we wish to address is much more precise: the consequences, for Latin American religions, of twentieth-century capitalistic modernizations, especially among the urban popular masses, and the corresponding socioreligious dynamics. But the genesis of Latin American capitalism, just as the genesis of the popular religions, can be situated in the fundamental trauma occasioned by the arrival of the Europeans in these lands. It becomes necessary, then, in this initial chapter, to enter into the social, cultural, and religious problems stirred up by the process of conquest and colonization. These strokes will paint a comprehensive portrait to which we can thereupon refer for an analysis of recent social and historical dynamics.

### The Conquistadors and the Religion of the "Other"

The arrival of these scarlet horsemen, in their shining helmets and armor, their weapons vomiting fire and destruction, constituted an unprecedented, fantastic image for the indigenous cultural universe. And contact with these strange inhabitants of certain exotic islands of the Oceanic Sea, supposedly subjects of the sovereigns of Cipango, was equally unprecedented and fantastic for the Europeans (Todorov 1982:36-37).

Columbus was to be surprised by the goodness and submissiveness of the Taino Indians, and their docility in a formal acceptance of the Christian faith. The religion of the natives (antecedent to current popular religion) would posit no difficulty, but would only render the Indians meek and amenable to the immediate authority of Colón and his folk—and, after baptism, to becoming subjects of the Spanish empire. But we know that the contrary reading operated as well, and apparently with far greater force, as it walked the route of deeds. Indians who rebelled were now infidels and idolaters, and thus, according to prevailing theology, were enemies of the Crown. And so war was declared on them, and as prisoners of war they were made slaves. This seems to have been the case most frequently with the Caribbean Indians. In his letters Colón informs the king and the court authorities, as a fact in his favor, that many Indians had been reduced to slavery, and had even been sent to Spain for personal service. The religion of the natives predetermined them, in the view of the early conquistadors, to subjugation: either, by way of cultural ideology, to Christianity and the Crown or, directly, to slavery and servitude.[1] That is, the religion of the "other," according to the reading of the first conquistadors, far from constituting a major problem, became a great boon in the adventure of becoming acquainted with and exploiting these "new" lands.

Rejection of religion and culture would carry the day, however, in the later stage of the *Conquista*. For Cortés, the customs, beliefs, and rituals of the Aztecs and inhabitants of the Anahuac were aberrant—proper to barbarians and infidels (Cortés, n.d.). It is significant that, in his correspondence, along with reporting the Aztecs' human sacrifices, he calls their temples "mosques." Here we glimpse the Spanish mentality of the Reconquest, whose last crusade had met with success: the "Moors" had been expelled from Spain with the taking of Granada in the same year, 1492, in which Columbus had first trod the American coasts. Christianity, then, appears as an ideology legitimating the Spanish "conquest" imposed on native American religions and cultures.

With the conquest and colonization of America, the long march of European feudal society toward capitalism was taking its first step: the expansion of European domination to world dimensions. The plunder of the Aztec and Inca treasures, the production of cane for sugar, rum, and molasses, the traffic in black slaves, and the exploitation of a native work force in the mining of precious metals all enriched the Spanish Crown, which in turn repaid loans to Dutch, Italian, French, and English merchants and capitalists. According to official figures, 18,000 tons of silver and 200 tons of gold were transferred from America to Spain between 1521 and 1660. It is estimated that, in the same period, the native population fell by 90% in Mexico and 95% in Peru (Beaud 1981:19). In certain regions—today's Cuba, Dominican Republic, Haiti, and Uruguay—the original native nations were destroyed from the outset. In other regions, the drop in the native labor force, or their diminished "productivity," determined the "importation" of a slave labor force from the western coasts of Africa, and the intense slave trade that developed lasted three centuries.

The spirit of the *Conquista*, then, now contaminated with an unslakable thirst for gold (Guarda 1973:188ff.)—denounced by Bartolomé de las Casas, among other prophets—would tilt, over the course of the sixteenth century, toward desire for a total breach with pre-Hispanic civilization.

---

1. Native Americans controlled by the Spanish were declared enslaved after the conquest of Mexico in 1520. Their slavery was abolished, however, in 1533, and replaced by the regime of service and tribute known as the *encomienda*, or "commission"—commitment of lands and persons to colonists.

The *Conquista* was followed by the extermination of the priestly caste, that depository of ancient religious, magical, and political knowledge, and by the subjugation and evangelization of the Indians. Inspired by the propheticism of Joachim of Floris, the first Franciscans [to arrive in the New World] renounced all compromise with pre-Hispanic religions and beliefs. None of the rites and ceremonies described by Sahagún—despite their unsettling similarities to confession, Communion, baptism, and other Christian practices and sacraments—were seen as a "sign" that might serve as a bridge between the ancient religion and the Christian. Syncretism appeared only at the base of the social pyramid: the Indians were converted to Christianity, and at once they converted the angels and saints into pre-Hispanic gods.[2]

### Christianization and the Condemnation of Idolatry

The subjects of the Catholic monarchs had come to our continent for the conquest of pagan lands. It is not strange, then, that they should regard the religion of the heathen as inferior and adverse to the Catholic faith. This spirit of conquest on the part of Christendom would carry far more weight in the Spanish reading of the indigenous world than would the "spirit of the Counter-Reformation," whose reading code applied rather to the Christian order.

Sociologically, when a conquest occurs, the gods of the conquered survive but are regarded as idols or magic for the conquerors. The process of political and military conquest has repercussions on the religious field: that conquest is accompanied by a "spiritual conquest" (Ricard 1947), which in turn legitimates, stimulates, and endows with meaning the profane conquest itself. It is interesting to observe the religious rationality that articulates the field of meaning of this process. As Weber has suggested, in the historical development of religion, the evolution from a popular, magical religion to an official, priestly religion occurs primarily on the basis of a "rationalization" of the relationship of the human being with the divine. This process is attended with a twofold peculiarity: on the one hand, the systematic, rational idea of God and God's relation with human beings is imposed, and on the other, religious conduct in this world is "irrationalized" by reorienting it toward otherworldly

---

2. Octavio Paz's synthesis of this process in his "Prefacio" to the book by Jacques Lafaye (1973).

religious ends (Weber 1964:344-45). Worship ceases to be a mimetic ritual operating by magical coercion and addressed to "spirits or demons": it comes to be a symbolic ritual operating through supplication, sacrifice, and worship addressed to the gods.

Methods of Christianization of the heathen, while surely conceived in order to convert those heathen, are also conceived in order to reproduce the faith and to renew the adherence of subjects to the Church. Accordingly, two kinds of "Christianization" can be distinguished:

*Ad extra*, having the heathen as its object: by means of the villages, missions, doctrines, new Christian villages or "reductions," and accompanied by "testimonial" in terms of "good example" or "bad example";

*Ad intra*, for Christendom's members, including Christianized native Americans: through catechesis, confraternities and brotherhoods, "testimonial," boarding schools for Indian children and youth, Christian teaching in schools and universities, ongoing formation of Iberian and native families.

Given the prevailing colonial system and the regime of the *patronato* or "patronage," there could only be inconsistency: on the one side, manifold efforts on the part of the colonizing state to gain hegemonic control, and on the other, models of evangelization and civilization proper to the missionary purpose. But the rejection of the indigenous religion, even in the presence of a partial, timid inculturation, marked an ever greater distance between official religion and the religious expressions of the dominated groups.

## Religious Response of the Indian and Mestizo

Miguel León Portilla, for Mexico, and Nathan Wachtel, for the Andes, have shown that the sixteenth century was the age of conquest and violent death and of the fragmentation and dissolution of the great pre-Columbian civilizations—an age of collective grief for the native. Accordingly, the impact of these changes on native American consciousness has been qualified as the "view of the defeated." Further studies have shown us that natives underwent a period of rapid acculturation—of facile collaborationism with the Spaniard, and commitment to the dominant system along with the dissolution of their own society and culture. Burga (1990) has shown that, in the face of the crisis and changes of the seventeenth century, the Andean utopia was conceived. The native populations—and their outcast mestizo intellectuals or impoverished chiefs—presented the indigenous as an alternative, and had recourse to laughter and fiesta in order to ridicule the history of such an absurd collapse. The utopia was ritual, desacralizing the system and idealizing the indigenous.

Although no exact date can be given for the origin of the multiplicity of current religious beliefs and practices in the popular cultures and subcultures of our continent, we can at least indicate that it was tied to the process of syncretization. At the base of the social structure, native Americans and mestizos, blacks, mulattos, and *zambos* (of mixed native American and black or white blood) generated a dynamic of religious creativity through which, from their own linguistic and symbolic universe, they invented a new religious expression in order to confront their new situation. The peoples sought to account "in their own way" for the traumatic experience of domination and subjection:

1. To account for the colonial regime and economic exploitation of this "Christian" nobility that was committing every kind of atrocity upon them;
2. To account for the various manners in which the Church, whether by compulsion or by persuasion, managed to baptize them in order to incorporate them into colonial Christendom.

The colonial undertaking restructured the preexisting social system through and through. The entire indigenous cultural structure of social relations and material and symbolical production was profoundly modified, with the accompanying destruction not only, directly, of the native American beliefs, rites, and symbols but of the very basis of the maintenance of these in the earlier social system. Wherever the Spanish and Portuguese had succeeded in imposing their own system of domination—on the basis of a systematic occupation of lands, the destruction of the old political system, and the forced introduction of feudal relations and a productive regime orientated to the markets of the metropolis, the mother country—colonial society entered a phase of transition to a mode of production wholly strange to indigenous society. The natives' response, in their daily and global practices alike, was not long in coming, and the process of breach with, resistance to, and adaptation to and integration into the changes that were occurring brought its own response on the religious plane.

The religious response of the subordinate groups took various forms. It depended on the type of relationship established with the conquistador, the type of their insertion into a particular structural relationship, the geocultural or georeligious area in question, the kind of traditions and customs at hand, and the subordinate groups' capacity for open or covert resistance to the cultural invasion.

As for specific responses to the religious component of the dominant new regime and culture, we may distinguish at least four tacks:

1. A rebellious attitude and reinforced attachment to the old divinities;
2. Submission to and integration into colonial Christendom;
3. Active resistance to the colonial order, with messianic overtones;
4. Partial submission, with an acceptance of Christianity, but with measures taken to assure the survival of ancestral beliefs in a syncretic way. This last attitude is more significant for an understanding of current expressions of popular religions on the continent.

### Rebellion

Indeed some chroniclers see the cause of native American rejection of Catholicism in that religion's connections with the oppressive power. Anchieta interpreted the evidence as follows.

> What most terrifies the Indians, and induces them to flee the Portuguese and consequently their churches, is the tyranny [the Portuguese] use with them, obliging them to serve as slaves lifelong, separating wives from their husbands, parents from their children . . . [Anchieta 1964:52]

In step with the solidification of Hispano-Lusitanian domination, the initial military resistance shifted to the symbolical plane: refuge in myths was complemented with ritual practices that concealed the survival of the old beliefs. This mythology assembled earlier elements and re-created them, endowing them with a content frankly subversive of the prevailing colonial order (Irarrázaval 1990:38-41).

But this open rebellion was ephemeral. It manifested only in the first reaction of a society now in process of subjugation and dissolution through integration into the colonial system. When open rebellion was no longer possible—in the form of rejection of the dominant religion—it then began to unfold by way of belief and clandestine religious practice: latent rebellion. Azzi declares:

> Perhaps this would be the deepest reason for the native inconstancy so frequently denounced by the missionaries . . . The

Indians would accept the Christian faith for a while, but then would return to their old usages and customs. [Azzi 1983:159]

### Submission to Christendom

There were cases in which the destruction of the old beliefs and the process of acculturation were profound. The Indian "went white," to form a new (inferior) "stratum" of colonial society and therefore of Christendom.

The principal means by which colonial society integrated the Indian was the system of production, which was centered on the *encomienda* or on *mita*. As we know, the social and economic institution of the *encomienda* characterized the colonial organization of Spanish America. It consisted in a "distribution" or "entrustment" of Indians by the Crown to a deserving Spaniard, accompanied by the fixing of a rate of tribute that the *encomendados* ("entrusted," "committed") Indians must pay the beneficiary of the grant, the *encomendero*, and the specification of a fiscal obligation to the king on the part of the *encomendero*, as well as the latter's duty to "take in charge the temporal and spiritual well-being of said Indians."[3] Thus, the *encomendero* was obliged to see to the catechizing and indoctrination of the Indians, defraying the cost of supporting the needed number of missionary priests and catechists and maintaining the churches and chapels out of the tributes received. The *mita* consisted of forced labor in the mines, performed by native Americans parceled out to the *encomenderos* (Konetzke 1971:184-86).

Despite the fact that the *encomienda* was such an extensive system and in mining regions was so closely tied to slave labor, it nevertheless seems clear that its effectiveness for evangelization was minimal.

### Resistance

Not infrequently, native groups that mounted armed resistance, and thereby preserved their territorial sovereignty, managed to ensure the survival of their social organization and to preserve intact their ancestral traditions and rituals, as in the case of the Mapuches of Araucanía. Another form of resistance was flight from the control of the Spaniards and colonial society. In numerous regions of the rain forest (Paraguay, Ecuador, Brazil, Peru), the most frequent form of

---

3. Leyes de Indias, book 6, title 9, law 1, p. 263 (cited in Hernández 1990:253).

passive resistance on the part of the natives was to shut themselves up in some remote territory. Among the Tupi-Guaraní of Brazil and Paraguay, leaders or shamans arose who proclaimed the imminent destruction of the world and led their followers through the forest in quest of the "Land without Evil," a place of paradise. This meant, if only by way of symbolism, the last defense of their way of life, and of their ethnic and religious identity.

At other times, the conditions of colonial oppression were so harsh as to generate uprisings among the native Americans and other subordinate segments, such as the mestizos, blacks, mulattos, and poor Creoles. In Brazil, during the era of the *Conquista* and colonization, four movements of penetration by the Portuguese are registered, each meeting its own native resistance: the Tamoio Confederation and the Potiguara war along the coast; the Guaraní war in the south; the Açu war, the Piauí war, and the Cariri Confederation in the hinterland; and in the Amazon cycle, the Manau war, the Mura war, and finally Cabanagem's great war (Prezia and Hoornaert 1989). Native American revolts and rebellions were invested with a forthright messianic content, and thus were altogether and substantially of religious and symbolical inspiration. In the first years of the colonization, when the evangelization of the natives was still sporadic and superficial, these rebellions simply reasserted traditional religious and cultural values. This was the case, for example, in the general uprisings of the Quijos in Ecuador (1562, 1578). The last was led by influential shamans of the region who, inspired by dreams of the "demon," proclaimed war to the death on the Spaniards, threatening to transform those who refused to obey into "toads and snakes." In this rebellion, a number of villages were destroyed, missionaries were violently persecuted, and churches were burned down (Muratorio, 1982). In the south of Peru, to cite a particularly meaningful instance, between 1560 and 1570 the Taki Onqoy occurred, a native American uprising of combined political and religious inspiration. The Quechuas rejected the invaders' demands, and dreamed of a *pachakuti*, an overtumbling of the world, with the reestablishment of order and an end of abuse and disorder.

As the "colonization of souls" neared its close and the ancient religions no longer constituted a formal system, native rebellions were no longer directed against the dominant religion; on the contrary, Christian significates and symbols were adopted in an attempt to defend subjugated interests and rights. Noteworthy in this regard is the Tupac Amaru rebellion, toward the close of the eighteenth century in Peru. The native chieftain of that name rose up against colonial abuses in defense of the Indians but, instead of reasserting his own religious traditions, declared himself a Christian and the defender of the Church against the abuses of the *hacienderos* and *encomenderos*. He even won the support of certain clerics, and their charismatic leadership was interpreted by the natives as providential. For many, Tupac Amaru was a kind of native American Moses, who through his acts of insurgency would lead his people to a land of promise ringing with echoes of the most distant past (Mires 1988:15-58).

### Syncretism

But the most frequently occurring phenomenon was the one we have already mentioned: the colonization process destroyed the reproductive bases of pre-Columbian religion by destroying the old indigenous society. It was in this period of transition—when, slowly and gradually, the logic of mercantile capitalism was being imposed on colonial society—that the most noteworthy syncretisms were produced.

On the ruins of their own tribal society, and on the basis of the new social relations of class being imposed by coercion, the inhabitants responded by accepting Christian baptism (in varying degrees of motivation and internalization). Thereby this process—interwoven with that of biological and cultural mestization—set the stage for syncretism in the religious field.

This syncretism, about which we shall have more to say further on, was also based on a process of symbolical production that—generally speaking—presupposed peculiar semanticization. We refer to the reinterpretation of the significate of the content, rites, and sacred images basically received as elements of a new religion—Christianity—in which one accepted *baptism*. The signifiers—God, Christ, the Virgin Mary, the saints—were accepted, but on the basis of a shift in the corresponding code of signification. A dovetailing with ancestral religious significates enables the Indian or mestizo to reintegrate the new components of the symbolical world into available codes of interpretation—the only way in which the native American could render legible, in cultural terms, this "conversion," which entails such a radical cultural mutation. Becoming "Christian," in large part, was to accept the culture of the other, the dominator. And yet this culture had to be accepted harmoniously, lest its subject fall victim to a cultural schizophrenia. Syncretism, then—not in the form of a crafty Indian strategy, but out of sociocultural necessity—was the most useful process that could be invoked in order to resist the peril of an anomic disintegration that, as a matter of fact, in many cases did occur, leading thousands of natives to suicide (Duviols 1976:92).

## Paradigmatic Case: The Virgin of Guadalupe

Although, in the transition to the colonial class society, the human relations of the native American world were dismantled, its relations with nature were not substantially modified. Religion played a central role as mediator in the reading of the natural world. That reading was "Christianized" to the extent that the missionaries could replace traditional practices with "Christian" significations. The cults of the old gods, now "baptized" into saints, were celebrated in chapels built on the very sites where the temples of these gods had been destroyed. The patron saint's festival replaced worship of the protective divinity of the clan. The dances and festive demonstrations with which missions and masses terminated were a reproduction of rituals of the past. "Indeed, these various forms of popular piety had identical functions in the various religious systems, despite the variety of forms" (Houtart 1989:173).

A paradigmatic example of mestizo syncretism is that of the Virgin of Guadalupe. According to the oldest known account, composed in the Náhuatl language, the *Nican Mopohua*, the Virgin Mary appears to a young Christianized Indian sharecropper, known as Juan Diego, whose uncle lies on his deathbed. The Virgin appears on the Tepeyac in 1531, ten years after the conquest of Tenochtitlan. She sends Juan Diego to the palace of the archbishop of Mexico City to inform him of her desire that a shrine be built in her honor on the Tepeyac. The archbishop refuses to listen, and the Virgin reappears. On a third occasion, the miracle occurs: the Virgin commands Juan Diego to pluck roses, there in the drought of the desert, and carry them off in his cloak. Juan Diego returns to the ecclesiastical authorities and empties the roses from his cloak, and the image of the Virgin appears miraculously imprinted on the cloak. The archbishop is convinced, and the shrine is built.

A great deal has been written and spoken concerning the extraordinary case of the Virgin of Guadalupe, her mysterious apparition (Lafaye 1985), and the fervent devotion she inspires in so many millions of Latin Americans. What is worthy of note in the mythical account is the enormous number of symbols it involves. The Virgin emphasizes to Juan Diego that she wishes to show her love, her compassion, her eagerness to help and defend the Indians, that the Indians "may trust me to hear their lamentations and remedy all their miseries, sufferings, and sorrows." The Virgin appears on the Tepeyac, the ancient Aztec sanctuary on which crowds gathered to worship Tonantzin, goddess of land and fertility. "It seems a satanic trick, for the purpose of disguising idolatry," Sahagún will one day say. The profound significance of the myth of Guadalupe lies in its combination of a Christian representation, the Virgin Mother of God, with a pre-Hispanic divinity, Tonantzin: the result is a sacred being who gives life and protection in the face of the traumatic experience of a culture (represented by the dying uncle) toppling under the onslaughts of an oppressive foreign invader. And yet we are dealing with a religious symbol of the dominator—someone who actually appeals to the supreme authority of the Church and obliges that authority to accept her message. The Virgin/Tonantzin, protectress of the Indians, inaugurates a new era: a Christian sanctuary rises on the ruins of a pre-Columbian one, but the religious significance of both cults merges in a new one, offering to the life of the mestizo a meaning born of the moribund Aztec culture and the life-giving, positive face of Christianity as the religion of the conquerors. Juan Diego can now be integrated into colonial society with the certitude that, on the religious symbolical plane, he can count on a powerful ally in the face of the humiliation and oppression of which he is the object on the part of the "Christians." The sense of symbolical protest residing in the myth merges with its reidentifying functionality, and with its meaning for the sense of life and history.

Many have been the apparitions of the Virgin (Vargas Ugarte 1956) in various regions of America. And the Latin American map is saturated with syncretic expressions that, from the sixteenth to the eighteenth centuries, succeed one another in a dynamic of astonishing religious creativity. With the introduction of African slaves, especially in tropical and coastal regions where there were large plantations, native/Spanish syncretism would soon be considerably influenced by the African cultures and religions that had now come to America's shores.

Especially worthy of note is the mythic (or mythified) and syncretic origin of, among other regional devotions, various contemporary ones: for example, Our Lord of the Miracles (Peru), Our Lady of the Apparition (Brazil), the Virgin of Charity of Cobre (Cuba), Our Lady Most Pure (Nicaragua), the Virgin of La Tirana (Chile), the Virgin of Copacabana (Bolivia), the Virgin of Caacupé (Paraguay), the Virgin of Chiquinquirá (Colombia), Our Lady of Itatí (Argentina), Our Lord of Chalma (Mexico), and so on. As we see, the response is complex. It gathers up a variety of earlier religious traditions, and in each region characteristic contributions are made and particular attributes ascribed. The antecedents of the current popular religions reach back to points in time antedating by several thousands of years the misnomer "discovery." Of course, there was popular religion before the process in question, both in pre-Columbian cultures under the domination of the great Meso-American or Andean civilizations and in the culture contributed by the Spanish soldiery and commoners of the first Iberian wave. But it is a fact that they all merged in processes of subsequent cultural creation and reproduction.

This original "religious response" on the part of colonial society's subordinate classes and groups across the Ibero-American continent, along with considerable contributions and sedimentations from the past, is at the origin of the syncretisms of the current manifestations of our popular religions.

As we have seen, the prism of "popular religion" enables us to approach the history of Latin American culture from another flank. In the dialectic of the semantic opposition (that is, real opposition) between popular and official religion, we discover, in a critical view, that we can no longer speak schematically of a simple homogeneous polarity. The dynamics of cultural history have left sufficient traces for us to be able to assert that even "official" culture, through condensation of the contradictions of history, also hosts counterpoised expressions. Both the myth of Guadalupe/Tonantzin and that of Saint Thomas/Quetzalcóatl (we follow Lafaye 1985 here) become symbols and standards of Mexican nationality—of a rejection of, and breach with, New Spain. But the fact that only Guadalupe—a Marian mythology proper to the creativity of persons of mixed Iberian and native American blood—becomes a collective image that has endured to our very day as a symbol of the religious, cultural, and national identity of the Mexicans and all Latin Americans is itself palpable proof that culture's generally lasting "creases" originate, in the majority of cases, in the popular cultures. As Octavio Paz says, with as much truth as exaggeration: "After more than two centuries of experiments and failures, the Mexican people no longer believe in anything but the Virgin of Guadalupe and the National Lottery."

## Is It Meaningful to Look at History?

All that we have said up to this point is crucial for an understanding of the past. But one doubt assails us. What relevance does an understanding of the past have for an analysis of the popular religious reality of today?

Considerations bearing on the historical framework in which popular religions have developed can be enormously enriching.[4] But they will be misleading if they are taken simply and solely in terms of the study of a prelude extrinsic to the problem. We have not sketched a historical evolutionary arc external to the popular religious phenomenon; we have glimpsed substantive elements of the actual historical genesis of that phenomenon. We shall find it impossible to understand the phenomenon in its trajectory through the twentieth century unless we have reconstituted the roots of yesterday, which continue to generate their sap in the age of today. We may assert, then, that the cultural contraposition obtaining between the religion of the dominated and the religion of official culture abides, under very diverse modalities and across a very broad spectrum of colors, to our very day.

As a corollary, we may conclude that the study of the religious phenomenon, especially in the matter of "popular religion," offers a new angle from which to observe the whole cultural confrontation underlying the polemics of the first five hundred years and forming the basis for articulation of the meaning, the signs, and the entire culture of what we today call Latin America. However, even though what we have outlined here constitutes a datum of the sociocultural reality of our continent, and in spite of the broad consensus of a certain intellectual community in this regard, it is also a fact that a positivistic bias rules in a goodly part of Latin American social science, and that the view of that science, seemingly so interested in the themes addressed, cannot altogether conceal its conviction that it is dealing with an altogether marginal question, one that has already been solved.

For an important current of contemporary social science, it is no longer very meaningful to examine the past in order to discover vestiges of a religious expression on the way to extinction. Current processes of capitalistic modernization, and the advance of contemporary science and technology, lead to a secularizing process past repair. At the very moment when these processes penetrate, and work their effect on, the underdeveloped countries, the cement of religious tradition is cracking and crumbling. Religion subsists as cultural rubble, deprived of any historical relevance. Religion is an affair of yesterday. Its autumn looms.

---

4. See Dussel 1986; Hoornaert et al. 1983, Hoornaert 1991; Marzal 1988; Salinas 1987.

This is one of the most debated questions in current sociological reflection on culture and modernization in Latin America. Indeed, the dispute over "modernization," so heated in the 1950s, has recently come in for renewed interest. Now, however, the topic arises in a different conceptual framework. Today we are assisting at the conceptual debate between the postindustrial "modernizing" interpretations and the "postmodernist" critique, which is partly the child of a disillusionment with the progress occasioned precisely by "modernity."

Standing in the background of the discussion of the relevance of the religious phenomenon on our continent, then, is the debate over Latin American culture. The definition of religion and of popular culture in terms of conceptual theory constitutes a mediating framework that conditions the interpretation of the whole religious phenomenon. It is not surprising that studies on popular religion in Latin America should have multiplied to the extent that they have over the last fifteen years. And having just commemorated a milestone in our common history, we find that an analysis of what is occurring with the processes of capitalistic modernization and religion—especially popular religion—in Latin America constitutes an unsuspected mine of material for reflection.

# Chapter 2

# "Popular Piety" and the Sociological Mirror

One is struck by the keen interest taken by intellectuals today in "popular piety" and culture. Notwithstanding aristocratic prejudices toward religious "folklore" or the "picturesque," "extravagant," and "vulgar" elements found among the people—and in spite of a systematic neglect, or symptomatic rejection, of cultural and religious themes on the part of a certain functionalistic, technocratic rationalism—we observe today, on the Latin American continent, a broadening, earnest concern for a methodical, rigorous approach to the cultural and religious expressions of the people.

## Renewed Interest in the Culture and Religion of the People

The interest in investigating this ensemble of topics arises from the fact that, for so many scholars, it makes up one of the most important defining facets of the proper essence and cultural identity of Latin America. Not unconnected with the development of intellectual interest in these themes are precisely the experiments in renewal conducted by the churches over the last twenty years. Just as germane is the work being done in recent decades in popular sectors by agents of education and social change. The crisis of the democracies, the collapse of the popular alternatives and of the left, the advent of the regimes of authoritarian bureaucracy marked by the reimplantation of a profoundly antipopular neoliberal capitalism have led intellectuals and social agents in the 1980s to—among other things—rediscover working with the grassroots. In the task of rebuilding a damaged social fabric, new practices and values have surfaced, and a new perspective has solidified. An attempt is now being made to rescue old facets of the culture and religion of the popular classes. World-wide changes after the 1989 fall of the Berlin Wall indicate that cultural and religious themes must not again be ignored in the analysis of reality.

The privileged position once enjoyed by structuralist analyses of the dependency of Latin American countries on the capitalist center is no more. Intellectual eyes have turned to the social subjects, who, in the last instance, make history. It has been rediscovered that—even under the worst conditions of oppression—peoples do not entirely lose their ability for thought and action in the framework of a cultural creativity endowed with relative autonomy.

The prioritization of the *popular subject* not only has had obvious political, and even philosophical, connotations but also calls for an approach to that collective subject, the people, in all of its complexity. From the halls of academe to the marginal urban barrios, for more than a decade now, we have begun to hear of the need to recover an appreciation of popular culture: its art, its folklore, its social and political organizations, its family, its education, its everyday life, its economic organizations and organizations for survival, its communications networks, its recreations and pastimes, and so on. A study of the *popular worldview* is also under way: its language, its styles of thought, its cultural and symbolical "grammars," and its other categories, including, of course, its religious beliefs and practices. This study has frequently been done in fertile interaction between intellectuals and the people through processes of popular education or through a combination of research and activity.

### "Popular Piety"

In the case of "popular piety" or religiousness, we are dealing with an object of study that has aroused the interest of the authorities of the Church—bishops, priests, religious, and theologians—since the 1960s. Recently, however, the topic has become the object of a heated intellectual debate. A new appreciation of popular piety in Latin America is rekindling polemics concerning our continent's "cultural substrate" and the actual or illusory influence of the processes of secularization. This new appreciation is also sparking a return to the theoretical debate over modernization and alternative historical projects for the Latin American peoples (Johansson 1990, Irarrázaval 1990b, Beozzo 1990, Parker 1989, Brunner 1985, Morandé 1984).

The churches of the region have played a relevant role in the defense of human rights in recent decades. Their social action in milieus of poverty and their prophetic and political gestures in quest of solutions that would enable the Latin American peoples to recover their democratic traditions have constituted them as a political actor sui generis, and that actor has come in for broad analysis at the hands of political science. But a major interest has been aroused by the presence, much more imposing in the 1980s, of Christian masses and their leaders embarked upon processes of resistance and of popular struggles for liberation—an area that had been the preserve of the Marxist left with its irreligious theory. Religion, then, as a not indecisive element in the cultural field of the Latin American people and a strategic one in the struggle for sociocultural and political hegemony, has become an area of growing concern for social science and for society as a whole.

In Latin America, the multifaceted complexity of the topic "popular piety"[1] has already been studied with some thoroughness. Innumerable studies have been devoted to the theme recently, and the bibliography continues to grow by the day, which of course is what makes it possible to embark on a synthesis and overview such as we are undertaking in the present work. Studies on certain religious manifestations of the people, however, especially those relating to daily life and its underlying worldview in the common sense of the popular masses, are not so numerous. True, we have accumulated an enormous quantity of knowledge concerning the beliefs, rites, myths, moral attitudes, customs, and traditional religious organizations of the peasantry or aboriginal groups. Likewise enjoying a growth spurt are studies on the new urban popular religious expressions, such as Pentecostalism and the Afro-American syncretic cults, the spiritists, or the sects. However, the bulk of the essays, notes, descriptive observations, and empirical studies on "popular piety" on our continent have dwelt on the more massive, spectacular, and extraordinary aspects of the piety or religiousness of the masses: popular shrines, pilgrimages, mass devotions, religious dance and song, religious protest movements, and

---

1. For the complexity and variety of manifestation of popular religion in the different historical dynamics and sociocultural contexts, and for the theoretical and methodological problems arising from this complexity and variety, see Bastide (1974), Isambert (1982), Lanternari (1982:121-43). While disputable on certain points, Enrique Dussel's attempted synthesis is also quite interesting (Dussel 1986:82-94); we have developed the theme in a previous study (Parker 1987b:52-92).

so forth.[2] There has of course been no dearth of historical studies. In the vast majority of cases, these essays and studies have been done in terms of a pastoral or theological interest. While not rare, rigorous scientific studies (anthropological, historical, psychological, and sociological) have not been sufficiently taken into account in the search for arguments to be used in the theoretical debate on the subject.[3]

In this chapter principally, as well as in other, later chapters, we shall adopt certain avenues of theoretical approach, of a sociological nature, to the concept "popular religion." This concept, as we shall see, is far more appropriate than that of "popular piety" or religiousness for a scientific treatment of the phenomenon of the popular religions in Latin America. The object of study that arouses our interest, then, is "popular religion" as a manifestation of the collective mentality, subject to the influences of a process of capitalistic modernization and its manifestations in urbanization, industrialization, education, and changes in productive and cultural structures. The conceptual proposal and hypotheses of investigation and interpretation that we shall set forth are founded on certain theoretical contributions from the sociology of religion and the sociology of knowledge, as well as on studies—mainly those having an empirical basis—done in recent years in Latin America.

### Sociology and Popular Religion

Whenever sociology fixes on cultural and religious reality as an object of study, it tends to generate a process of major epistemological contradictions. In order to study these realities, sociology must reduce their complexity to analytical and functional categories, and it cannot study them unless it operates in this manner. But in so doing, sociology dissects a complex reality, thereby rendering an adequate understanding of it impossible. Indeed, the dilemma is of a deeper epistemological order. Since its origins in Comtian positivism,

---

2. There is an abundant bibliography on "popular piety" in Latin America. A recent bibliographical summary, while not altogether complete, can be found in *Teología y Vida* 1987. The bibliographies of Vidales and Kudo (1975:85, 127-32), Süess (1979:199-210), Parker (1986a:531-48), and Johansson (1990:289-302) may also be consulted.

3. On the various Latin American focuses of "popular piety," see Vidales and Kudo (1975:63-85), Süess (1979:51-160), Arias (1977:17-37), Richard (1980:41-45), Scannone (1985:55-67), and Johansson (1990).

Durkheimian functionalism, Marxist materialism, or Weberian comprehensiveness, the problem of the values and ideal components of the social has been posited in terms of dependent variables of these elements, to be elucidated and understood in function of "social factors." Even apart from any consideration of the idealistic or materialistic, structuralist or historicist options involved here, it can scarcely be denied that sociological rationality, on the strength of its methodological logic, has a tendency to a certain reductionism when it comes to values, the esthetic, and the religious. The problem appears to reside in the rationalistic Enlightenment premises shared by all of these focuses, which, at the moment of grasping, explaining, and understanding the complexity of the profound mystery of the religious, show themselves to be insufficient, and from certain standpoints, myopic. In his essay, *Cultura y Modernización en América Latina* (1984), Pedro Morandé diagnoses—correctly, in my judgment—the problem by questioning the underlying epistemology of these focuses. Unfortunately, however, Morandé's conclusions and proposals are very questionable, even erroneous. Having executed a critical analysis of the conceptualization prevailing in the modernizing formulations of North American sociology and Marxist sociology when they broach the subject of religion, the author comes to the determination that the two currents are of a common stamp. "In the one as in the other, religion belongs to the stage of pre-awareness, of pre-Enlightenment. In a word, religion does not belong to modernity. If there is religion in modernity, it is simply as an obstacle to the development of the latter, or as a fetish impeding its full realization" (Morandé 1984:138). Involved here is the question of the capacity of our social sciences, in their current state, to apprehend in cohesive fashion the reality of religious symbolism among the Latin American people. Could the social sciences' modernizing paradigm be altered? How could these sciences develop a focus that would enable them to strike a dialogue with Latin American philosophy and theology? We think, with Morandé, that to address this set of problems will involve more than a change of emphasis with regard to the object of study, or even a change of the object of study itself; also, and mainly, it will mean changing our epistemology. Without pretending to have reached an altogether satisfactory solution here, we may observe that this is the central motivation that guides our study and our proposal for reinterpreting that "different logic" of which we shall speak in the last chapters of this book.

Taking up the challenge we face when speaking of sociology and religion, we must refer first of all to the social conditioning of all knowledge. It will never be without utility, or superfluous, to return to this epistemological question. Any process of cognition, whether of the cognition of common sense, or of scientific cognition, occurs in a social context and is historically situated. This conditioning obeys a multiplicity of factors, but ultimately it depends on a *class-influenced sociological* conditioning. The latter flows from the peculiar character of the social class in which the cognition in question develops. Mannheim called this factor the *perspectivity* of cognition (Mannheim 1954). It operates in simultaneity with the proper *cultural-linguistic* conditioning of the semantic and semiologic structures of the particular era and social group in question, as well as of those structures that transcend sociohistorical barriers and are proper to universal languages and metalanguages. Thus, there is no timeless, absolute truth in social sciences, although this does not mean, as Schaff argues (Schaff 1973:283-318), opening the doors to relativism, since objectivity is possible and any scientific undertaking seeks to progress to higher levels of the relative truths that form objective cognition.

This antecedent epistemological consideration serves as an introduction to the following issue: the "socially situated" nature of any development of theory, especially in the human sciences, calls for a recognition and explication of the specific mediations and conditionings operating in each case. Any development of theory in sociology—a sociology that means to rise above either a self-sufficient or a dependent intellectual mode of production—seeks the reformulation of theoretical conceptual frames that, as they receive the contribution of accumulated knowledge, avoid falling either into a sterile dogmatism or into an empiricism deprived of all horizons. What is wanted, then, is a development of heuristic conceptual frames that will be open to the enrichment of scholarly cognition by social praxis—but, above all, open to the new questions arising from a sociocultural reality that, like the popular, passes by way of language and thought categories at times rather foreign to the academic and intellectual language, practice, and world of the "social scientists." For the latter are generally of extrapopular origin and operating at some remove from the life and immediate experience of the Latin American popular sectors who live in misery and oppression. For purposes of this heuristic enterprise, the "predominant sociological way of seeing the world" (Lazarte 1990) will have to be abandoned, and an attempt made to maintain the rigor of a "scientific" focus without reducing the existent to what can be rationally explained, quantitatively measured, and analytically condensed into abstract theories. In these terms, we

shall have to initiate our study under the aegis of a twofold "epistemological break"—the classic break with denigrated "common sense,"
of course, and a new break with the classic paradigm of an "objectify-
ing sociology": that is, a break with the *predominant sociological common sense*.

For decades now, Latin American social science has been a social
way of producing knowledge whose content, instruments, and processes of specialization come to us from a cultural and scientific universe that stands at a distance from Latin American reality: the European and North American intellectual world. We have nothing
against Western sociology; but a warning is necessary concerning the
dependent character that, generally speaking, has characterized the
intellectual production of Latin American sociologists. This is particularly important when it comes to a focus on religion.[4] Although
there are other, earlier, antecedents, the sociology of religion in Latin
America has pretty much sprung from the root of initiatives of pastoral renewal arising in the 1950s, of European origin especially (France,
Italy, Belgium). "Religious sociology," then, was born under the sign
of its dependency on European religious sociology, in the framework
of definitions of theoretical and empirical problems proposed by the
institutional church itself.

## Latin American Sociology and the Debate on Popular Religion

In Latin America, the initial debate harks back to the theories of
modernization of the early 1960s. The dichotomy between "traditional
society" and "modern society" was the pivot of a theory about the
transition in which the continent found itself. All modernization and
development, according to this theory, involves some form of "secularization" of society. This was the period in which Creole sociology
developed, under the theoretic influence of the paradigm of the sociology of modernization. Cultural anthropology had provided this sociology with the key category of interpretation of Latin American reality: the "traditional versus modern" category (Marzal 1967, 1979)
that Redfield had generalized on the basis of his "folk versus urban"
categories.

On this basis, the Catholic religion is identified with traditionalism—that is, is identified as an obstacle to development and modern-

---

4. On the focuses and trajectory of the Latin American sociology of religions,
see Maduro (1978:50-63) and Parker (1992b).

ization.[5] Even Catholic sociologists champion religious renewal in order to foster those changes that require a "spiritual life less contaminated with the traditional myths of the rural world" (Houtart and Pin 1965). If we closely observe the consequences, for an analysis of the religious causes of Latin America's social lag by comparison with the developed countries, of the Weberian thesis on the Protestant ethic and the spirit of capitalism, we can posit the same thesis in the following simple terms. Catholicism reinforces a traditional ethos that leaves no room for innovative models on the part of the elite classes— a middle class, a business elite, a governing political elite, and so on—that would have responsibility for ushering in the modifications necessary for Latin American "feudal" society to wrench loose from the obstacles that prevent it from following the developmental path, a route along which it suffers considerable lag by comparison with the European or North American countries.

From this viewpoint, Gino Germani suggested a name for the type of reaction to change mounted by the Latin American elite: "ideological traditionalism." Germani is referring to an acceptance of technological and economic innovations accompanied by a rejection of innovation in the political, educational, and religious orders. This type of reaction to change on the part of the Creole elite, according to Germani, while very widespread, is doomed to failure, due to its internal inconsistency (Germani 1962:112-16).

Then came the theory of dependency, which analyzed the mechanisms of our continental lag through the explanation of an external dialectic: the Latin American countries to a large extent contributed their surplus to the development of capitalism in the central countries. Religion, in this analytical framework, was discounted, and the Weberian and neo-Weberian theses were criticized for adopting reactionary postures that missed the real explanations of the structural causes of underdevelopment in the dependent capitalistic countries of our region (Gunder Frank, 1978).

In the contemporary debate, especially in the ecclesial field, analysis is once more under way on the interrelation between religion and culture. To some eyes, the phenomenon of religion is behind the times, given the inevitable process of secularization; accordingly, the Church

---

5. Fals Borda, for example, declared that the role of religion in peasant life gave rise to an "ethos of passivity." The industrial revolution in Latin America in the twentieth century had not developed as it had in Europe in the nineteenth century, because "the needed transformation of beliefs, attitudes, and motivations, that is, the 'ethos' of the population, had not yet matured in Latin America" (Fals Borda 1961:17). See also Houtart and Pin (1965:58).

ought to embark upon an internal renewal, and thereby be able to evangelize these secularized societies of Latin America (De Carvalho 1983). According to a more radical version, embraced by revolutionary Christians of the 1960s and now abandoned, Christianity is a factor for decisive change, but on condition that it discharge its "superstitious" and "magical" ballast: in a word, on condition that it present itself as an emancipatory consciousness stripped of all alienation, that is, internally secularized, disengaged from its matrix and tissue of ritual symbolism and from the popular, native roots of that matrix and tissue. An ethical religion, a formal one, an incentive for action, a utopia rationalized by motivations in terms of the secular political, was supposedly in order.

Although, since the beginning of the 1990s, Latin American social science is making friendly gestures toward religious thematics, actually, under various theoretical frameworks, the thesis of secularization as an inevitable process still carries a certain weight in Latin Americans' sociological view of religion. We shall deal extensively with this problem in our next chapter.

At the other extreme, popular religion is defended against the rationalism of the dominant culture, whose articulating axis is said to lie along the lines of formal rationality and functional ethics. Religion is presented as the essence of Latin American culture—as the "Catholic" substrate that will afford the possibility of salvaging popular originality and autochthonous cultural identity. The structuring nucleus of the religious sense does not reside in the linguistic articulation of the symbolical field, we are told, but basically in a ritual and sacrificial articulation. The sacrificial sense present along the complex, varied ritual gamut of expressions of "popular piety" allows the religion of the people to be proposed as the "counterculture" to the ongoing Enlightenment as a rationalistic culture based on the word (Morandé 1986). The apogee of popular piety is identified with the colonial baroque. Here we are dealing with a very widespread thesis among theologians and scientists of culture having ties to ecclesiastical circles, especially to the contemporary Catholic field.

## Renewal of the Sociology of Religion

The transformations that have occurred in Latin American societies under the military regimes, a new dependency of Creole societies on transnational capitalism and the regressive consequences of that dependency for regional development, and the crisis of the Marxist socialistic alternatives during the 1980s make it possible to appreciate, in the trajectory of the sociology of religion on our continent, the influence of the intellectual about-face that has been executed by a number of groups among the progressivist elite. Democratic solutions are now sought for the crises of the societies, and a breach is appearing in the wall of a Marxist dogmatism that, in the past, characterized a certain leftist element. The renewal of social thought in the 1980s sought liberation alternatives which, within an anticapitalistic option, would avoid technological, bureaucratic developmental styles and be immune from the negative experiences of the communist societies. However, the crisis of the real socialisms of Eastern Europe has cast its pall over the panorama of skepticism, with an assist from the relative failure of revolutionary experiments in Latin America. Some speak of a crisis of utopias; others attempt to reformulate old longings for change in the framework of a more real and concrete situation. This cloud of uncertainty and searching will doubtless thicken in the decade of the nineties.

Against the background of this renewal of the sociology of religion on the Latin American continent, we can appreciate a change of objective, focus, and attitude. Adopting a much more favorable view of the religious and cultural expressions of the Latin American people, sociology is forthrightly incorporating the culture and subjects of the social processes as an object of study, discarding the structuralist focus that had dominated in Latin American sociology since the close of the 1960s. The new attitude is the function of a quest for the recovery of the more profound popular cultural identities; it also stems from a rebellion against the cold, cerebral, anti-emotional formalism of the Enlightenment, which was reflected in the technologically scientific, repressive rationality of the developed societies and transnational capitalism. In Latin America, the rediscovery of the popular cultures' potential for protest and resistance, a potential that is present as well in their religious expressions, represents in part this intellectual climate, with its neo-Romantic nuances, which imbues the new refractory spirit of a certain intellectual elite.

As a consequence of this new intellectual climate, favorably inclined toward the religious and cultural expressions of the people, the number of studies on popular religions has grown considerably. A large majority of these have their orientation in a focus whose vertex of theoretical analysis is located in the series of problems that arise in the study of the social classes. These studies adopt contributions from Marxism, but frame them in the dynamics proper to the cultural and religious field—entailing a reelaboration, along these lines, of the contributions of classic writers like Durkheim and Weber, with the latter's theory being updated by Bourdieu's.

Thus we can maintain that a new systematic theoretical framework is emerging for the study of popular religion and culture in Latin America. Here we identify our own effort as an attempt to delve deeper in the direction sketched by Otto Maduro, who, nearly two decades ago now, proposed a reformulation of the sociology of religions for our continent (Maduro 1978).

## A Nonreductionistic Conceptualization of the Religious Element

In light of what we have now set forth, it will be observed that we are dealing with an effort of theoretic conceptualization calculated to transcend the reductionistic standpoints so common in sociology today. In order to make progress in this task, we must face up to a threefold challenge in the development of a sociological theoretical framework for urban popular religion in Latin America.

In the first place, we must maintain a *critical distance* from the theoretic conceptual contributions of European and North American sociology of religions—acknowledging its value and contributions, but making an effort to redevelop its concepts in order to give a consistent account of the specific phenomena of *Latin America*. Thus, the focus should be scientific and objective, but—in full awareness of the social conditioning of scientific process—must, in adopting value premises and rendering them explicit, purify the analytical moment of any potential contamination. Once the "data" of the problem have been reconstructed, the conclusions will need to be rigorously orientated in terms of the theoretical framework and its value premises. This focus presupposes the use of a serious, verifiable, and trustworthy methodology. We must have heuristic and even hermeneutic procedures that will be intersubjective, consistent, and solid. We shall have to abandon the objectivist pretensions explicitly present in positivistic scientificism and underlying the other approaches whose paradigm is infused with an Enlightenment rationality and its reductionism of the symbolical, the affective, the nonrational, and the mysterious.

In the second place, our focus must manage a certain independence of the church and its institutions, lest our analysis be slanted by the evaluations and interests proper to the church institution. The latter do not always coincide with those of the subject under investigation—in this case, with popular religion, which, precisely, is characterized as an instance of the manifestation of the religious field distinct from the official and institutional field. Indeed, any sociology that means to contribute to pastoral theory and practice must take its distance on the basis of a critical framework of analysis and interpretation. Otherwise it would not be free of confessional contaminations that would block its objectivity.

Finally, an adequate theoretical framework must seek to adopt the class conditioning and linguistic conditioning attaching to any type of cognition, even, of course, to sociological cognition. Only in this fashion will the scholar of popular culture and religion be able to take up, in all of its magnitude, the sociocultural difference separating that scholar from the forms of thought and categorization that characterize the popular *common sense*.

Any theoretical perspective of a sociological type entails a methodological moment of great importance for an understanding of sociology's epistemological breadth and limit. Sociology must recognize, in the case of an object of study such as the religious, that it must not overstep the bounds of its own competency by erecting itself into a self-sufficient science. The complexity so marvelously and irreducibly present in the symbolical paraphernalia evoked by faith and mystical fervor, the numinous, miracle and mystery, illumination and asceticism, is too rich for this. Sociology must adopt a systematic and methodic option that "brackets," as phenomenology does, faith as God's revelation and gift to human beings.

The phenomenon of faith needs to be analyzed in all its nakedness. An operational definition of the religious must inform any process of investigation, but that definition cannot rest exclusively on an analysis of functionality. It must also refer to content (Houtart 1977:267). But sociologists must not define this content themselves, under pain of slipping into theology. "Faith" must be analyzed as a religious phenomenon, in all of its symbolical density, in the framework of a sociological focus that assigns a value to the substantive element of culture, but a framework in which the supernatural is taken solely as an enunciated reference and rendered symbolical reality by its actors themselves, not as a reality with an extrasociological density of its own. While it is pertinent to speak of a reference to the transcendent in the constitution of the symbolical texture of society, we have no intention of referring here to considerations of a philosophical or theological order, which escape our methodological and theoretical perspective.

Generally, from a comprehensive sociological viewpoint, the religious phenomenon appears in the field of communicational significations and languages of a collectivity whenever that collectivity sees itself existentially confronted with a "limit problem." The problem of the *limit situation*, from the standpoint of the rationality of the actors, has to do with the solution of the actor's great life contradiction. How can I ensure the reproduction of life on this earth and beyond it? How can I overcome the limitations imposed by the scarcity of resources, how can I overcome the dangers flowing from contingency, and their assault on the prolongation and enhancement of that life? But the *limit situation* from the standpoint of the collectivity has to do with situations threatening the collective life, either immediately or in historical time. This limit, accordingly, which is experienced by the actors as collective incertitude, calls for the establishment of a *social nexus* of a ritual symbolical order—a *sacred cosmos* calculated to provide the opportunity of generating not only meaningful links that strengthen the community but also collective representations that will furnish the collective actors, or society, with a *collective meaning*. We refer to a meaning that will incorporate the effort of social production and reproduction into a more transcendent framework, whether in order to recall a foundational origin, or to preserve and legitimate the present order, or to transform the present into a qualitatively different approaching future.

Understood as a collective undertaking of the production of meaning—entirely apart from its social functions in the constitution and regulation of the social human being with that being's corporeal, natural, social, historical, and cosmic surroundings—religion is a primary component of the field of cultural symbolism belonging to a group or society. This component, from the standpoint of its significations, makes an explicit reference to an extraordinary, metasocial reality: the sacred, the transcendent, the numinous. This numinous reality, whose time/space is transhistorical, maintains a variety of relations with habitual, normal (profane) spatiotemporal reality. The type of articulation prevailing between the two dimensions is not something that can be conceptually defined a priori, or in "clear and distinct ideas," as a Cartesian mentality would have it; rather, it must be studied historically, case by case. This transcendent, suprahuman reality—so defined by the actors—its discourse, and its practice can be personalized (gods) or not (supranatural, nonanthropomorphic entities). With it the actors can establish various kinds of relations and interchanges, and—inasmuch as we are dealing with a suprareality, generally endowed with superior powers, transcending individual and collective human abilities—the interchange will always operate by means of semiotically structured, codified relations, with the greater or lesser intervention of cognitive intellectual components or of affective ritual ones expressed in gesture. In either case, the ambit of interchange between human beings and these sacred powers can be analytically distinguished in terms of their symbolical semantic mediation by way of (1) cognitions and representations, (2) rituals, (3) ethical norms, and (4) organizations. The symbolical paths in question create a meaning that, in turn, institutes and regulates conduct. Since the production of a transcendent meaning bound up with the problem of limit is at the basis of religion, the series of significative structures in question are articulated around semantic oppositions reflecting the life contradictions of these concrete individuals and their culture—good/evil, order/chaos, heteronomy/autonomy, prohibition/prescription, dependency/liberation—which in their own turn can be synthesized in the great contradiction of life and death.

## On Popular Culture

Obviously, in terms of what we have stated, the mere mention of popular religion as a concept calls for an antecedent clarification of what we are to understand by popular culture. After all, we know religion to be a very significant component of that cultural reality.

In the context of the modernized capitalistic societies of Latin America, the concept of "popular culture" must not be confused with that of a "culture of poverty," in the phrase coined by anthropologist Oscar Lewis (1969:xliv-lvi). The latter concept refers to a specific, immigrant (in the sense of immigration from the countryside to the city), marginalized subculture subjected to disintegration and anomie. And as can be demonstrated, within popular societies and groups a number of different subcultures subsist, many of these enjoying full integration, formal and real, into modern capitalistic society. Nor can Latin American popular culture be identified with the Gramscian concept of subordinate culture (Gramsci 1954, 1972, Portelli 1974), much as that theory might incline us to the reformulation we suggest. At the core of the Gramscian conception, we discern a value judgment pronounced upon the "inconsistency" and lack of systematicness of popular culture; but this judgment can be refuted, on the basis of a different interpretation of the "logic" underlying popular thought, as we shall see in chapters 9 and 10. Furthermore, this Gramscian view legitimates the supremacy of the "organic intellectuals" in the shaping of a new popular culture, which opens the way for a "Leninist" rereading, with all of the error entailed in that political theory in its approach to the articulation between culture and politics in a complex society.

By "culture," we understand the series of significative collective practices based on the work processes maintained for the satisfaction of the whole gamut of human needs—these collective practices being institutionalized in structures of signs and symbols transmitted by a series of vehicles of communication, and internalized in habits, customs, and manners of being, thinking, and feeling.

In so-called primitive societies, the division of functions is based on a basic structural homogeneity. In developed societies, the tendency to structural homogeneity engenders a tension toward a hegemonic culture that represses diversity. By contrast, in our underdeveloped societies, subject as they are to processes of increasing heterogenization, a varied, differential insertion of the culture-generating groups into global social relations gives rise to a cultural differentiation. This differentiation will be more or less accentuated in proportion to the degree of generation, by the structural heterogeneity, of institutionalized differentiations of areas of both production and reproduction of cultural symbolism.

There is more. In the dependent societies of the Third World, a cultural excision will occur in the global society by reason of its uneven structure and development. In uneven structures—in which the division of labor does not follow technological criteria, but is determined by a differential access to scarce goods of power, capital, property, and prestige—such cultural diversification will be exaggerated in dominant and subordinate areas of cultural production and reproduction. Thus, popular culture is that broad cultural production by society's subordinate classes and groups. While this production is a dominated cultural one, it is by no means an invalidated one, nor is it wholly subjugated in its capacity for resistance and innovation, as we shall see, in the creative ability of the people when it comes to religion.

## The Religious Element in Popular Religion

We are convinced that certain approaches used in pastoral theology to define the nature of popular religion tend to obfuscate a clearer view of things. I refer to the "judgment" handed down, implicitly or explicitly, when popular religion is analyzed. Popular religion is immediately qualified as "traditional piety," or as "ignorant," "superstitious," and "pagan," by contrast with official "religion," which is judged a priori as "authentic" and "true." In order to analyze the nature of the phenomenon, we shall have to consider it as a factual, and not a normative, reality, as we prescind as far as possible from ideological and theological presuppositions. J. C. Schmitt acutely emphasizes that it serves no purpose to assert a priori that the ritual behavior, the piety, and the beliefs of a twelfth-century peasant are naive, puerile, or "prelogical" (Schmitt 1986). We concur with Nesti that the important thing, on the contrary, is to understand how all that has come about, and what it actually represents in a given social structure (Nesti 1980). However, in order to maintain consistency with our epistemological and theoretic options, we must not forget that certain value judgments underlie our own approach—in this case, value judgments favorable to a positive reevaluation of popular religion. Therefore, while in a first instant our focus must incline to objectivity, in an antipositivistic acceptation of the same—in a second instant theoretical reflection can authorize a renunciation, in our propositional and prospective concern, of the artificial "axiological neutrality" so eagerly proposed by Weber in his own methodological focus, which, he pretends, is noncommittal. This, even apart from any imperfections in the present text, explains why, in the last part of this book, our sociological focus reverts to the social.

At all events, we shall have to undertake a careful examination of our conceptual categories if we are to purify them as far as possible of *ethnocentric* connotations—which our focus does not entirely escape, as scientific and rigorous as it claims to be. As Pedro Ribeiro de Oliveira insists, in an article reporting the broadest investigation of popular Catholicism on our continent, the one conducted by FERES, this risk cannot be entirely avoided.[6]

A theoretical proposition of the first order which we are in a position to make is that "popular religion," qua symbolical product of historically and structurally situated social groups, is not a reality *in itself*, either as a universal ahistorical reality or as an autonomous, phenomenal category free of all social conditioning. Popular religion subsists in a multiplicity of manifestations, which we reduce conceptually to a unitary term, but to which in actuality a huge heterogeneity attaches, both from the morphological and semiotic viewpoints (in its representations, myths, beliefs, and rites) and from the socioreli-

---

6. Ribeiro de Oliveira (1972). The FERES investigation was carried out by various teams in 1969-70 in various countries: (Mexico (IMES), Colombia (ICODES), Venezuela (CISOR), Brazil (CERIS), Chile (CISOC).

gious (institutional), sociocultural (as expression of culture and world-view), social (being of various ethnic groups, classes, and subcultures), and historical (having various configurations in various eras and conjunctures) viewpoints.

Precisely on the basis of all that we have now posited, the prevailing, too extensive concept of "popular piety," popular religiousness, must be called into question. The term "popular piety" corresponds to a concept too equivocal, slanted, and lacking in rigor to be used by social science. In the first place, by "piety" sociography usually understands the mean or average "religious feeling" of a determinate population. This is very indefinite, being based on quantitative studies of a concept as subjective as "religious feeling." In the second place, the concept of "piety" connotes a negative semantic content when it is opposed to "religion." That is, the expression "religious feeling" denotes an ensemble of beliefs, rituals, and religious practices that "deviate" from the pattern established by official orthodoxy. To a large extent it implies a negative sentiment or prejudice toward the phenomenon. At the same time, the adjective "popular" is never appropriately defined or explicitly related to the social and cultural structure of a given society, but simply denotes a generic reality spread widely throughout the population; that is, it refers to something "vulgarized" and generalized. Finally, works and studies written on "popular piety" from a descriptive or phenomenological position regard the phenomenon in a critical fashion, referring it exclusively to the religious field—thus, apart from its broader sociocultural and historical context. Such studies thereby reify a phenomenon emptied of its social and cultural conditionings, which in no case can be regarded as external variables, since they contribute to the development of constitutive elements of the phenomenon's internal significative structure.

What seems positively to define a conceptual environment for our object of study is its semantic relationship with its contrary: nonpopular religion. We refer to what sociological and historical tradition calls *official religion* (Vrijhof and Waardenburg, 1979), frequently also called institutional religion, the religion of the elite, or priestly religion. Now, the complexity of the relationship obtaining between popular religion and official religion is a reflection of the simultaneous complexity of class relations in a stratified society, of the degree of institutional development achieved in the religious field, and of the real symbolical relations prevailing among cultures and peoples, interethnic encounters, and transcultural intersections.

Following Lanternari, we can assert that all popular religion is generated in a dialectic with official religion and culture. Of course, we may not reduce the significate and the multiple manifestations of the phenomenon to that dialectic; but the latter enables us to reconstruct, from a sociological and historical viewpoint, our object of study and to develop our analyses consistently. Indeed, within any civilization of complex stratification—that is, having differential ethnocultural classes and groups in relations of domination and dependency—together with the institutional development of a religious production of beliefs and theologies, myths, rituals, and religious organizations, with specialists operating as interpreters and guardians of the officially defined religious ideas, an opposed phenomenon occurs:

> Religious or magico-religious currents finally spring up and develop that will be contrary to the dominant ideology, but that will still maintain a dialectical relation with it. Thus it is that, wherever a religion of a priestly or aristocratic elite dominates, or else a state religion, and even a system of institutional churches bound up—implicitly or overtly—with economic and/or political interests, there spring up and develop through a spontaneous process, by way of response, forms of religiousness that may be called "popular." [Lanternari 1982:137]

These popular religions are collective manifestations that express, in their own particular fashion—in particular and spontaneous form—needs, anxieties, hopes, and aspirations that have no adequate response in official religion or in the religious expressions of the elite and dominant classes.

### The Popular Element in Popular Religion

Thereby we glimpse a dimension of enormous importance for the empirical analysis of popular religion: its character as a phenomenon inscribed within the religious field (Bourdieu 1971, Maduro 1978). But not only may we distinguish popular religion in relation to the subject "religion": we must also consider the adjective "popular," which in this case determines the nominal subject in order to complete the framework of conceptual definitions. And adopting Lanternari's suggestion, we must here give an account of the dialectical character with which the phenomenon is shot through—its dialectical nature, which proceeds from the fact that, qua expression of religious symbolism and culture-shaping element of social groups, popular religion is an ingredient of the culture or subculture (heterogeneous and plural) of the popular and subordinate groups of a society marked by a clear class differentiation. With Gramsci, then, we may reject a universalistic, ahistorical conception of culture (see Gramsci 1972, Ricci 1977, Portelli 1974). There is such a thing as cultural stratification. There is an official culture, corresponding to the privileged and hegemonic classes; and there is a popular culture, corresponding to the subordinate and dominated classes. But inasmuch as all human beings are subjects of culture, there is always particular cultural—and religious—production, however dependent and subordinate its form. This means that, implicitly or explicitly, in the distinct cultural models and forms—including their explicitly religious components—*conceptions of the world* are generally locked in open or underground combat. It is not a matter of postulating a class reductionism, since a relative autonomy is ascribed, and ought to be ascribed, to these cultural expressions, which are not, as Godelier reminds us, merely "the icing on the cake" (Godelier 1978)—not merely an expression of epiphenomenal structures from which it is all but impossible to prescind, but components of the actual content of the particular social relations in question. The ideal is part of the real. Thus, in resolute abandonment of a narrow, antihistorical mechanicism, we must also acknowledge the function, the significate, and the influence that the components of culture—and of the religious—might have in the shaping of practices and the constituting of "infrastructural" relations.

The relative autonomy of the cultural and religious becomes manifest as we move beyond the narrow schema of class differentiation. Thus, we may observe that many elements of the dominant culture have been appropriated by the popular culture—which, we must not forget, is a subordinate culture (García Canclini 1982). Thus have many other popular elements—purified of their "vulgarity" and "obscene rusticity," of course, so incompatible with "refined" official taste—come to shape an official culture. How many folkloric elements—however eviscerated by a consumer society that "mercantilizes" them and transforms them into objects of "exportation" for the enticement of tourism—have come to be incorporated into the artistic cultural legacy of the Latin American nations?

In the case of popular religion, the matter is clear enough. As we can see from the empirical investigations that have been done, it is rather difficult to draw a narrow line between what is popular religion as authentic expression of the subordinate classes and groups, and popular religion as expression of the "mean" or average manifestations of the gross believing public in a mass society. The difference between an official, institutional religion, of priestly mold and inspiration, and popular religion is more precise: their operational delimitation is feasible. On the other hand, in Latin American countries, with their Catholic majorities, there are certain religious traits common to the upper and middle classes and the working, subproletarian, peasant, village groups and the mass of unemployed and underemployed. Available data indicate rather the presence of a *continuum* in religious manifestations[7]—but a spectum whose difference in frequencies marks not only quantitative distances but, at certain points, imperceptible qualitative leaps substantively marking off the meaning structures that bestow consistency on the particular religious expression corresponding to each class or class fraction. Thus, for example, in all social classes we observe practices of devotions and votive offerings made to the saints, but it is a fact that these practices tend to augment considerably as we descend the social ladder—where we find ourselves in the context of the popular culture—and, on the contrary, tend to diminish considerably in the upper strata, where they occur in the context of a dominant and bourgeois culture.

It is perfectly logical to suppose that the ensemble of religious representations of one class or class fraction should be ordered according to an in-depth, nonvisible meaning structure capable of being apprehended, analyzed, and explained in terms of *religious models*, and that that structure should be a totality composed of a set of relations among "relational elements" (Parker 1986a). The different religious models present in the collective mentality have no wholly defined empirical limits; however, differentiations in meaning are indeed established. Accordingly, one and the same element—for example, the ritual practice of a promise made to a supernatural mediator (who can be the Virgin Mary as mediator with God) involving a pilgrimage, votive offerings, and strict fulfillment of the promise in order to obtain the "miracle"—may register as a practice with a lady of the upper aristocracy as well as among homemakers living in extreme poverty on the urban periphery. But while the ritual and the religious representations connoted by the ritual are formally similar, the profound significate may be very different, since in each case it will be inscribed as an element within a broader meaning code that is de facto very distinct: the mentality of the aristocrat has recourse to

---

7. Büntig's research in Argentina shows an interesting example of this. See Büntig (1970, 1973a).

reasonings and theories, to processes of codification and decodification, very different from the reasonings and categories of the people—even apart from the differences in the set of contextual conditionings that determine life in the one case as in the other. In sum, although the religious element, as part of the cultural field of the classes, does not always maintain a direct correlation with the *objective class situations* of the actors, at least it occurs in correspondence—complex correspondence, and not immediate, via the mediation of the field of practices—with the *class positions* (Bourdieu 1966) of the actors, and this not in external fashion but on the basis of its role in the constitution and internal configuration of the different class positions, as we have argued and shown at greater depth in an earlier study (Parker 1986a).

## Renewed Effort of Analysis

The great impact today of new religious movements of a spiritualist or sect type, or of their esoteric mystical manifestations, on a "postmodernist" focus whose neoconservative slant leads it to cheerfully reinterpret the vitalist emergence of the religious at the heart of a "secularized society" is obvious. Nevertheless, those same movements, and a reactionary return to "tradition" in Catholicism—a tradition whose reappearance is owing not only to "backlash" in the official institution but to the influence of the popular cultures themselves—arouse a concern and growing anxiety in those theorists whose paradigms of interpretation had been riding the crest of the vanguardist wave of the 1960s and 1970s. How can popular liberation be achieved now, in this sea of traditionalism and religious alienation?

In the face of the crisis of the Enlightenment paradigm, the crisis of a Westernizing philosophy, a new paradigm is emerging which seeks a reencounter with the cultural and religious roots of the Latin American people in the framework of great changes effected by the current process of transition from a technologically scientific society to a "technotronically" information society. And the decisive problem of this age is precisely how to rescue the ethical elements that have emerged in the practices of the new social movements (Gomes de Souza 1989), and how to find new forms of inculturation of new values—how to face up to the process of scientifico-technological transition—without breaking with the underlying ancestral wisdom of the culture and religion of our peoples. The new intellectual elite—now perhaps less well supplied with totalitarian utopias—including among them the sociologists of religion, have a vastly more extensive terrain over which to work in the study of the renewed events of religious culture. Thus, they did not hold aloof from the debate that flared up anew in the context of Latin America's fifth centenary.

With a view to an in-depth approach to the Latin American religious phenomenon in the framework of worldwide transition—a globalization process that reinserts the poor countries of the Third World into the new international division of labor—one must understand the nature, characteristics, and depth of the structural transformations of our societies. And at the heart of these societies, we must understand the articulation of their representations, practices, and religious institutions, inasmuch as the social actors are actively and passively involved in a new scenario, and their motives, longings, and needs are being affected. Faith, in its manifestation dialectically mediated by the daily series of concrete historical practices, will be an expression of this new, emerging culture. Modernization and the changes it generates do not necessarily threaten religion; indeed, religion is undergoing a revitalization. The subordinate classes and less favored sectors in this process will now orientate themselves toward the religions, in a quest to renew their energies and their motives for aspiring to new forms of a common social life.

After all, it is through the window opening out upon the religious dimension that we are enabled to discover, more acutely and in more pristine form, the flow of ideals, values, and lifestyles that, in multiple fashion, today shape what we define as Latin American culture. Not that we intend stubbornly to maintain that that culture is settled solely upon the pillars of religion. It is only that the religious folds in the tissues of meaning of that culture, and the signifiers operative in the religious factor, are elements indivisible from the actual symbolical shape of that culture. We ourselves have no wish—indeed, it would be precisely only wishful thinking—to baptize Latin American culture from without, as the yearners for "Christian culture" fruitlessly and anachronistically attempt to do. On the contrary, with eyes that seek objectivity and dispassionate analysis—although with a commitment to prioritizing the view "from below," the view of eyes that peer out from amidst the popular masses of the continent—we cannot but recognize the fact that faith constitutes an initial baptism. Under its manifold formations, even when displayed in baroque fashion, even when battered by various ethnic cultural waves, even under an apparent threat provoked by a modernizing "secularization," this faith is a point of departure around which a whole network of symbolical systems in the Latin American cultures is being structured.

## PART TWO

# TRANSFORMATION

*It would be in order to ask ourselves whether sociology today, which has contributed so effectively to the disenchantment of the world by assisting in the transformation of the transcendent into a "rumor of angels," to use Peter Berger's felicitous expression—in a word, that sociology which has been so effective in destroying the worlds of fantasy and appearance in the name of scientific truth and reason—will have anything to give the human beings flailing about in the meaninglessness of the modern megalopolis, clawed to death in the grip of a system that extracts from them the best that they have, their best years, their strength, their creativity, only to vomit them out as refuse when they are finally exhausted, robotized, imbecilized, annihilated as human creatures. Will sociology have anything to offer these human beings?*

Rolando Lazarte

# Chapter 3

# Modernization and Religion: The Changes

The deep religious sense of the popular masses—even in the great metropolitan cities—would seem to undercut theses that posit the teleological and irreversible nature of an intrinsically secularizing capitalistic development. A closer examination reveals the staying power of traditional expressions of religion among the Latin American people, as José Comblin (1972) showed so brilliantly some time ago. But the observer is also struck by what happens sociologically in the area of these expressions precisely where, according to the parameters of the theory of secularization, religion among the people ought to be in particular danger: in the large cities of our developing countries. This question deserves a thorough study, based on the most substantial data available.

## Modernization and Recent Progress

One of the most significant structural mutations undergone in Latin American capitalistic societies over the last sixty years has been the process of urbanization and industrialization at work in these societies. The process is a concrete, historical one, and dependent on international processes whose consequences in the field of cultural symbolism are evident.

Certain comprehensive social indicators for Latin America show that considerable progress has been made in the relative development of the countries of our region. As we observe in graph 1 on page 44, considerable progress was made in Latin America between 1965 and 1985 in per capita consumption, net enrollment in primary education, and life expectancy at birth. This is outstanding progress, by comparison

*43*

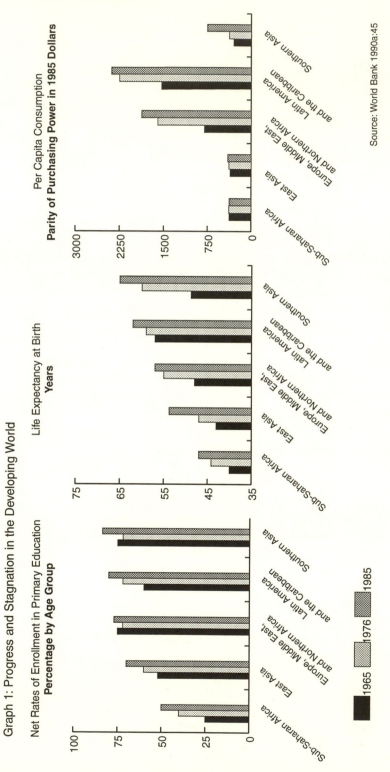

Graph 1: Progress and Stagnation in the Developing World

Net Rates of Enrollment in Primary Education
**Percentage by Age Group**

Life Expectancy at Birth
**Years**

Per Capita Consumption
**Parity of Purchasing Power in 1985 Dollars**

Source: World Bank 1990a:45

with advances achieved in other regions of the Third World.

Relative progress in the living conditions of the Latin American population, especially in countries of greater relative development, is observable in graph 2 below in the upward curve of life expectancy at birth, which, for Latin America as a whole, rose from 51.8 years in 1950-55 to 66.3 years in 1985-90. In addition, infant mortality dropped, from 12.51% for 1950-55 to 5.51% for 1985-90 (*Business International*, 1990:2).

Progress in the literacy rate of the population between 1945 and 1990 can also be observed (graph 3, page 46). Between 35 and 45 years ago, the rate of illiteracy in the population was 44.9%. Thanks to a growth in primary-school enrollment, along with the institution of literacy programs and adult education, and as a result of modernizations in the school system and society at large, by 1990 the rate of illiteracy in the region had dropped to 17.2% overall, and in nine countries to 10% or lower.

Graph 2: Life Expectancy (1950-90)

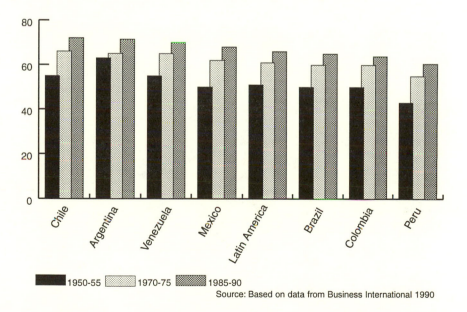

1950-55    1970-75    1985-90

Source: Based on data from Business International 1990

Indicators of the urbanization process at work in the region—a process under way in some countries by the beginning of the century, and accelerating with the crisis of 1930—show a constant rise in the proportion of the population who live in urban agglomerations. As we see in graph 4 on page 47, between 1960 and 1990 the urban population of Latin America rose from 36.4% to 46.6%, and in the more urbanized countries[1] from 61.9% to 77.5%.

The percentage of the population living in localities of 20,000 or more inhabitants rose in the more urbanized countries from 32% in 1950 to 60.1% in 1980—in some cases, to 65% or more, as shown here in table 1.

Table 1: Population Living in Localities of 20,000 Inhabitants or More

|  | 1950 | 1960 | 1970 | 1980 |
|---|---|---|---|---|
| Chile | 42.6 | 50.6 | 60.6 | 81.1 |
| Argentina | 49.9 | 59.0 | 66.3 | 70.3 |
| Brazil | 20.3 | 28.1 | 39.5 | 67.6 |
| Venezuela | 31.0 | 47.0 | 59.4 | 67.3 |
| Colombia | 23.0 | 36.6 | 46.2 | 65.4 |
| Uruguay | 53.1 | 61.4 | 64.7 | 65.0 |

Source: Sosa 1989:745

Graph 3: Decrease in Number of Illiterate Persons (1945-55 to 1989-90)

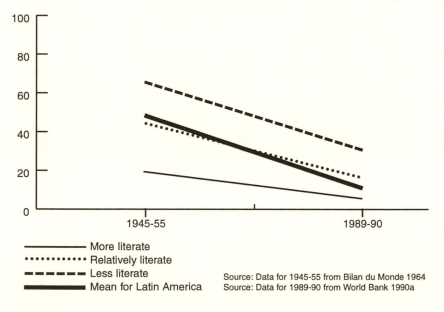

More literate

•••••••••• Relatively literate

▬ ▬ ▬ ▬ Less literate

▬▬▬▬ Mean for Latin America

Source: Data for 1945-55 from Bilan du Monde 1964
Source: Data for 1989-90 from World Bank 1990a

---

1. Argentina, Uruguay, Chile, Venezuela, Brazil, Cuba Puerto Rico, Mexico, Colombia, and Peru.

## Uneven and Heterogeneous Development

Urbanization in our countries is characterized by the accelerated demographic growth of social agglomerations, by urban centralization, and by spatial segregation in a progressively uneven social structure. This is the historical result of the particular forms and rates of integration of the Latin American economies into the world capitalist market. In step with the advance of capitalism in the central countries, effects are felt in the peripheral countries. In Latin America, as in other parts of the Third World, urbanization is not the product, as it is in advanced capitalism, of the impact of internal industrialization. Characterizing the modality of the urbanization process on the continent is a frank disparity between a relatively high level and rate of urbanization, from 1930-40 onward, and an obviously lower rate of

Graph 4: Process of Urbanization in Latin America (1960-90)

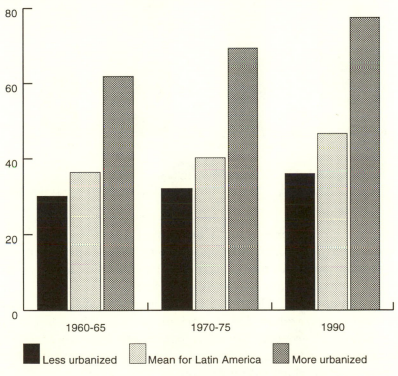

Source: Based on data from World Bank 1990b

industrialization (Davis and Casis 1957, Castells 1978, CEPAL 1983). The impact of dependent industrialization does not occur through a growth in industrial employment, and the system shows itself incapable of absorbing the labor power that emigrates from the countryside, expelled by the crisis and backwardness in forms of production and land occupancy. In rhythm with a decrease in the size of the economically active population in the rural sector, the population employed in the industrial sector grows. But as we see in graph 5 below, that growth is insufficient, and occurs at a much lower rate than the growth of employment in the tertiary sector of the economy.

Graph 5: Evolution of Distribution of Employment in the Principal Countries of Latin America (1950-80)[2]

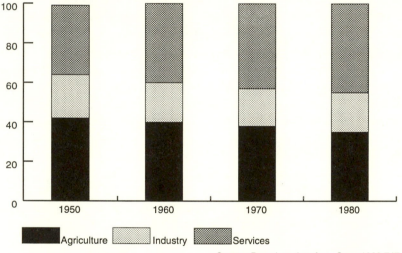

Source: Based on data from Sosa 1989:747

Another characteristic note accompanying this process of "tertiarization" of the Latin American economy is that, with the growth of an economy subjected to great structural inequalities, the so-called *informal sector of the economy* increases as well.

This is an unmistakable trait of Latin American development and peripheral modernization. Labor markets are insufficient to absorb the growth in the economically active population. With the high rate of population growth, the new ranks of labor grow more rapidly than the number of employment opportunities. This generates an excess

2. The countries considered were Argentina, Brazil, Colombia, Costa Rica, Cuba, Chile, Mexico, Panama, Uruguay, and Venezuela.

in the work force, issuing in a growth in the ranks of unemployed and underemployed. The original urban population lives alongside an ever greater mass of "relative overpopulation": persons unemployed or underemployed, or employed in nonproductive activities and informal services (Touraine 1977, Cockcroft 1983). Here the masses have sundered their ties with rural society, and live in spatial, social, and cultural segregation (Quijano 1972, Paviani 1985) in the peripheral belts of the great Latin American metropolises.

The structural logic at the root of this relative overpopulation lies in Latin America's prevailing capitalistic model of accumulation, a model dependent upon the dynamics imposed by transnational capitalism. It is not, however, a matter of a mechanical dependency that would explain the situation by solely exogenous reasons, as in the—now classic—theories of dependency (Gunder Frank 1978, Amin 1973). The process is a complex, multidetermined one, and is influenced by the internal dialectic of Latin American societies. These swelling segments of "urban poor" and the extreme poverty generally—which, far from shrinking, tend to hold even or grow in the countries of Latin America and the Caribbean—are the result not only of a dynamic of growth and accumulation dependent on the international capitalist market but also of the particular historical formation of each society's social relations, national state, and social and political struggle (Parker 1986a:45ff.).

In view of all of this, when we speak of the informal sector[3] of Latin American society, we do not understand it in dualistic terms, since the marginalized do not make up an autonomous, self-sustaining, and assimilated system, but a system interrelated with the formal dominant system of the economy. This interrelation obtains in the form of the subjection of these sectors of the economy to capital, which means that the interrelation is a function of the growth of the more advanced sector, and thus of the concentration of wealth and consequent growth of inequalities. In other words—in cultural terms—there is no "marginal culture," or "culture of poverty," on the basis of a system of its own, a system that would be exempt from the influence of the economy, society, and dominant culture.

Those who find themselves in this particular group are inserted into the labor market in very differentiated fashion. They constitute heterogeneous segments: there are individuals engaged in low-income self-employment, and there is a multiplicity of forms in the social organization of work in which noninstitutionalized produc-

---

3. For an interesting critical review of the concept of "informal sector," see Hugon (1980).

tive units (that is, localized outside of the capitalistic formal productive sector) predominate. All of the workers in these segments are involved in backward, precapitalistic, and subcapitalistic forms of production in which there is only a formal submission of labor to capital. Individuals and families organized in economic micro-units, filling in the chinks in the system and performing economic activities disdained by the modern capitalistic nucleus, compose a significant fraction of the work force in nearly all of the countries of Latin America (table 2, below).

## Those Who Are Invisible in the Economy

It is difficult to study the "poor" sectors without noticing the controversy that rages over the conceptual and operative definitions of "poor" and "poverty" (Labbens 1978). Adopting the findings of one of the most elaborate studies done on Latin America, however, we may

Table 2: Latin America Work Force to 1980

|  | Informal Sector* | Wage-Earning Sector[‡] |
|---|---|---|
| Bolivia | 50.9 | 38.2 |
| Equador | 37.9 | 47.6 |
| Guatemala | 33.1 | 46.9 |
| Peru | 32.0 | 45.1 |
| El Salvador | 30.1 | 59.2 |
| Brazil | 27.6 | 65.3 |
| Panama | 24.6 | 63.3 |
| Colombia | 18.7 | 53.5 |
| Mexico | 18.4 | 44.3 |
| Venezuela | 15.1 | 64.1 |
| Costa Rica | 14.8 | 75.2 |
| Chile | 8.8 | 66.7 |
| Uruguay | 8.0 | 69.4 |
| Argentina | 6.3 | 71.2 |

* Percentage of work force in urban and rural nonmodern informal sector
[‡]Percentage of work force in wage-earning work forces, according to occupational category

Source: PREALC 1990:281

state that, for eleven countries of the region, "at the beginning of the 1970s, 40 out of every 100 Latin American families were poor, with a poverty incidence of 26 out of every 100 families in urban areas, and of 60 out of 100 in rural areas" (Altimir 1981; see Di Filippo 1982). That is, according to this study there were at that time some 110 million poor in Latin America. In 1990, according to World Bank 1992, about 108 million persons lived below the poverty line in Latin America, that is, 25.5% of the total population, while by 1990, for the totality of the developing countries, the index of population below the poverty line had reached 29.7%.

The percentage of the population living in poverty in terms of consumption has diminished in recent years; still, due to the increase in population, the drop in the absolute number of poor has been, and will continue to be over the next years, more modest. World Bank 1992 forecasts 24.9% (126 million) poor in Latin America for the year 2000. According to Kanbur, "Progress in the reduction of poverty has slowed during the 1980s, and in some countries has been reversed" (Kanbur 1990).

Other sources, however, indicate a greater number of poor, and one is led to conclude that the World Bank report has underestimated the actual number of poor in the region. The Regional Conference on Poverty in Latin America and the Caribbean (Conferencia Regional 1991:463), with its high-level representatives from the countries of the region, declared, on the basis of a technical report of United Nations Development Programme (PNUD), that "*270 million Latin Americans, or 62% of the population, live in conditions of poverty*, and the majority of these form the group with the greatest number of needs."

Table 3: Poverty in Latin America (1985)

| | Extreme Poverty | | Poverty | |
|---|---|---|---|---|
| | Millions of persons | % | Millions of persons | % |
| Latin America | 50 | 12% | 70 | 19% |
| All Developing Countries | 633 | 18% | 1,116 | 33% |

Source: Kanbur 1990:209

The nonorganized and noninstitutionalized sectors of the work force, generically denominated the "informal" sectors, do not exhaust the concept of "invisible sectors," but are contained in these latter. In the majority of the countries of the region, systems of statistical information are incomplete and inadequate for an understanding of the structural and dynamic dimension of even the informal sectors. As for any measurement of the other invisible segments, it is practically nonexistent, and only appears in isolated inquiries and investigations of a local nature.[4]

By contrast with the lack of information, the invisible sector, composed of the masses of poor who are unemployed, underemployed, or precariously employed in the formal economy, on the whole has considerable importance in the countries of the region, since they develop alternative "survival strategies" to those of the formal job market. "The relevance of such segments is limited neither to their absolute volume nor to their relative weight, but also includes their alternative role with regard to the survival forms of their members" (Max-Neef et al. 1986).

In order to speak of subordinate classes and groups, then—that is, in order to speak of those who fundamentally live in an absolute or relative situation of poverty—one must also speak of their particular capacity for an active response to their unfavorable situation in society. We are dealing not with numerals, but with human subjects who have adverse surroundings to face. As their income is insufficient, their employment insecure or unstable, and social security or health insurance not commonly available to them, their living conditions are precarious and unhealthy, and their objective situation of misery becomes traumatic in the degree of incertitude it entails. It is perfectly reasonable that these individuals, who have the greater part of their basic human needs unsatisfied, should seek, at times in great anxiety, the means and mechanisms to satisfy them, thereby ensuring the subsistency—that is, the continuation and reproduction—of their lives. The so-called *survival strategies* (Parker 1986a:61-63, Rodríguez 1981, Lomnitz 1975, Razeto 1983) of the poor groups, then,

---

4. The "invisible" sectors are out of reach of "the capacity of prevailing systems of information, evincing once more that, from the viewpoint of analysis and policy formulation, these systems seem to take account only of what can be measured. Lacking any adequate theoretical basis for an approach to these ambits, demographic workforce accountings and national registers are deprived of a basic orientation for the production of relevant measurements" (Max-Neef et al., 1986:65-67).

are social forms of collective action that must be acknowledged and appreciated as a phenomenon having profound repercussions on the construction of a way of life and on the worldview of the groups that make up the majorities in the population of an underdeveloped continent.

## Exhaustion of a Style of Development

The development of Latin American capitalism was particularly discouraging in the 1980s. According to reports furnished by Comision Económica para la Americalatina (CEPAL) (1990, 1992), the magnitude of the economic and social deterioration registered in the Latin American and Caribbean countries during that decade justified calling it the "lost decade."

The crisis of the 1980s in Latin America marked the exhaustion of a style of development that had permitted great industrial and urban growth over the course of more than three decades, but that had achieved neither a tendency to greater equity, nor the materialization of an endogenous capacity for technological innovation, nor a structural change in the region's mode of integration into the international markets (Fajnzylber 1989).

Consequently, the typical structural and conjunctural tendencies of *peripheral modernization*, of which we have made mention in this chapter, have contributed, as a whole, in one way or another, to the increase both of relative poverty and of extreme poverty (a phenomenon occurring especially in urban areas). In general terms, CEPAL estimates that in 1980 some 112 million persons were living below the poverty line (35% of Latin American and Caribbean families). That number rose to 164 million in 1986, or 38% of all families.[5] PNUD's estimates for the end of the 1980s raised the figure to 270 million poor: that is, 62% of the Latin American population would by that time be living below the poverty line. Programa Regional de Empleo para la America Latina y el Caribe (PREALC), for its part, estimates that between 1980 and 1985, owing to the implementation of struc-

---

5. The data of the CEPAL report (CEPAL 1990:36) differ considerably from the data of the Second Regional Conference on Poverty in Latin America and the Caribbean (based on PNUD estimates), as well as from the World Bank data for 1990, which we have listed above, pp. 44 and 47. The difference is no doubt due to the differences in the various institutions' operational definitions, in their technical criteria for classification and definition, and in their use of indicators for assessing poverty.

tural adjustment policies, the proportion of expenditures for education and health in the overall budget fell by 3%, while direct unemployment grew by 8.1%, with a per capita income drop of 12% in the
region. These indexes translate into a 6% extension of poverty, which
means that the number of poor during these years rose from 120 million persons to 160 million (PREALC 1988).[6]

This deterioration in living conditions, especially for the sectors
and classes of the lower strata, has accentuated frustration, crises in
family relations, tensions, and expressions of social violence, particularly among popular youth, some of whose manifestations are the
growth of delinquency, drug addiction, and various forms of moral
degradation and/or rebellion. Thus, we can scarcely be surprised at a
growth in the stream of migration from Latin America and the Caribbean to the United States and Canada.

Simultaneously, the peripheral capitalistic economic growth model
has occasioned the appearance, among entrepreneurial economic sectors in these years, of small enclaves enjoying elevated rates of concentration of wealth and levels of productive modernity on a par with
those of the developed countries. This concentration has occurred especially in sectors of the nontraditional financial and exporting bourgeoisie. But this modernization occurs in a society on the edge of the
system, and is subject to its own contradictions: thus we may characterize it as *peripheral modernization*. In general, there is no denying
that certain indicators of modernization, such as those that we reviewed initially, as well as certain macroeconomic balances achieved,
indicate, in the long term, progress in the region. However, this contrasts with the development lag in these countries by comparison
with the development of highly industrialized countries, and demonstrates the precariousness of our economies and their dependence on
the transnational system, as well as, on the internal level, the broadening social gap in the distribution of income and access to markets.
The region's "flourishing market economy" limps along on one leg,
owing to the growth among us of inequalities, exclusion, and exploitation. The segmentation of the consumer market escalates.

---

6. A recent document of the United Nations Development Programme (1994)
stated: "During the last twenty years poverty has increased in Latin America.
Following the estimates for the seventies and eighties and the beginning of the
nineties, there were more than 112 million poor people in 1970 and more than
170 million in 1986. They increased up to more than 196 million in 1990. The
people living in misery surpassed 93 million. In more than twenty years more
than 84 million Latin American inhabitants entered the world of poverty" (p. 64).

### Capitalistic Modernization and Cultural Change

Steeped in the historical and structural processes that we have analyzed, the cultural field, including the religious field, sustains changes.

This peripheral urbanization and industrialization occurs on the foundation of a national and international process entailing an uneven, concentrating, and excluding development that increases structural heterogeneity. Thereupon, in diversified and heterogeneous fashion, it exerts an influence of its own, transforming mentalities both in the various expressions of official culture and in the plurality of cultures and subcultures of the middle classes and the various popular groups, ethnic aggregations, and classes, rural as well as urban. In turn, this change of mentality generates new cultural models, and the latter institute new social practices that have contributed, consequently, to historical and structural change in recent decades.

Up until two decades ago, sociology simply adopted uncritically the North American theory of modernity in its approach to the topic. According to that theory, the step from a traditional agrarian society to a modern urban and industrial society inevitably entails the *secularization* of values. Gino Germani declared that the process of secularization "constitutes a basic change, a necessary (but not sufficient) condition for the rise of a modern industrial society" (Germani 1969:15).

In this understanding of a modernizing change, religion would have less and less importance in social life, and would be replaced by wholly secular values and norms having no reference to supernatural realities. The deterministic, mechanistic analysis of a Creole Marxism too attached to certain classic postulates of orthodox Marxism concurred. In that era, religious sociology was disturbed by the study and conceptualization of secularization (Poblete 1975), and sought to bring more clarity to a new process which was seen as inevitable and which constituted the greatest of all of the risks confronting the pastoral activity of the Church. A certain theology and pastoral approach are still traumatized by the danger of "secularism" on our continent. Since then, sociology has abandoned secularization as a central theme of study, although the problem does call for a reconsideration in the light of the new background, and we shall undertake that reconsideration in our next chapter.

## Are the Latin American People Secularized?

The criteria of positivism and the resulting sociographic warp dog the steps of the sociology of religion as well, which frequently attempts to quantify qualities, as in the case of "secularization." Statistical data are a valid, but only relative, indicator, and ought to be taken only as providing illustrations for the development of more qualitative descriptive pictures. Let us review certain data with a view to a subsequent comprehensive sketch of the phenomenon of secularization.

The classic indicator, "Sunday practice," is still prioritized as the yardstick of religious adherence. However, this indicator ought to be used and analyzed critically. Otherwise, the observer runs the risk of identifying "nonpractice" with "religious indifference," and that will distort the panorama. A great number of those defined as "nonpracticing" in terms of the Church's official practices may actually be very religious persons; but they live and practice their popular faith under extraecclesial formulas, and thus come to be classified statistically as "indifferent." The same occurs with the classification "nonbelievers," so common in polls and census data. In-depth studies, when it comes to "nonbelievers," especially when these studies are done among popular groups, show that, in the vast majority of cases, the category "nonbelievers" is made up of religious dissidents—dissident, usually, from the region's hegemonic Catholicism. Actually these persons are believers—persons who have become "secularized," in a way, through a rationalization of their beliefs and rites, but who, at critical moments, when the meaning of their lives is under stress, have no hesitation in having recourse to the transcendent, without complexes or doubts.

In Latin America, a person listed as "nonpracticing" in terms of official canons is, in all likelihood, a "popular practicing" person, and only occasionally a "religious indifferent." Just so, the "nonbeliever" is very probably a "dissident believer," partially secularized, as available surveys show.

For this reason, the indicator "atheism" would seem more adequate when it comes to measuring secularizing influences, in a classic sense, among the Latin American population in general and in the urban popular sectors in particular. However, the concept of "secularization," as we have already posited, must be subjected to a critique, with a view to its reformulation.

In terms of the comprehensive data indicated by the *World Chris-*

*tian Encyclopedia*,[7] the proportion of Catholics on our continent up until 1980 was overwhelmingly majoritarian. However, this percentage had fallen since 1900—in eighty years—by 3.6%. We observe, in table 4, a rising trend in the percentage of the population who profess Protestantism. What is noteworthy is that the rise of atheism is the most moderate of all of the increases throughout this period of time. As for "other religions," among which we should have to include the Afro-American syncretic religions and the sects, recent decades have seen growth here.

Table 4: "Population by Religion" in Latin America (in thousands)

|  | 1900 | | 1970 | | 1980 | | 2000 | |
|---|---|---|---|---|---|---|---|---|
| Christians | 62.00 | (95.1%) | 263.30 | (93.0%) | 341.90 | (92.2%) | 556.70 | (89.9%) |
| Catholics | 60.00 | (92.3%) | 254.00 | (89.7%) | 329.00 | (88.7%) | 533.00 | (85.9%) |
| Protestants | 0.95 | (1.5%) | 8.30 | (2.9%) | 11.70 | (3.2%) | 22.40 | (3.6%) |
| Anglicans | 0.84 | (1.3%) | 1.00 | (0.4%) | 1.20 | (0.3%) | 1.30 | (0.2%) |
| Other Religions | 2.82 | (4.3%) | 11.10 | (3.9%) | 16.30 | (4.4%) | 34.20 | (5.5%) |
| Nonbelievers | 0.37 | (0.6%) | 7.30 | (2.6%) | 10.80 | (2.9%) | 24.80 | (4.0%) |
| Atheists | 0.01 | (0.0%) | 1.30 | (0.5%) | 2.00 | (0.5%) | 4.30 | (0.7%) |
| Total Pop. | 65.20 | (100%) | 283.00 | (100%) | 371.00 | (100%) | 620.00 | (100%) |

Source: Barrett 1982

A study of the overall panorama for the countries of Latin America reveals that, despite what modernization theory might postulate, there is no simple proportion between the degree of urbanization and industrialization and the increase in the number of nonbelievers. Countries displaying higher indices of modernization—that is, countries with more urbanization, industrialization, and primary education (Argentina, Uruguay, Chile, Venezuela, Mexico, Brazil, Colombia, and Peru, in that order)—do not reflect a secularization in direct correlation with that degree of modernization, if we measure secularization in terms of the aggregate of "atheists" and "believers having no reli-

---

7. The data listed by this encyclopedia are based on population censuses and various polls of religious affiliation and membership for the population of all of the countries of Latin America and the Caribbean.

gion." As we may infer from table 5, a country with indicators of modernization even as high as those of Argentina do not show a corresponding degree of secularization. Somewhat the same thing occurs with Mexico and Venezuela. The cases of Chile, on one side, and Peru and Colombia, on the other, reveal a certain correspondence between relative degrees of modernization and secularization. However, the case of Brazil, by reason of the complex configuration of its indicators, raises doubts whether, precisely in the cases just mentioned, secularization is the result of simple and solitary causal variables.

When we consider what occurs with religious indicators for the seven principal countries of Latin America, we observe that the percentage of the population reached by a "secularizing" current does not strikingly increase between 1900 and 1980. On the other hand, the growth of Protestantism in Latin America, as well as of the number of "dissident Catholics" and, in a lesser proportion, of sects and other religions, is a matter of common knowledge. The involution of majority Catholicism as well as of the native American minority religions, which by the last quarter of the twentieth century have lost the importance they had at its beginning, is clear (see graph 6, p. 59).

Table 5: Comparative Rates of Modernization and Secularization

|            | Modernization Index | Secularization Index |
|------------|---------------------|----------------------|
| Chile      | 0.670               | 0.110                |
| Argentina  | 0.695               | 0.033                |
| Venezuela  | 0.634               | 0.041                |
| Mexico     | 0.621               | 0.066                |
| Brazil     | 0.603               | 0.014                |
| Colombia   | 0.593               | 0.019                |
| Peru       | 0.592               | 0.019                |

Source: Indexes calculated on data given in World Bank 1990b, Betancourt 1988, Barrett 1982

An internal comparison of available data reveals that, in certain European highly developed capitalist countries, where Catholicism or an analogous religious culture (Anglicanism) is in the majority, the proportion of nonbelievers is greater than in the industrialized and urbanized countries of Latin America (see graph 7, p. 59).

## Graph 6: Religious Affiliation in Latin America in the Twentieth Century

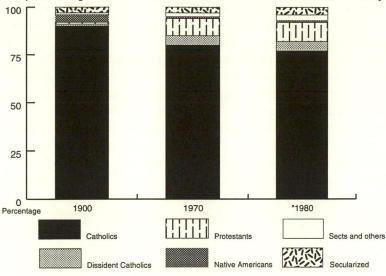

Source: Based on data from Barrett 1982

## Graph 7: Nonbelievers in Western Europe and More Industrialized Countries of Latin America

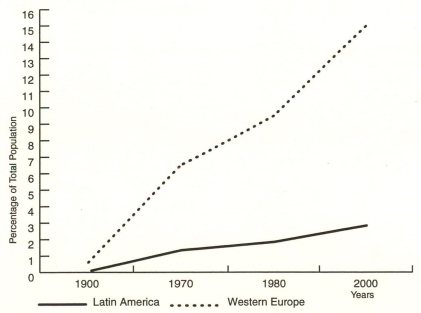

In the countries of developed capitalistic Europe that are of Latin culture and Catholic in their majority, in 1980 the mean percentage of nonbelievers was above 9%. In the United Kingdom, an Anglo-Saxon country, cradle of the industrial revolution and of Anglicanism, the same mean prevails. Meanwhile, for the largest countries of the Latin American continent, whose indicators of modernization are relatively elevated, the number of nonbelievers averages less than 2.5%. It seems clear, then, that with the advance of capitalistic modernization in the European countries, a process of growth in nonbelief indeed occurs, but that there is no such process in our countries (see table 6, below).

While the proportion of nonbelievers advances at a very slow pace in Latin America, the percentage of believers who abandon Catholicism but retain their belief, by contrast, registers a constant gain, in step with the index of urbanization and modernization on the periphery, in unbalanced and underdeveloped conditions.

Table 6: Percentage of Nonbelievers in Western Europe and the More Industrialized Latin American Countries

|  | 1900 | 1970 | 1980 | 2000 |
|---|---|---|---|---|
| *Europe* | 0.53 | 6.58 | 9.38 | 14.95 |
| Belgium | 0.8 | 5.8 | 7.5 | 13.8 |
| Spain | 0.0 | 2.2 | 2.9 | 5.5 |
| France | 0.3 | 12.0 | 15.6 | 22.9 |
| Italy | 0.2 | 9.0 | 16.2 | 23.5 |
| Portugal | 0.0 | 2.3 | 4.6 | 10.0 |
| United Kingdom | 1.9 | 8.2 | 9.5 | 14.0 |
|  |  |  |  |  |
| *Latin America* | 0.10 | 1.69 | 2.13 | 3.60 |
| Argentina | 0.2 | 1.5 | 1.7 | 2.4 |
| Brazil | 0.1 | 1.0 | 1.4 | 2.5 |
| Colombia | 0.1 | 0.6 | 0.9 | 2.3 |
| Chile | 0.2 | 6.0 | 6.6 | 8.5 |
| Mexico | 0.1 | 1.7 | 2.8 | 4.8 |
| Peru | 0.0 | 0.4 | 0.5 | 1.5 |
| Venezuela | 0.0 | 0.6 | 1.0 | 3.2 |

*Source:* Barrett 1982

To conclude, on the whole, the data analyzed in this chapter, bearing on the peculiar processes of peripheral modernization from Latin American capitalism and demonstrating the absence of an accompanying persistent, frank tendency to secularization, suggest new questions. The data indicate that, while a certain percentage of the population is influenced by secularizing currents—in the classic sense, that is, as determinative of a decline in the weight of religious symbolism in the makeup of cultural models in daily and public life alike—this phenomenon occurs rather as a mere countercurrent to the central trend. That central trend, as we have seen, consists, on the one side, of the persistence, however eroded, of Catholicism and, on the other, of the growth of new religious expressions of various kinds, especially among the Latin American popular masses. In the context of a Latin American society subjected to a peripheral, heterogeneous, uneven modernization, a modernization characterized by a self-exhausting style of development, the religious element, instead of being stifled, would seem to be transformed. What may we expect in the future?

Why would religion in Latin America persist in spite of the processes of modernization that have been such a part of our experience in recent decades? Would it not be because, in a peripheral society, the gradual, linear disappearance of the religious element from a culture is remarkably slow? What are we to understand, then, by a "process of secularization," in light of the historical, structural, and religious reality of Latin America?

In the following chapters we shall attempt to approach the problems posed by these questions in all of their magnitude and complexity, with the understanding that the answers will not always be unambiguous nor always entirely satisfactory.

**Chapter 4**

# Capitalistic Modernization and Religious Resurgence

As we have observed, in Latin America the religious element has real weight in the makeup of society's symbolical field, and manifests that field in all of its magnitude. While an abundance of studies is available on the religious phenomenon and the process of secularization in the region, we still need to delve into the sociological relationship between, on the one hand, the various forms of religious expression prevailing among the popular sectors and, on the other, the process of our societies' urbanization and industrialization, together with the secularizing effects of that process. This in-depth investigation will require us to enter once more, in light of contemporary changes, upon a theoretical discussion of the secularization process and then to analyze the peculiar nature of Latin American capitalistic modernization. At that point we shall be in a position to understand, and to seek to explain, our continent's religious transformations.

## Secularization and Popular Religion in Latin America

In Latin America, as we have seen, theories of secularization meet with greater difficulties than they do when they are applied to European countries. On our underdeveloped, dependent continent, secularization processes have acquired different characteristics from those of the corresponding European processes. In part, these characteristics obey the historical and structural evolution of our particular processes of capitalistic modernization; and in part, they are a response to Latin Americans' cultural *pathos*, which prevails in a special way in our popular cultures.

A glance at the sociological interpretation of "Catholicism" in Latin

*62*

America from the 1950s up to the time of the Medellín Conference (1968) indicates that the key concern of pastoral theory and activity—and of religious sociology, their unquestioning servant—was secularization. The religious reality of the Latin American masses was studied either from a quantitative sociographic, or else from a functionalist, perspective. Sociologists' preoccupation was that of the Church—which was in consternation at the "decline of the religious spirit and the penetration, little by little, of laicism and materialistic currents" that were undermining the "Christian marrow of society" and "supernatural inspiration" and rendering sacramental life ritualistic and skeletal (Pin 1963:35).

Two years before Father Godin published his celebrated *La France: Pays de mission?* ("France: A Mission Country?"), in 1943 (cited in Pannet 1974), Father Hurtado had asked, in his own book, "Is Chile a Catholic Country?" *(¿Es Chile un país católico?)* Hurtado was disturbed by the contrast between massive expressions of popular piety and scant sacramental practice. Cultural practices did not translate into practical life through a family, professional, and social morality. Even Pin, on the basis of the best investigations and observations since the 1940s, in his famous *Elementos para una sociología del catholicismo latinoamericano* (1963), detects a considerable decline in sacramental practice, especially with respect to Sunday mass, confession, and marriage.

Today the panorama does not seem to have changed substantially. The data indicated in a recent publication on the world religious situation, while not entirely comparable and trustworthy, indicate, for Argentina, Brazil, Colombia, Chile, Mexico, Peru, and Venezuela, a considerable decline in Sunday practice, especially in urban areas; but elsewhere the rate of participation in the Sunday Eucharist is very high.[1] However, these indicators are only for the Sunday practice officially prescribed by the Church. From an "ethnocentric" viewpoint (Ribeiro 1972:573), it is logical to expect a drop in the level of official practices as an indicator of secularization in urban society, since a rise in the index of secularization there would be associated with a greater distance taken from the Church as an institution. Ignored, however, is a little-studied subcategory of (official) non-practitioners, where the data belie a comprehensive secularization: that of "popular practitioners," with whom devotional and tutelary practices

---

1. Taking the data cautiously, we may assert that, while Catholic rural practice may reach 60% or 70%, in large cities it is always lower, and never as high as 22%, with a mean of approximately 10-12%. See Barrett (1982).

occupy a central place in life, while the constellation of sacramental practices is relegated to a secondary level.

Up until 1968, studies on the sociology of religion, and specifically on popular piety in Latin America, addressed their theme via the methods of ethnology, with culturalist or functionalist methods calculated to indicate the degree of religious density as a cultural phenomenon and as a phenomenon of adherence to the Church—that is, as a specifically religious phenomenon—with popular religious practice being regarded as dysfunctional as far as change and modernization are concerned.[2] The accent was on the "folkloric," the "mystical," and the "extravagant" (spontaneous, uncultivated forms of piety) so widespread in poor, mainly rural, milieus. These studies found inspiration in the past. The survival of the past in the present was erected into an absolute norm. The view was a static one. These studies failed to capture precisely the dynamism of the social and religious transformations under way in the various countries of the continent (Comblin 1968:10). Furthermore, they implicitly pronounced a value judgment upon an object of study: religious practice was evaluated on the criterion of a "pure" Catholicism, which did not exist in practice. The sociological category into which those persons fall who define the "purity" of the expressions of faith in question is that of the religious elite, whose authority is legitimated extrasocially (its reference and foundation being a hierocratic power). Thus, they become empowered to define truth in terms impervious to any social criticism.

Despite the variety in the typology of Latin American Catholicism applied by the various authors of this current, we discern a shared concern, although a concern not always explicitly and coherently expressed. That concern is with the secularization processes. Ribeiro distinguishes three great typological approaches prevailing at the beginning of the 1970s—approaches resting on differing principles, on whose basis a particular combination of elements of Catholicism composes each type of that Catholicism. Pin and Büntig establish their type on the basis of motivations; Camargo, Bastide, Lalive d'Epinay,

---

2. F. Houtart and E. Pin, in their relevant *L'Eglise à l'heure de l'Amérique latine* (1965), exemplify this position. Referring to the cultural level and personality type of the devout who participate massively in pilgrimages, missions, and ritual devotions, they state: "It is not certain that it corresponds to the cultural level or personality type that the city needs, and that tomorrow's elite will have to possess . . . One thing seems to us to be rather clear: one cannot rely on a participation in those cults and devotions for the founding of a spirit of renewal and progress, unless the content of those cults and devotions undergoes a renewal" (pp. 165-66).

and, in a certain sense, Pin and Büntig do so on the basis of adaptation to comprehensive elements of the social structure (especially the rural and the urban); and Acevedo, Comblin, and Rolim look for factors of differentiation on the basis of the processes of the spread and historical realization of Catholicism (see Süess 1979:61-112). But all of these typologies and studies embrace the thesis that Latin American society is in a process of transition from the traditional rural and religious to the modern urban and secularized. This concern, and the decisive weight of the theory of modernization in vogue up until those years, can also be observed in the way in which FERES's broader comparative investigation into popular piety in 1969 and 1970 posed the problem that structured its theoretical framework.[3]

Religious sociology was only adopting the position on secularization proposed by one of the most influential Latin American sociologists of the 1960s, Gino Germani. Germani, for his part, had uncritically accepted the theory of modernization developed by other authors, such as Apter, Eisenstadt, and Almond. For Germani, the secularization process constituted a necessary (although not sufficient) pathway to the rise of modern industrial society (Germani 1969, Gomes de Souza 1982:160-61). This concept thereupon became an object of concern on the part of the sociology of religion, which saw in this secularizing modernization an inevitable challenge to the pastoral activity of the Church (Poblete 1975).

One of the topics coming in for heaviest emphasis at the General Conference of Latin American Catholic Bishops held at Puebla (1979) was *religiosidad popular*, popular piety. The Church's new awareness of popular piety had been aroused at Medellín (1968); but at Puebla, more mature reflection was brought to bear on the subject, nor were polemical interpretations lacking (Alliende 1979, Lozano 1979).

The view put forward in the Preparatory Document of the Puebla Conference was that the axis of contemporary transformations in Latin

---

3. The research on popular piety in Latin America was carried out in 1969 and 1970 in Mexico by IMES, in Colombia by ICODES, in Venezuela by CISOR, in Brazil by CIRES, and in Chile by CISOC. (See FERES-AL 1969.) So also a most outstanding sociologist—because of his empirical studies on popular religion in Argentina—A. Büntig, posed the question in the following terms: "But secularization, objectively considered, is an irreversible cultural fact, although it does not occur identically everywhere. This means that all traditionally Catholic countries—Argentina among them—will have to confront, at different points in time, the reality of a minority Catholicism, a genuine leaven in the mass. . . We observe a secularization that is advancing at the accelerating rate of a waxing urbanization, while the search is on for a new face for the Argentine church" (Büntig 1970:61).

American capitalism was the passage from an agrarian, rural society to an industrial, urban society. That step entailed the growth of a rationalistic Enlightenment mentality, as well as of tendencies to secularization—in the face of which popular piety, of baroque mold, rose up in the Latin American cultural synthesis and prepared to do battle with secularism. Criticism was not long in coming. The main criticism (Gomes de Souza 1982) bore on the church document's mistaken view of capitalistic modernization processes. The document's faulty premise was that development in Latin American countries must of course follow a process similar to that of development in the United States or Europe, which were regarded as models and final terms of the process. The imbalances and particular complexity of our cultural and religious processes, subject as they are to the contradictory and uneven influences of a dependent capitalistic development, were ignored.

The treatment ultimately accorded the theme of "popular religiosity" at Puebla (1979) was by and large an advance over that of the Preparatory Document, if only unevenly so. In tandem with a forthrightly positive appraisal of "popular piety," certain disputable theses were accepted, such as the indissoluble connection between Catholicism and the "profound substrate" of the continental culture. Nor were the thematics of secularization addressed with adequate balance: instead, we heard warnings against the threat of "secularism" entailed in capitalistic modernization. However, Puebla's positive reappraisal of the faith of the poor, their "evangelizing potential," and the yearnings for liberation rooted in popular piety stand out as gains in the Church's interpretation of popular religion.

Current pastoral approaches to the phenomenon of secularization take into account all that has been gained in terms of a positive reappraisal of "popular piety" between the Puebla Conference (1979) and the most recent Conference of Latin American Bishops, held at Santo Domingo (1992).[4]

The conclusions of the Santo Domingo Conference (1992) embrace the results of the reflection on popular piety that the Catholic Church has entertained in recent decades. Popular piety is accepted as a "privileged expression of the inculturation of the faith," the fruit of a racial

---

4. Recent years have seen a multiplication of studies and essays on popular religion in Latin America, and the bibliography on the subject is growing by the day. See the recent bibliographical material assembled by Johansson (1990), and Parker (1986a:531-48). See also Arias (1977), Dussel (1986), Johansson and Pérez (1987), Morandé (1984), Parker (1992a), Richard (1980), Samandú (1989a, 1989b), Scannone (1985), and Vidales and Kudo (1975).

and cultural intermarriage, and a manifestation of the wisdom of the people—although there is a concern, in the Santo Domingo Final Document, to reject the "syncretism," and deviations from the authentic Catholic faith, of popular piety. As for the bishops' reflection on the secularization process, its appraisal as a positive process of modern consciousness (nos. 153, 252) is striking, and a criticism of secularism as a negative phenomenon challenging pastoral activity appears more nuanced. However, there is no absolute consistency in the bishops' overall diagnosis of the two phenomena, secularization and the upsurge in popular piety. They appear in the bishops' reflection as disconnected processes. Underlying the entire diagnosis in whose light the document's theological reflection unfolds and its pastoral recommendations are made is a certain ambivalence between a positive appraisal of autonomous sociocultural processes and the defense of the dogmas of the faith and of the Church.

As we review the reflection of the past decade, we are struck by Marcelo de Carvalho's position (1983) to the effect that, in Latin America, technological development cannot be assimilated to secularization. Just as in Islam, especially in the Iran of the ayatollahs, or in overdeveloped Japan, a capitalistic power, the impact of advanced technologies has worked no detriment on the hegemony of religion in society, so too with Latin America. Carvalho offers an acute analysis of the profound, irresistible impact of modernity, whose strength is in inverse proportion to the weakness and fragility of the religious basis of social legitimation. In certain respects, something of the kind occurs on the Latin American continent, says Carvalho. Here, secularization occurs by way of development, a consumer economy, and a consumer propaganda that attempts to make life into a market, functionalizes it, and introduces into it an instrumental rationality.

This rationalization makes itself felt in the pressures of a "technified," bureaucratized life, in secularization at the hands of political ideology, in the school system, and in the media, which today reach into the furthermost corners of society. All of these influences give persons a "set of meanings and values proper to cultures and societies that are not theirs but that attract them and spawn conflict by virtue of the contrast between their underlying critical thought and people's simple, naive beliefs" (De Carvalho 1983:2).

Secularization fragments religious hegemony; and while it does not efface religious awareness, it softens its imprint on people's lives. As education broadens, religious indifference broadens as well. Thus, education fills all vacuums of ignorance and challenges irrational thought.

Carvalho's position is only partially correct. Throughout the present work, we are attempting to show that the secularization process is a very complex one, and that it hosts contradictions, which prevent it from effecting the irremediable loss of all religious sense in the life of the popular classes.

Instead of justifying Carvalho's position, empirical and historical evidence tends to support Dussel (1986), for whom the Latin American people in their daily lives gain sense and meaning for the world and their lives, their families, their work, for life and death, not from the educational system and the culture of the mass media, or even from the parties of the left, but from their own particular religious forms.

We intend to show that the problem of secularization and popular religion is more complex in Latin America than might at first appear. True, religious syncretism is a typical element of Latin American popular Christianity (Marzal 1986). But it is erroneous to conclude by way of diagnosis that, in the face-off with contemporary secular modernity, the religious vitality of popular syncretism offers little stability (De Carvalho 1983:1).

### Modernization and Religion

Following Weber, we readily observe, in the economic field as in the political, the decisive institutional vectors of modernity, and therefore of "secularization."

Historically, the modernizing institutions par excellence have been *modern industrial capitalism* and the *modern bureaucratic state*. To a large extent they still are, though a number of important developments have now to be taken into account. The most important of these is that since the industrial revolution technological production has acquired an autonomous dynamic (and rationalizing force) of its own, which is no longer necessarily linked to the particular economic arrangements of capitalism. [Berger et al. 1973:102]

In terms of modern consciousness, one can distinguish certain primary vehicles of modernization and certain secondary ones (Berger et al. 1973). The former, Berger explains, are the industrial world, the bureaucratic apparatus of state, and technology. Among the second we find urbanization, the primary school, and the media (as well as other vehicles of modernization). This distinction between primary and secondary vehicles of modernization is analytically necessary, it is true; but from the standpoint of what is occurring in today's society, that distinction is insufficient for a description of the secularizing characteristics of forms of modernization. In the concrete, whereas the industrial organization of labor and modern state bureaucratization are indeed agents of rationalization and provoke "disenchantment," this does not hold for modern informational and electronic technology, which has a qualitatively distinct symbolizing power. In the case of the modality of modernization at work in Latin America, we shall first need to review the peculiarity of the processes of urbanization and industrialization involved. In and of themselves, urbanization and industrialization are agents of rationalization; but at the same time they are agents of transformations that, whether for structural, practical, or historical reasons or simply by virtue of the relative autonomy of the collective subject when it comes to producing religious models, do not occasion the dissolution of the religious element. Along with studying the so-called heterodox factors at work in the modernizing evolution of Latin American society, we must analyze the peculiar process by which the information revolution, which is wreaking such havoc with the entire symbolical field of certainties and paradigms in which modern society placed its highest hopes, is penetrating our continent.

According to the Durkheimian thesis, it is the need every society has for cohesion that roots the appearance of religious bonds in a collectivity. Now, these bonds of meaning may be either explicitly or implicitly religious (invisible religion). Whether, in a given instance, the activity of symbolization, ritualization, and reference to the transcendent order be called "religion," or whether it be some form of mythology or ideology substituted for religion, the important thing is to analyze and evaluate the composition of the religious field in each concrete society, together with its various legitimating (or delegitimating) functions there, and to be able to understand that particular society's evolution from a premodern situation to modern society. But from the point of view of the construction of each social group's symbolical field, in the framework of a social formation having a differentiated and complex system of stratification, as in the case of the contemporary social formation, the distinction between the religious and the nonreligious enjoys a much stronger relationship to the peculiar construction of a worldview by a given group or class. The distinction between the religious and the nonreligious enters into the reconstruction, made by each social group (the popular classes, in this case), of nature, the social, and the meaning of life, on the basis of that group's particular needs and processes of symbolization and language.

Religion in Latin America seems to be privatized, as Luckmann's theory posits. But it is privatized in a qualitatively different way from the privatization that typifies it in the developed bourgeois world. The structuring nucleus of classic capitalistic social relations—that is, the relation between capital and labor—in all parts of the world has been secularized, in the sense that it no longer requires a religious legitimation. As a consequence, in the highly developed countries secularization has extended to other spheres of reality, and religion has been polarized toward the more private and more public institutional spheres, especially toward the state and the family. Religion, then, performed certain ideological functions, and revived as a supplier of meaning to the various groups of a more and more pluralistic society. But with the information revolution, that panorama is tending to change, and we shall analyze this change below.

In Latin America specifically, although this polarization toward the public and the private is indeed verified, it occurs not in society at large, but only among a certain upper class and intellectual elite. For the broad majorities—the popular sectors and middle classes—the religious is reproduced in family space, but does not become completely privatized. It continues to fulfill important meanings and functions for the popular culture.

Religion can tend to become pluralistic, as Berger observes (1973) and as we have asserted, and we shall develop this below. But it does not thereby lose its structure of plausibility and its capacity for the symbolical reinforcement of legitimations in terms of *nomos*. We mean this not in the sense that economic and political relations would require and reproduce religious legitimations, but only in the sense that the symbolical weight of the religious in the construction of the meaning of life—in the construction of *nomos* as protector from the absurd,[5] in the reconstitution of meaning amidst uncertainty, in the gen-

---

5. We differ with Peter Berger's position and think that the activity of the sacred cosmos is not reducible to a legitimation of the ordering *nomos* of life significates. To this "protection" of a dynamic, ever precarious social construction (a concept basically implying a conservative view of the reproduction of the significative order) a creative, transforming function must be added, generative of alternative visions of the world, utopias (a concept implying a dialectical view of the reproduction of meaning). While the function of the reproduction of the significative order falls mainly to the various institutions of the social order, the transformative function of that significative order, the utopian generation of new significations—new alternative *nomoi*—rests, as a dynamic and ever creative

eration of new hopes for the vast majority of the Latin American population—is a sociological and cultural fact fraught with unforeseeable consequences for the very construction of Latin American culture. Latin American society is shot through with a process of cultural and religious pluralization, resulting more from the transformation of the religious field and the social and historical dynamics of the social actors than as a direct consequence of a social structure being modernized in the classic sense. Recent "modernizations," however, insofar as these result in a growth of the informal sectors and the sectors that are "invisible for the economy," as well as by reason of the form assumed by the "technotronic" and informational revolution, have direct repercussions, revolutionizing the cultural guidelines.

## Sociological Effects of Latin American Urbanization on the Religious Expressions of the People

Classic theories of urbanization postulate that, with the disintegration of the feudal order and the rise of the capitalist mode of production, the "urban way of life" appears (Wirth; see Remy and Voyé 1976). The modern process of urbanization, we hear, arises from the introduction of the capitalist mode of production. Modern industry reorganizes the landscape and generates a new mode or manner of producing and reproducing economic, social, and cultural life. With the liberalization of labor power, the subjection of labor to capital, the concentration of the population in urban agglomerates, mercantilization, automatization, and bureaucratization, the rhythm of life is modified, and social relations become impersonal and anonymous.

Whereas the traditional piety of the peasantry has been oriented by a feeling of dependency on heteronomous divine forces—the classic theories say—which one sought to control and placate by means of magical manipulation, the piety of the modern proletariat will be more manageable. The proletariat depend on their labor and on social forces, and this introduces the consciousness of a rational autonomy in their lives. Natural processes can no longer be influenced by magic or provi-

---

process, with the collective subjects, in the concrete historical movements and practices of determinate social groups and classes. The privilege of the structures, in this case, is that of the functions of reproduction of the order; the privilege of the social subjects, especially those of the subordinate actors, whose interests coincide with a will to change, is that of the transformative functions of the cultural and religious models.

dence. Thereby ceases the characteristic "providentialism" of traditional piety (Prien 1985:294-98). The people's rationalism is no longer invested with a religious faith, which comes to be supplanted by ideological substitutes.

This functionalist theory of the secularizing changes of the processes of capitalistic urbanization may be partially valid under certain concrete conditions. But it betrays its inadequacy to explain the processes of secularization at work in the particular conditions of underdeveloped urbanization in Latin America, especially in view of the complexity introduced by recent sociocultural transformations.

In nearly all Latin American countries, a process of capitalistic modernization has occurred that brings with it a process of secularization of the political and ideological fields (Míguez Bonino 1974). However, despite the change introduced by transformations in productive forces, the step from "traditional" society to "modern" society, with all that this entails in terms of rationalization and a "disenchantment of the world" (to use Weberian terminology) is verified only in the most superficial layers of Latin American cultural diversity, and primarily in the culture of the elite and of dominant groups— precisely in that "lettered" and "enlightened" culture characterized by an accentuated degree of permeability to the instrumental rationality of a modern capitalistic consumer society. Still, in the case of the modernization of the national states in Latin America, as with almost all of the non-Western countries of the Third World, the modernizing guidelines of state bureaucratization coexist with, and at times are intertwined with, traditional guidelines in social relations in the political field. Actually, the bureaucratic state as such does not become established in Latin America. Instead, traditional bonds are reinforced, such as clientage, cliquism, caciquism, and so on. This is explained not only by the existence of a diversity of frames of reference prevailing between modern bureaucracy and its client[6] but by the configuration of the informal networks of Latin American bureaucratic organization, which contributes most frequently to the re-creation of bonds of interaction of a traditional type.

---

6. "The client of the bureaucracy has no need to enter into the reference framework of the bureaucrat in order to enter into interaction with him . . . This may mean, simply and plainly, that a great number of persons continue to expect miracles from the state, with absolutely no understanding of the mechanisms that would be needed in order to work those miracles" (Berger et al. 1973:125).

## Peculiarity of Urbanization and Plurality of Religious Models

The structural dynamics occasioned by capitalistic modernization in Latin America—with the peculiar "urbanization" from that phenomenon, along with increased tertiarization of the economy, heterogeneity and structural inequalities, and the growth of the informal sector—condition the restructuring of class relations and the class position of the popular groups in society.

The structural transformations that we have characterized in the foregoing chapter have as a consequence a heterogenization of the urban popular classes in Latin American countries. Together with the classic proletariat, we find another proletariat, one typical of the less developed sectors of industry, commerce, and transportation. Here is a proletariat with very few skills, receiving paltry remuneration, without unions, and without social security. Simultaneously, the "invisible" sector broadens, swelling with an immense mass of subproletarians who ferret out very diverse occupations in the informal sector of the underdeveloped economy. Street vendors, independent laborers, domestic servants, impoverished small entrepreneurs, and so on, appear. This phenomenon is accompanied by a "relative overpopulation," of huge proportions, of chronically underemployed or unemployed. Further, there is the misnamed "inactive" sector—homemakers, students, and retired—which is actually active, and which makes up a very important segment in the popular sectors. Concentrated in the peripheral population is an enormous mass of popular families, urban "heaps," obliged to eke out a subsistence in conditions of extreme misery and abandonment, without social opportunities and the satisfaction of their basic needs.

This heterogeneity of class situation tends to generate an equally heterogeneous field of cultural and religious representations, roughly corresponding, through the intermediary of the collective actor's field of practices, to that actor's class positions.

With the majority of the urban popular sectors living in conditions of such extreme misery and exploitation, only partially integrated into the dominant capitalism and its way of life, religion of a traditional mold takes on a new meaning. The working-class sector integrated into capitalism, on the other hand, with its higher rate of primary-school enrollment and its incorporation into neighborhood and union organizations, will tend to see its beliefs and rituals rationalized. But the life of the working world will be only partially exposed to the modernizing influence of industrial technology upon consciousness, and given the relative autonomy of the religious field, various religious models will appear that are either more influenced by ethics or else *internally* secularized (Isambert 1976b). Religion, however, will persist as a latent source of meaning in their worldview.

In the case of the subproletariat and the mass of urban poor, with their lower school enrollment and generally greater availability to the influence of their original peasant culture, it is their social marginalization that will determine the ensemble of practices conditioning their view of life and of faith. Difficult conditions of existence, that is, the nonsatisfaction of their vital needs, will lead them to attempt a series of strategies that—through the reinforcement of their bonds of solidarity—will generate a network of practices calculated to ensure their survival (Lomnitz 1975). Hunger and lack of housing, clothing, and health services will lower the thresholds of uncertainty. The gravity of these afflictions will be in inverse proportion to the availability of employment. Accordingly, certain interpretations have generalized the theory of a "culture of poverty" (Lewis 1969, 1988), which postulates the disintegration and anomie of the poor as a source of irrational behaviors (see Prien 1985:819, Büntig 1970:99, Süess 1979:92). And it is true that popular culture appears to be characterized by a certain "immediatism," by a spirit of "one day at a time." The reason for this, however, is not so much an incapacity for rational foresight on the part of those who live in a situation of poverty; it is rather their capacity for effective adaptation to structural conditions of domination, which render their daily life so unstable.

Social and cultural uncertainty is fertile soil for the growth of a piety characterized by a strong sense of dependency on supernatural powers (Marzal 1970). Recourse to the Virgin, the saints, the Holy Spirit, and the departed souls or the spirits in the form of religious magic, whether in the guise of traditional Catholicism, popular Pentecostalism, or syncretic cults such as *umbanda*, compensate for, and symbolically replace, what the dominant society in effect refuses to supply: attention to health, means of survival, institutional satisfaction of needs (Bentué 1975). The life of the subproletariat in the city is subject to the cycles and imponderables of social dependency, and has severed its direct relation with nature, since it no longer depends on natural cycles. Now it must face the uncertainty of the changing "social world" of the urban industrial consumer society upon which it depends. The recurring cycle of employment → unemployment ⇒ misery has replaced the cycle of planting → rain ⇒ harvest. The subjective sense of dependency upon unmanageable external conditions is still there, however, and through symbolical recourse to the mediation of the transcendent, one can still attempt to render these conditions "manageable" and thereby reduce the threat of meaninglessness. In this fashion, the piety of the masses in the city becomes a sort of "symbolical survival strategy" (Parker 1986c), contributing to the reproduction of the meaning of life by reinstituting in the enterprise of survival, on the basis of a tutelar and favorable sacred cosmos, the *nomos* that removes, among these marginalized classes, all insecurity and all threat of destruction both of the order of meaning—and of life itself.

### Information Revolution, Threshold of Uncertainty, and Religion

With the advent of the postindustrial society, the technological scientific revolution which we are experiencing is transforming the world in nearly as decisive a fashion as did the industrial revolution that began at the close of the eighteenth century. Together with the revolution in productive forces, the whole cultural edifice begins to teeter and sway.

Graph 8: Three Industrial Revolutions

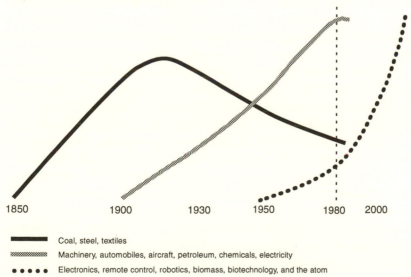

1850          1900          1930          1950          1980   2000

━━━━━ Coal, steel, textiles

▨▨▨▨▨ Machinery, automobiles, aircraft, petroleum, chemicals, electricity

●●●●● Electronics, remote control, robotics, biomass, biotechnology, and the atom

Source: I. Kerkhofs: "Panorama des valeurs en Europe: Permanence et adaptation," Colloquium, L'Ethique dans le débat public, January 1989

One of the core processes typifying this qualitative leap by contemporary humanity resides in the progress of information and communications technology. There are, of course, three other terrains where this leap is taking place: automatization and robotization, nuclear energy, and biology (microbiology, genetic engineering) (see Schaff 1987). With the progress being achieved in electronics, the world of communications has been substantially altered: we need only mention, by way of example, television and the other audiovisual media, electronic and satellite communication, the information revolution, the world of personal computers, and remote-control technology. As we observe in graph 8, on page 75, with the crisis of 1930 the first phase of the industrial revolution, based on coal, textiles, and steel, was on the wane. Since about 1980, the second phase of the industrial revolution (electricity, chemistry, mechanization, the automobile, oil, the airplane) has been losing headway, and the relevance of the third phase—in electronics, remote control, robotics, biotechnology, biomass, and the atom—is on the upsurge.

## Technotronic Modernization and the Reenchantment of the World

Changes in the systems of production have a direct repercussion on transformations in the systems of signification and symbolization. Today's social imagination[7] is radically different from the one that, up until two decades ago, characterized the mentality of our familiar capitalistic modernization. An analysis of the various spheres of daily living in modern postindustrial society, and of their influence on the representation of objects and of human needs, will have to be resituated in the context of this basic mutation in the productive systems.

We stand at a turning point in history. The new revolution continues to be characterized, of course, by a replacement of the classic productive factors: labor, natural resources, and capital. But now a fourth factor, and a decisive one, supervenes: the information revolution. Information is now processed as "informatics"—that is, information converted into bits. For the first time in seventy-five years, the factory has been reinvented from the ground up. The conventional forms of the organization of production, the characteristics of the work process, consumer guidelines, and other aspects of social,

---

7. This consideration upon the "social imagination" (G. Durand's concept) takes its inspiration in Maffesoli 1990.

political, and cultural life are under critical review (Gatto 1990).

In turn, dizzying advances in the use of time—cause and consequence of the productivity in question—spark an acceleration in the subjective sense of time and engender an ensemble of needs in the area of communication and symbolization. Productive needs, for their part, determine processes whose complexity grows because they entail a "proliferation of variety" in the modalities of economic activity, and this in turn determines a multiplication of the relations of linear and nonlinear variables to be considered. In sum, the notion of a linear, predictable time has been shattered. "The symmetry of historical time has been broken" (ILPES 1986). Accordingly, as the planning theoreticians, astonished at these changes, declare, the ability to plan is diminished because of the reduction in predictability and the lowering of the threshold of uncertainty in social processes (Costa-Filho 1990).

With the remarkable increase of labor productivity and the growth of leisure time, a new consumer sector has opened and is rapidly being filled by the new technologies. The appearance of the "mass society," by contrast with the culture of the elite that characterized classic industrial capitalism, is a contemporary phenomenon and is based on the fact that the market has now broadened, no longer in quantitative terms alone but qualitatively, as well. In what sense do we mean "qualitatively"? We are thinking of the phenomenon of absentee investment, which is replacing the typical capitalistic mechanism that once upon a time revolved around ownership as the articulator of the other systems of needs.

As social production and the historical evolution of capitalism meet basic needs more and more completely (in the developed countries), in step with that progress, new needs arise—for new objects of merchandise generated under the patronage of the revolution occurring in the current productive structure (see Parker 1991a). And suddenly we see a peculiar type of merchandise—"technotronic" merchandise— whose value in terms of utility not only generates the satisfaction of material ownership and social position but simultaneously offers the opportunity to satisfy needs of a far more profound and qualitatively different kind: needs of the symbolical order. That is—to invoke Maslow's progressive schema of the scale of needs (see Maslow 1963)— we are dealing with object goods that present themselves as (real or fictitious) satisfiers of higher needs: functional substitutes for the institutions of socialization in traditional society. Modern means of communication—a television set, a videocassette player, a personal computer, or a cellular telephone, to cite a few examples—do more than merely enable the subject to enter more easily into contact with other subjects. That is, they not only act as means of communication between a "sender" and a "receiver"; they become veritable "electronic icons," with all of the ambiguity of their sacred content (Cox 1979): they become tremendous and fascinating. They constitute symbolical merchandise that actually makes it possible to "reinvent" an entire, radically distinct world, a world that transcends the restricting confines of daily life, and in that sense merchandise that "changes the life" of the receiver/subject. The use value here is "symbolical." That is, the utility in question is no longer merely that of the functionality of goods, but now spills over into the possibility of a "creative" entry into a "different world" (if only in appearance, since what it often generates is a new passivity, a new form of alienation). Here the "use" does not consume the good; it consumes the life of the subject—but it does so in a seeming act of productive "transformation" (transforming the "nature" of the everyday into a "second nature"), the "Brave New World" of the cultural industry. This new world is reenchanting our old world with new fantasies and mysteries, incidentally producing new social and collective identifications, and assembling new ensembles—quantitatively scattered and isolated in the crowd, in the "mass," it is true, but engendering, by virtue of the emblematic or symbolical nature of this new type of "symbolism-producing" merchandise, new feelings of "belonging" and of social solidarity. The need to be integrated into this "new world" of "technotronics," the new electronic religion,[8] thus becomes a "basic" need—that of being reintegrated into the new, emerging world, a reintegration occurring on the basis of the satisfaction of basic needs and the competition for the acquisition of the goods of social "distinction."

With the growth of productivity and mass production, this "technotronic" type of goods becomes gradually more accessible in the globalized market. Then, as the masses have more and more access to this new merchandise whose use value is symbolization, there is no longer any "need" to invent new worlds: such worlds come readymade, at the accessible, inexpensive exchange value of this new merchandise. The need to own something, including private property, is no longer as decisive as it once was, or is so only in appearance. What is decisive now is this new need to share in the "New World" symbolically produced by technotronic merchandise.

Admittedly, in postindustrial society, another, nontechnotronic, type of merchandise acquires this symbolizing capacity as well: drugs, sports, martial arts, or Asian-style cults, for example. In this fashion,

---

8. Religion, from *re-ligare*, to "re-link": the need to "connect" with an electronic icon that is invested with transcendental power to create and regenerate various worlds.

as technological science gradually penetrates the everyday of contemporary life, far from any functionalization of life at the hands of that science, life finds itself "resignified."[9] We need only think, for example, of the enormous creative energy invested in the production of television material, such as films produced for television and especially the television serials, like the familiar Latin American "teleseries." Access to the "New World" is not always direct. It frequently occurs in vicarious terms, through the mechanisms of communicational symbolization.

We are faced with a new reality, then, and in this new reality, one thing is certain: daily life has ceased to be "humdrum," "flat," and "disenchanted." Today, in this new world, life's routine is broken, filled to overflowing with new fantasies—almost like actual dreams—entertained by a society whose utopian aspirations have dozed off and whose alienating dream presents itself as the new utopia. The quantitative, the extensive, "having more," no longer presents any problem. Now we face a system of needs in function of which human beings must "change worlds"—participate as spectators at an undertaking of symbolical transformation in which their secret yearnings are transmuted into "needs" to be satisfied only by this new market of technotronic goods.

Thus, a new sociological fact characterizes the closing decades of the twentieth century. With recent modernizations, technology—unlike earlier technology, with its power of "disenchantment"—is generating a dialectic of *secularization/sacralization.* Secular goods are transformed by the modern technotronic industry into new myths, entailing a "resacralization" of the very spaces of functionality introduced by technological scientific rationality itself. The resacralizing vectors of this emerging society are displacing the traditional religions, to be sure. And yet, on occasion they engender spaces in which the old religions are actually regenerated through internal transformations or new religions and religious movements emerge.

## Underdeveloped Capitalistic Modernization

The impact of this "informatic" capitalistic modernization becomes much more dramatic in underdeveloped societies by reason of the peculiar nature of their historical processes. Such societies are dependent on the world markets and system. Furthermore, they are characterized by an internal structural heterogeneity. Add to these

---

9. See an interesting debate on the impact of modern scientific technology on the cultural life of East and West in L. Morren (1989).

considerations the fact that the three industrial revolutions analyzed above occur in parallel and in complex conjunction, and we see that the complex modernization of which we speak occurs in the context of an extremely uneven society.

In the underdeveloped and peripheral world, processes unfold in a qualitatively distinct way from the manner in which they have developed in other societies, whose modernity has come to them in the past. In modern industrial or manufacturing activity, as in the formal and modern sector of the Latin American economy generally, the modernizing process does not occur in such a manner as to affect the awareness of the laborers as a group, who work there in identical fashion. This is because, on the one hand, the system is modernized in a differential way and does not require that the workers as a group have the same preparation and qualifications and because, on the other hand, workers in the modern formal enterprise, while subject to modern technological relations with that enterprise, can enter into these relations without participating fully, or with minimal participation, in its modern, Enlightenment ethos. The ethos of the classic industrial modern enterprise is characterized by a cognitive frame of reference having its roots in the Cartesian paradigm, where the pragmatic meaning of technology supposes a causal relation in terms of the patterns of Newtonian mechanics. But with the informatic revolution and the change in the paradigms of contemporary physics, that ethos of the modern, formal enterprise is being rapidly transformed, thereby impinging on the consciousness of those who work in that enterprise. Furthermore, the tendency of the services sector to grow, together with the growth in the informal sector of the underdeveloped economies, determines a twin process. On the one side we have the reproduction of nonmodern, traditional productive forms, and on the other, the emergence, in parallel, of productive forms of very advanced informatic technology, with its complexity-fraught rationality, which raises levels of uncertainty, demolishing the "instrumental" paradigms of predictability with which productive forms were invested in the earlier, Cartesian industrial mentality. In both spaces, the world appears as less manageable, more arbitrary; thus, a symbolical niche is generated in which there is greater probability of a resurgence of the mysteries that for centuries have tormented human consciousness.

The modernization of society and of the economy, which has been so rapid in recent decades in nearly all of our countries, from Mexico to Patagonia, betrays the presence of a struggling, secularized society. But this is only the tip of the iceberg. Coexisting with urban landscapes of modern buildings and shining skyscrapers are the millions of dismal, wretched shacks and hovels that stretch across the cities and countryside of our lands. Structural heterogenization translates not only into a tertiarization of the economy, into the widening poles of uneven local and regional development, into a very broad diversity of technological development among enterprises, and into very diverse levels of the productivity of labor in the economy; structural heterogenization also translates into a growth in the informal economies and their marginal markets, semilegal and illegal. All of these infrastructural processes engender conditions for nonmodern social practices—not by virtue of automatisms or determinisms deriving from a "reflex theory" (now in disuse), but through the dialectic of the daily, concrete practices of production and reproduction on the part of the subordinate subjects who escape the market and its logic of exchange value.

As long as the comprehensive logic of accumulation continues to operate, according to which the needs of ownership constitute the key to the system, the popular classes will—in general terms—have their basic needs unsatisfied. Meanwhile, the powerful classes succeed in reaching a market that need by no means envy the markets of the metropolises.

The popular classes are in a doubly prejudicial situation. They do not have their basic needs satisfied, and the mechanisms of economic adjustment impoverish them still further; nevertheless they receive the influence of a market and its marketing—which, often enough, they seek to resist, overtly or unintentionally—that simultaneously spawns the needs of position and symbolization. And the more traumatic the situation of misery and exploitation, the stronger the tendency to seek a "way out" by the purchase of goods of symbolical use, be these the technotronic (television sets, videocassette players), the traditional "secular," such as drugs, gambling, drink, or the traditional religious, such as the revival of magico-religious practices and rites.

But in the dialectic of history, all modernization is the vehicle of contradictions whose manifestation can occur as processes or utopias of countermodernization. In that case we are dealing with an underground dynamic. We refer to counterprocesses that host the seeds of alternative sociocultural constructions—on the basis of the rebuilding of the past (reactionary), or of the building of the future (revolutionary)—although conditions today may not be adequate for their realization, if indeed they ever will be. In our era, the culture industry produces this new symbol-producing merchandise, and although what it sells in the market is "canned culture, in pieces" (exchange value), still, by its "uses and readings" (use value), it takes up the task of reviving the fantasies of ritual symbolism—the magic and the mystery—in a word, the mythic background of humanity, a background now functionalized in terms of the logic of exchange. But the human mentality in these modern surroundings rebels and turns its gaze toward the old gods in a ceaseless spiritual quest. Thus, the reenchantment of the world, in the light of the crisis of this modernity, engenders movements of piety—principally nonreligious (or secular) in developed societies, and specifically of a religious kind in the societies of the Third World.

In Latin America, the "higher needs"—religious needs—once upon a time so out of favor or even called into question as alienating (and having alienating functions, indeed, in many concrete instances), appear and reappear as the source of a "system of needs" now reassumed by the human. This is a system of needs that can be found in the world of objects and transactions which, in consort with other contributing elements, weave the warp and woof of popular culture, of that popular culture that has fallen between the cracks of the system and is integrated only marginally into the contemporary formal market, where merchandise and its exchange value and the modernizing ethos of industry reign supreme.

Indeed, industrial workers, doomed to a dire fate because of deindustrialization, are only partially exposed to the modernizing dynamics of the world of labor and its classic technologies. Like the "invisible" majorities, they are exposed to the new technotronic technologies and their resymbolizing capacity. Because of these unbalanced, "heterogenizing" processes of modernization occurring in Latin America, the social majorities are under constant threat of failing to ensure their daily subsistence, and so their symbolical world must be strengthened through the legitimations of the sacred cosmos in order that they may be protected or have new energies infused into them. This explains why the popular culture appears, in many concrete cases, as a partially resistant culture or, in others, as a counterculture to the official dominant, modernizing culture. In the world of the object-goods of this popular culture (goods not necessarily having an exchange value), the religious object is resignified by the popular culture in alternative codes to those commonly assigned it by official religion. In the case of the popular cultures, the "electronic icon" tends to be obfuscated by real "religious icons" of those cultures' own symbolical production.

## Dynamics and Complexity of Relative "Secularization"

In conclusion, we may assert that the processes of capitalistic urbanization in the Latin American situation, by virtue of our continent's underdevelopment and dependency, do not automatically lead to a process of secularization that would dissolve the whole religious sense of the popular classes. Our structural transformations tend to "modernize" certain spheres of public life, especially under the influence of primary schooling and the media. But in parallel and complex articulation, there are two additional processes. First, the new forms assumed by the economy in these countries broaden certain conditions of exploitation and marginalization, suffered by vast popular masses, that predispose these masses naturally to resist certain secularizing factors in the modernization that has been implanted. And second, the introduction of the revolutionary cultural guidelines of the new technologies gives rise to spaces of mythic/symbolical resignification: those guidelines "cook up the right kind of soup" for the revitalization of religious practices and beliefs. In other words, capitalistic modernization and its pluralizing, ever more complex, logic create conditions for a "secularization" in the classic sense, yes; but in the same movement they provide the wherewithal for the dialectical defeat of that tendency in the "resacralization" of modern life. That resacralization is accentuated, in the form of a qualitative leap that transmutes it, in the underdeveloped and dependent countries through the very contradictions and paradoxes upon which the modernizing processes in these regions undergo their evolution.

At the same time, the concrete historical shift in the churches, with their "preferential option for the poor," has fostered—at least to some extent—a reencounter with the network of daily practices maintained in the popular cultures. This fosters conditions under which the religious traditions of the churches are transformed. The transformation is still a doubtful one because of the involution of the orientations of Catholicism toward a more conservative (yet populist) politics and of the aggressive penetration of fundamentalist denominations and sects in recent years. In particular, the Catholic Church could lose its major influence among the popular masses more integrated into the modernizing processes, by reviving religious traditions of doubtful future effectiveness because of a spirit of rigidity in adapting to change.

To be sure, the structural evolution introduced by the processes of capitalistic urbanization and industrialization have an influence on the religious field. In the instance of the Latin American popular classes, as we have seen and shall see more in depth further on, the religious sense is not vanishing, but is being transformed. Surely there is a gradual rationalization of religious beliefs and practices among the people, and these beliefs and practices depend on the class conditionings of their subjects. But the subjects' religious convictions tenaciously resist, on the strength of a passive or active acculturation, and reproduce a religion transformed in its expressions and significates; or the subjects creatively invent new religious responses to the challenges of structural, cultural, and historical changes, as we shall likewise see in coming chapters.

After all, the field of religious symbolism is not only the orientator but also the result of the practices of the social actors. The latter act in the space delimited by structural conditionings, but when structures change by reason of economic or political factors, phases of disorder are produced in very unstable, insecure conjunctures. This provokes the unraveling of the prevailing coherencies of religious symbolism and the emergence of new concrete practices that generate, and are legitimated in, new symbolical representations.

Thus, an adequate sociological understanding and explanation of the transformations under way in the religious expressions of the Latin American people must take account, simultaneously and complementarily, of the structural and historical dynamics in which the actors live and move.

Accordingly, the ensemble of sociological factors that we have just described issues in a process of secularization that should be understood much more as a process of *transformation of religious mentality* than as an irreversible decline in the faith of the people. Again, we shall analyze this phenomenon at greater depth in the chapters to follow.

The transformations in question go in two directions, but in mutual dependency. On the one side, on the basis of a more or less common Catholic tradition we see a *pluralization* of religious expressions among the popular masses. On the other, we have a *relative rationalization* of beliefs and rituals, especially in groups more exposed to the modernizing urban ethos. But we must not forget that these two tendencies in the transformation of the popular religions are processed by the people's *religious creativity*, which—under the stimulus of modern informatic technology—can tend to re-create a fervor of religious symbolism much more inclined to the festive, the multitudinous, the magical, the mystical, and to the messianic aspirations latent in the—implicit or overt—potential for protest residing in popular symbolism. This last factor sometimes acts as the detonator of new popular religious models, broadening the spectrum of religious expression, and sometimes it weakens this tendency; but in any case it blocks a certain type of secularistic and rationalistic rationalization by stirring up the religious embers that, at various temperatures, smolder in the popular mentality.

## PART THREE

# LIFE

*Nobody ever got drunk on the basis of an intellectual understanding of the word "wine."*

Anthony de Mello

*Be this, then, thy consolation,*
*For this is a thing that's sure:*
*From here to Glory I fly.*
*See there!  Ah, there at the gate*
*The angels of Paradise await me!*

*Need I not open that gate*
*For my parents, and brothers and sisters?*
*Let them only show, at their death,*
*That they die all contrite*
*For tasting Eden!*

*Mourning?  Not for me!*
*No need, for I am in bliss.*
*I go now to the Lord of Sinai,*
*That God to beseech*
*For those who linger below.*

Adolfo Reyes, popular poet

# Chapter 5

# Popular Faith and the Meaning of Life

The popular religion of Latin Americans is alive and well wherever they live. As far off as Stockholm, political refugees of the Southern Cone (Chile and Argentina) anxiously seek out a priest to baptize their children or schedule a wake. The Month of Mary and novenas are everywhere, even in the most scattered locales. It is scarcely strange that the more than forty million Latins of the North American population maintain their customs and religious rituals with faithfulness and devotion.

## Faith: Central and Diversified

It is becoming more and more common to meet, among the inhabitants of the poor neighborhoods of the Latin American city and countryside, small communities of faithful or chapels brimming with a fervent, renewed faith. Indeed, there is a very broad spectrum of expressions of that faith. The faith of Chicanos and Mexicans in the inner city, or on the edges of large North American and Mexican cities, and the faith of the South American exiles in Europe are surely different. The faith of young persons whose leftist militancy has been inspired in a religious mystique contrasts with the faith of the *volados*, the "flown" young drug addicts, who are utter outcasts as far as official urban society is concerned, although they may share the same inspiration in a secret youth counterculture. In turn, the Aymara or Quechua miners of the Andes (in Oruro, Potosí, Cuzco, La Tirana), with their dances and expressive rituals, with their devotion to the Virgin (the *Pachamama*, the "Earth Mother"), and with their ancestral beliefs, do not much resemble the members of the many Pentecostal congregations of São Paulo, Bogotá, Quito, born again in the Spirit, with their frenzied worship and ecstatic glossolalia, who are multiplying as well in the marginal neighborhoods of nearly all of the great capitals of Latin America. These experiences, in turn, differ from those of the Afro-Cuban *Santería*, or Haitian voodoo, or the mass manifestations of Salvadoran Catholicism that have made Archbishop Oscar Romero a veritable popular saint. All of these manifestations, however, in all of their diversity, share the common traits of a popular counterculture that stands over against the official, dominant culture, and are independent of that culture.

All of these phenomena are expressions of a very wide gamut of manifestations, but they all reveal one thing: the ability of the people, on the basis of their common sense, in the midst of their diverse situations and experiences, to re-create religious meaning. Just as it is impossible to speak of "the popular worldview," as if it were one, consistent, and homogeneously distributed, so it is unthinkable to employ the category "popular religion" in a simple, univocal way, as if by the simple operation of conceptual abstraction we could blur the real differences that make up the texture of concrete religions and cultures. But the plurality is not absolute or chaotic. Still, there exist certain identifiable common traits, however impermeable to typology, in the sense of a cultural and religious grammar common to all of the subordinate sectors.

To all of the proper cultural paraphernalia of the people—oral tradition, ancestral roots (native American, African, and Iberian, among the majority of Latin Americans), class styles, historical memory, and, finally, popular creativity—must be added the various social and cultural influences of official society: churches' socialization, the influence of the school and the media, on one side, and the influences of the "vulgarization" of official culture by means of the popularization of science, technology, and philosophy, on the other. All of this merges in a dynamic process—via the field of the popular actor's daily, concrete practices—shaping an original popular vision and practice, which many times have a strange appearance to the eyes of official culture and its intellectual elite. It is a submerged, bobbing, unevenly distributed worldview which does not always show its actual roots and whose blossoms, although not of the fragrance and species so finely cultivated by high culture, are of a peerless vitality.

By now we have come to recognize that the Latin American people have a profound religious sense, manifested, as we see, in differential and complex fashion. This religious sense is part of the common popular sense—not, however, in the form of some static component, but having a dynamism of its own, accentuated by changing historical circumstances. True, particular conjunctures foster these expressions. But they constitute an incontestable fact, and they stand as a living refutation of the thesis that popular piety is merely some traditional, archaic thing, surviving only among the peasantry of the countryside.

In many urban conjunctures, public, massive demonstrations of faith are very much in evidence. A piety that seemed confined to the private sphere needs only a favorable concrete event as the catalyst to make it blossom with uncontainable force (Gogolok 1986). The common sense of the broadest majorities of Mexicans, South Americans, Central Americans, Caribbeans, and so on, hosts a secret hope in the supernatural forces that signify a symbolical opportunity of survival, sometimes of cultural resistance, or in any case a wellspring of security and meaning not found in other, secular symbolical referents, be these ideological, artistic, or political, let alone in those proceeding from the official culture. As a "songstress"[1] of the people indicated to me one day, "Faith is the most sublime thing. Faith is the most important thing, even if you're out of the church. Faith is in everybody, in all persons."

## Religion and Popular Common Sense

The consistent, multiform presence of the figure of God in Latin America's popular religion appears to be the most salient fact of that religion. In research done in popular sectors, the proportion of believers in God varies between 96% and 99%. In terms of beliefs, in second place and very close to the figure of God comes Jesus Christ (between 95% and 97%), the central figure in a culture whose roots are in the Christian universe. Next, with less relative relevancy, the Holy Spirit (85-90%) and the Virgin Mary (80-84%) are mentioned, and here we should probably see the influence of the traditional catechism and its insistence on a triune God. What is sure, however, is that majoritarian popular religion believes cognitively, but with less intensity, in Jesus Christ (except the Protestants). By contrast, Catholics believe with greater devotion in the Virgin Mary, to the point that, for some scholars, the popular Trinity is constituted, in heterodox fashion, by the divine family: God the Father, the Virgin Mother, and Jesus the Son, in a descending/inferior divine scale. Belief in the saints is also very widespread in the popular mentality.

---

1. A woman of the people who devotes herself to folkloric music and song.

God, understood as Father and Creator, powerful and benevolent, caring for and remembering his children—human beings—"is the most basic reality of popular piety" (González 1987:59). A profession of faith in God, far from being the mere enunciation of a rational conviction, is the transmission of a vital experience. This is a constant among broad sectors of the popular culture. God is not only the original Cause of life, but the Force that sustains it. The faith of the social actors who live in a situation of misery and exploitation is not the product of a simple custom introjected in processes of early socialization and exteriorized as a rooted habitual attitude; faith here is the product of an experience of divine providence, although the verbal argumentations offered may not show this. These persons may report, instead, that they believe "because my parents taught me"; "because there must be a Supreme Being"; "because if I believe, I can save my soul"; and so on. Belief in God—and the weight of the Christian image of God is decisive here—is not, in this sense, a "traditional custom," a simple cultural trait. Nor therefore is it necessarily accompanied, in the popular common sense, by formal membership in the churches or religious institutions.

Up until the close of the nineteenth century, Christianity (in its Roman Catholic form) discharged a comprehensive function and was hegemonic in the cultural field and the mentality of the impoverished Latin American masses. Christianity, as we have seen, penetrated America with the *Conquista* and, together with the introduction of the Hispano-Lusitanian mercantile and military logic, had a profound cultural impact on pre-Columbian society. That society disintegrated, in some cases disappearing altogether through extinction or absorption. And yet the "indigenous element," with its particular worldview and its profound, deep-core religious sense, despite all of its disarticulation and subjugation, became a key component of emerging Latin American culture. Undeniably, the indigenous root is present —frequently in underground fashion (in societies such as the Argentinian or the Uruguayan), at other times openly (in Peru, Bolivia, Ecuador, Guatemala, Mexico, and so on)—in the hybrid culture of the subordinate classes, even in the large Latin American cities.[2] In those

---

2. Farrel and Lumerman, in research into popular piety in the supposedly most Westernized and secularized of Latin American cities, Buenos Aires, state: "The cultural nucleus that originates in native thought subsists today in the Creole population, which in our time has come to form the very core of the great city. And although it seems to have no direct relationship with the indigenous world, somehow underlying it is an ensemble of characteristics that it has carried with it since times long gone by" (Farrel and Lumerman 1979:20-21).

regions where the colonial enterprise once "imported" a slave labor force, the African cultural composition, with its strong animistic religious sense, feeds cultural roots as well and becomes an additional, integral component—*mulatto, zambo* (of mixed native blood), *caboclo, garífuna*, and so on—of the Latin American cultural hybrid.

This composite base (Hispano-Lusitanian, native, African)—with greater or lesser weight in function of each specific situation and the development of each region and country in terms of its cultural history—is the sociocultural base of the popular majorities (even of the proletariat). It constitutes an objective (although not always conscious) counterpoise to the culture of the middle classes and privileged minorities as well as to what is called the "national culture" (which is a great deal more influenced by an enlightened, bourgeois culture of European origin as well as, more recently, by transnational culture)—mass culture, the culture of the market and its "American way of life."

Practically all studies and reports on the religious mentality in Latin American popular sectors agree: faith is present as something per se evident—an unquestioned dictate of common sense (Parker 1986a:201-7).

## Urban Popular Religion

In typological terms, abstracting from its manifest heterogeneity, popular religion shares certain traits that set it apart from the more traditional religious forms, those of peasant origin.[3] To the extent that the masses living in the popular barrios consist of recently emigrated generations of peasantry, popular piety among them will preserve purer traits of rural religious forms, with all of the characteristic elements of their locale of origin. But as the population becomes settled in its urban habitat and is socially and symbolically incorporated into the urban way of life and urban values, its religion is affected. At this point, a transformation of religious consciousness occurs, without this meaning a complete abandonment of the deeper traditions of the group in question.

Indeed, available data and studies on urban popular religions in

---

3. See Arboleda (1983), Bentué (1975), Büntig (1969, 1970, 1973a, 1973b), Carutti and Martínez (1974), Gabaja (1972), Houghton Perez (1979), Irarrázaval (1978), Kudo (1980), Lalive and Zylberberg (1973), López (1972), Martínez et al. (1979), Parker et al. (1982), Parker (1986a, 1992a), Poblete (1970), Pollak-Eltz (1974), Rodrigues (1987), Rolim (1980), Zenteno (1972).

Latin America display, on the whole, a panorama that appears paradoxical to the eyes of an enlightened mentality. A secularist rationalization of the beliefs of the popular masses does not always occur with the advance of their social and cultural urbanization. In fact, magic and superstition actually undergo a revitalization. The growing influence of the Pentecostal movements, the Afro-American cults, and religious magic in popular Catholicism demonstrate that underdeveloped urbanization can also spark transformations of the religious field that, far from diminishing magic, symbolism, and religious fervor, increase them by stimulating religious creativity among the people.

In the case of so-called popular Catholicism, certain salient traits are verified by thousands of pastoral workers in their contact with the people in the urban periphery. True, this is only one particular model of popular religion among many; but it must be acknowledged, as empirical evidence further demonstrates, that it is without a doubt the most generalized and extensive one. In significant sectors of the popular masses, however, Catholicism manifests itself only in massive pilgrimages to shrines (generally those of the Virgin Mary or popular saints) and in certain "rites of passage" (baptism, First Communion, marriage, wakes), and not in weekly Sunday practice. A goodly part of popular Catholicism is "nonpracticing," in the sense that its devotions and beliefs develop independently of the official pastoral ministry and the various sacramental practices prescribed by the Church as an institution. Nevertheless, subsequent to the introduction of elements of renewal by Vatican Council II, Medellín, and Puebla, a new panorama in the parishes of popular neighborhoods began to be fairly common. Not only did lay participation in parish life grow; the little cells of renewal of Latin American Christianity that are the small base church communities began to proliferate (see Alvear et al. 1983, Gomes de Souza 1982, Perani 1981, Rolim 1980, Zenteno 1979).

Popular Catholicism is far less inclined to typical expressions of folklore or to public or mass expressions of devotion in the city than it is in the countryside. Urban religion seems to become privatized, and other spheres of life take over the "mass encounter" function: political meetings, sporting events, secular festivals, and so on. But the religious element is still manifested in popular daily life in families and in collective neighborhood celebrations (Month of Mary, Palm Sunday, Holy Week, parish life), as well as in the new devotions and popular rituals of the cities (urban shrines, votive offerings, processions, urban folkloric beliefs, and the like). Feasts of patron saints take on a different meaning in the city; but certain popularized practices subsist with greater intensity in the churches of large cities, such as the blessing of the palms on Palm Sunday. In the pious belief of oral tradition, the blessed branches are to be placed behind doors at home for good luck and to avoid evils and catastrophes.

"This piety is less exuberant, less expressive, less ritualistic. It is certainly less 'practicing.' Therefore it is more difficult to recognize and verify. But its roots are real and deep," Segundo Galilea (1977:16) once declared, and his intuition retains its validity.

In the context of urban life and of the values introjected from the media and the school by the inhabitant of the popular barrio, he or she loses direct contact with nature. In the city, workers or subproletarians are much more closely bound to a set of social institutions, and contact with the earth and its natural cycles is lost. Now the religious experience is mediated by sociocultural factors, and not by natural, biological factors. It is not surprising that these persons' forms of religious experience, their representations of God and of the bond of the supernatural with life, should also be transformed. Workers and subproletarians in the city no longer depend on imponderable natural cycles for their survival; now they depend on finding work or, by default, on their own "strategies" of subsistence. Their religiousness no longer constitutes a direct solution to their needs. It becomes much more a periodical piety, rekindled by certain moments of passage or by certain critical periods of life: the birth of a child, an illness, a tragedy, unemployment, marriage, death, and so on. "It is not always a matter of a continuous attitude; it is a matter of moments of greater intensity, very experiential, that stir the more or less latent embers of the popular religious soul" (Galilea 1977:17).

All of the ritual and devotional expressions, beliefs, and practices in question foster, on the basis of everyday life, a sense of the meaning of life in the popular subject. They do this by "resemanticizing" a common sense that must confront adversity at every moment. Beneath the hotchpotch of significants (rites, beliefs, myths, devotions, symbols, signs, words, expressions, and so on) lies a significate code in movement, constituting the core of that communicational field that is the religion of the people. This manifestation of popular religion is significant because it accompanies the evolution of life, while at the same time nourishing that life with a "more" of meaning. This sense of life—in a subject steeped in contradictory Latin American modern society and open to the invasion of the culture industry and its resacralizing effects—is reinforced by its peculiar way of decodifying the series of messages that it daily receives in its social life.

### Beginning of Life: Baptism

It would be unthinkable, in the popular mentality, to leave a baby without baptism. The identification between being a Christian and the social existence of the person is so powerful that the sacrament associating the two realities acquires an absolutely obligatory character for access to social life. Furthermore, baptism has a pristine meaning of symbolical protection: a baby cannot be left a "Moor" or unprotected in the face of adversities and evils.

When it comes to establishing the importance attributed to baptism by the Latin American people, it is interesting that, for Catholic baptisms, studies indicate a rate of over 90%. In Mexico, a survey of broad samplings over the last seven years of the 1960s in 24 different parishes of the country (not exclusively urban, as in Mexico City) yielded approximately the same mean proportions: 97-98% of the persons surveyed were reported as having been baptized (Mendoza 1979:37). In Chile, one of the most relatively "secularized" of Latin American countries, spot checks in six popular-sector parishes in 1987 and in 1990 report an average baptismal rate of between 96.4% and 98.3%. Let us note that, while we are speaking primarily of Catholic baptisms, the sacrament is basically shared by all of the Christian churches.

The following comparative data on birth rates and percentages of Catholic baptisms in various countries (table 7) are a good indicator of the importance of this fundamental sacrament—shared with all of the Christian churches—for the Latin American people.

As we observe, the difference between the overall raw birth rate and the coefficient of baptisms among Catholics is low, except in the cases of Nicaragua and Peru in 1975. We must note, however, that in the birth rate, the rates of neonatal mortality and infant mortality are not discounted, whereas we do not know whether this is the case for the baptisms. It is worth pointing out that, for 1987-88, the difference between the number of Catholic baptisms and the number of live births is lower. Thus, except for the case of Nicaragua (where the difference is up by 2.2 per mil.) we observe no tendency to a diminution in the number of baptisms among Catholics; on the contrary, we note a slight relative growth here. Given the percentage increase of Protestantism throughout Latin America and the Caribbean, the overall raw rate of baptisms (Catholics and Protestants together) may be presumed to have been maintained, or actually to have increased, in those years.

Table 7: Comparative Birth and Baptismal Rates in Latin America
(by thousands)

| | 1975 | | | 1982-1988 | | | |
|---|---|---|---|---|---|---|---|
| | Birth | Baptism (0-7 yrs.) | Diff. | Birth | Baptism (0-7 yrs.) | Diff. | Total Diff. |
| Argentina | 21.4 | 21.7 | -0.3 | 21.4 | 21.1 | 0.3 | -0.6 |
| Colombia | 33.8 | 26.6 | 7.2 | 29.2 | 25.3 | 3.9 | 3.3 |
| Costa Rica | 29.1 | 27.9 | 1.2 | 28.9 | 29.6 | -0.7 | 1.9 |
| Chile | 25.4 | 18.0 | 7.4 | 22.3 | 17.0 | 5.3 | 2.1 |
| Guatemala | 41.1 | 35.9 | 5.2 | 38.5 | 33.3 | 5.2 | 0.0 |
| Mexico | 37.5 | 35.6 | 1.9 | 29.0 | 27.6 | 1.4 | 0.5 |
| Nicaragua | 46.6 | 31.8 | 14.8 | 41.8 | 24.8 | 17.0 | -2.2 |
| Peru | 39.7 | 23.5 | 16.2 | 34.9 | 20.9 | 14.0 | 2.2 |
| Mean | 34.3 | 27.6 | 6.7 | 30.8 | 25.0 | 5.8 | 0.9 |

Sources: Vatican, Secretary of State 1975, 1988; United Nations 1990

As we know, since the period of the Conquest itself, baptism has been one of the rituals that are most extensive in time and space. In colonial Christendom, an attempt was made to distinguish and separate rites of initiation directed by clerics from autochthonous or syncretic rites of initiation. Generally speaking, although there were exceptions, during the first years of the colonization baptism was part of a coercive order. However, it has been adopted and adapted as a syncretic ritual by the people, in a mentality in which a goodly part of an original sense of Christendom endures.

The meaning given to baptism in popular sectors—in conformity with popular common sense—involves more than the official meaning of incorporation into the Church and access to a new life cleansed of original sin. In various cultures and subcultures, while the meaning of baptism may vary, it does so on the basis of a common significative matrix that is independent of the official one. For example, in the

Andean—Quechua and syncretic—culture, baptism is celebrated in order to make its recipients "be Christian," "be folk, and not mountain *chunchos* [buzzards]" (Marzal 1988). The answer was, at bottom, the same as that of displaced rural folk settled in Santiago de Chile when we asked, "Why do you have your children baptized?" There too the frequent reply was, "So that they won't be like little animals," "Otherwise they're little animals," or "To make them Christians." In a 1987 survey in Santiago de Chile, 65%, and in 1990 58.3%, of those interviewed answered in the affirmative when asked, "Do you believe that an unbaptized child is like a little animal and falls ill more readily?" Although persons of rural origin tend to assert this popular belief more frequently than do those born in the city, the difference does not seem particularly significant; by contrast, the influence of the primary-education variable is relevant.

There is an identification, in the popular semantic codes, between being a Christian and being a member of society. A person not integrated into Christianity is outside civilization. He or she remains in the state of nature, or "is like a little animal." It is actually the old Hispanic tradition that is being resemanticized here, according to which an unbaptized person "remains a Moor," with the assimilation of "Moor" to "little animal" or "mountain buzzard." It is difficult not to see here the residue of a mentality of colonial Christendom that tended to identify being a Christian with being a member of official society— with being a subject of the monarchs of Spain or Portugal, the defenders of Christendom. In the ideological version of colonial Christendom, an unbaptized person, the native American or the black, was an "idolater," and therefore to be excluded from the dominant society. In its most extreme version, such a one will be reduced to the category of "barbarian"—the lowest limit of the human condition— with an accompanying legitimation of the exploitation of natives and enslavement of blacks. In the popular version, however, the significate proper to the colonial culture is reinterpreted. In the popular version, being a Christian is interpreted as forming part of the popular, believing "us"—that is, simultaneously as "child of God" and "child of the people"—whereby the individual is dignified by the bestowal of personal identification through a personal name, with the connotation (not always precise and explicit) of popular identity, as opposed to the "otherness" of the dominant, modernizing culture.

Thus we have a symbolical reappropriation: a colonial ethnocentric significate (baptism in the colonial ideology) reverts to a popular ethnocentric significate (baptism in the context of the popular culture). The rereading in question is a collective rereading—not always conscious for the individual—of a very important component of the dominant culture, revealing a "resistant adaptation" on the part of the popular culture.

Baptism further constitutes, in popular Latin American culture, a factor interlacing social relations through that so deeply rooted institution, *compadrazgo*, godparenthood. (The baby's godparents have an importance in the ceremony as great as, or more than, the baby being baptized.) Baptism is an occasion for the establishment of alliances that, once upon a time, were alliances among extended kin; now they link family members, neighbors, and friends, thus constituting a broad system of ritual kinship. The importance of *compadrazgo* resides precisely in the fact that it establishes and sacralizes a traditional structure of social relations in the popular culture. For this same reason, godparenthood as a social relationship contains its ambiguity as well: while it reinforces the popular culture itself, it can also be a factor reproducing traditional bonds of subordination/dependency, both in the family structure and in the subordination of inferiors to their superiors in interclass relations (Codina and Irarrázaval 1987:28-29).

Baptism is also an occasion for festival—for a gathering of family members and friends. How can we fail to see here a factor of religious culture of enormous symbolical significance—an element of identification, self-dignification, and cultural resistance and the vehicle of the social relations that support such a weighty part of the framework of popular culture?

It is incorporation into the human world. By one's name, one accedes to personhood; through the collective rite, one accedes to the religious world, and that world is intimately associated with the self-identification of the social group qua popular culture—the world of the popular "we."

Not surprisingly, in the constitution of the popular field of religious symbolism, an element of the collective identity—enunciated in the lexeme "we"—is closely bound up with the profession of religious faith. In this way, religion in its popular form fulfills a symbolical function—that of managing threatening occurrences, reinforcing energies for survival, ensuring cultural resistance, and designing a common sense of "us," "workers," "poor," or "lower class," or "Christians," thus tracing a line of demarcation between this group and the "them," the "rich," and the "bosses," who are qualitatively foreign because they "don't believe in God or anything else" (Kudo 1980:69-89).

## Origin and Increase of Life: The Virgin Mother

Across our continent, popular religion is structured on the basis of shrines, pilgrimages, promises, devotions, votive offerings, and festivals. The Virgin Mary and the saints are the symbol, icon, and significate articulating these expressions. But beyond any doubt, it is the image of Mary, on the foundation of a Christian cultural background, that crowds out nearly everything else in the panorama of profound devotion.

The central position of the figure of the Virgin Mary is another characteristic trait of Latin American popular religion. For Evangelicals, of course, the figure of Mary either has no importance (one does not "believe in her") or is rejected. In research that we have done in Santiago de Chile, we have observed that, while only 75% of the population surveyed proclaim themselves Catholic, 83% assert "belief" in Mary. In popular religion, however much we may discern circumstantial indifference to and mistrust of ecclesiastical culture, we see a faith in the Creator, in the Virgin Mary, and in her Son Jesus Christ, to the effusive accompaniment of song, prayer, pilgrimage, and festival.

Unlike official theology, for which the concept of an intermediary between God and human beings is ontologically defined in terms of nondivinity, for the religion of the people categories are not so crisply differentiated. Indeed, popular faith seems to classify sacred beings not on the criterion of their ontological character, but on that of their sacred power; that is, it appears to classify them on the criterion of their capacity to intervene "miraculously" in the world of the living. We know the central place held by the "saints" in the popular pantheon. In the figure of the saints (among whom are included the Virgin Mary in her various capacities of advocacy, Jesus Christ, and the canonized saints) the dimension of intercessor before God is of far greater importance than that of a model of life. "The capacity for intercession is due to the saint's sharing, in some sort, by virtue of being a follower and messenger of God, in the divine power" (Marzal 1988:47).

It is power that counts, and therefore symbolical effectiveness—the ability to act in supernatural fashion and to produce mysterious realities that simultaneously fascinate and frighten. For the faithful popular devotee, the Virgin Mary is one of these "mighty" mediators. Not only is she the Mother of God; she is the Mother of all human beings besides, and she watches over these children of hers (González

1987). Her capacity for intercession before God the Father, in her quality as spokesperson of human beings' supplications and requests, is guaranteed precisely by her privileged place in the pantheon, a place in which she has comparative advantages over the other saints. It becomes difficult to assert whether, in the popular mentality, the Virgin is regarded as a female deity or merely as a very special saint. In any case, Mary as the most privileged of mediators belongs to the legacy of the popular religion of Latin America, especially of its Catholicism.

The Virgin, as the figure second in importance in the popular religious pantheon, in some cases is even above her son Jesus Christ. More importantly than being a virgin, she is the Mother of Jesus and of human beings. How could it be otherwise in this "heavenly family," which, for the popular imagination, is so difficult to represent under any other parameter than that of the classic earthly family of father, mother, and child?

As we know, in the high pre-Columbian cultures of Mexico and Peru, the presence of female divinities was bound up with fertility—especially in that we are dealing with an agrarian culture, a culture of the earth. Tonantzin—"our mother," for the Aztecs—was syncretized in the Virgin of Guadalupe, a native American Virgin, just as the *Pachamama* (Earth Mother) of the Quechua and Aymara has been syncretized with Mary (as Mother). Clearly, in the first colonial era at any rate, the image of the Virgin Mary, in the native and *mestiza* mentality, constituted the syncretic elaboration of a female deity linked to cosmic rhythms, vegetation processes, and agrarian rites. But just as surely, the official Catholic significate gradually imposed itself as the agrarian culture lost its force. After all, the Virgin is Mother, no longer as goddess of the fertility of the earth, but as refuge of the helpless. As Octavio Paz declares: "The situation has changed: it is a matter no longer of ensuring harvests, but of finding a lap. The Virgin is the consolation of the poor, protection of the weak, refuge of the oppressed. In sum, she is the mother of the orphans" (Paz 1990:7).

Over the course of the centuries, the official church has built imposing shrines to the Virgin, culminating in her "coronation" as "Queen" and "Patron" of various Latin American nations. Nonetheless, for the popular perception, the Virgin, venerated on every side in her most diverse advocacy capacities, is still the Mother of Jesus, who had her child in a stable and laid him in a manger, who fled to Egypt, and who was with him at the moment of his death on the cross. She is perceived as someone very close to the poor, a very human mother who is now in the glory of God and, from heaven, is still very simple and very near. "My dear little Virgin," "My sweet little *mestiza*" ("mi Virgencita, mi chinita") are her titles in the songs that, in all tenderness, accompany her dances in the Chilean North (Van Kessel 1977, 1988). For the Colombians, the Virgin is the "holiest of women," the "most beautiful of women," and a "miraculous mother" (Zuluaga n.d.).

The Virgin is the Mother who is always near, the figure who is at one with the origin of the life of the God-and-human-being, as she is at the origin of the life of all human beings: the diligent, maternal protector of the life of persons, especially of the "lowly and oppressed," as the Magnificat prays—of those who have lives most threatened and unsure.

Hymns sung by mine workers in the Andes in praise of the Virgin, but incorporating a powerful element of protest against the "bleeding" of the workers by the "mighty mine owners" (Van Kessel 1977:292, Uribe 1974:100), have nothing of "false conscience" about them. On the contrary, they demonstrate the compatibility between popular faith in Mary and a social consciousness on the part of persons who daily suffer the injustice of a system that, in the relationship of capital with labor, extracts violently from workers ("like a knife to the throat of the lamb") their very blood—the vital fluid that bears oxygen to the body, preserves its life, and protects it from diseases. The Virgin Mother, protector of the life of the "poor," is also their consolation in their objective class situation, and at the same time a subject of communication to whom one can send up a protest against the manner in which society threatens the life of these human beings.

## Progession of Life: Rituals of the Stages of Life

Just as human (social) life begins with popular faith, even though the biological (animal) life of the subject is already under way, so also faith acknowledges the origin of life in God the Creator and in the Virgin who cooperates in life's increase. Accordingly, faith accompanies the most relevant stages of one's personal life.

Generally, in the working-class neighborhoods and marginalized peripheral quarters of large Latin American metropolises, customs and practices are repeated in a framework that assumes various colors and hues, while everywhere appearing to have been painted by the same hand. The absolutely obligatory ceremonies are baptism, First Communion, and usually the *casamiento,* or wedding, and wake or wake party. These are practically the only reasons the people see for contact with the priest and the parish pastoral ministry. All of these ceremonies find in the fiesta a special dimension, which endows the ceremonies with a profound popular meaning.

The great French sociologist of religion, G. Lebras spoke of the " 'seasonal conformists'—the mass of people on the move, migrants for whom religion is defined by three rites: baptism, matrimony, burial, and usually children's First Communion—folk who enter a church only when the bell tolls for them, advising the parish that they must observe the customs of their ancestors" (cited in Pannet 1974).

We refer to the "rites of passage" (Van Gennep)—nonperiodic popular rites, elevated by the Church to the status of a sacrament. They help the subject to process subjectively and accept a change in social position: birth, puberty, marriage, death. The point is that the initiate is to receive a new status in the eyes of others, and a new way of being before others. After all, when the ritual is over, it may now be said that this person knows the secrets of existence, such as his or her own culture has codified them, and has thereby become responsible for transmitting that wisdom to the community. For the community, each rite of passage also constitutes a motive for coming together, for strengthening the ties of solidarity, for celebrating, and thus for ritualizing the passage of "one of their own" from one stage of progression to another in the social life of the human person.

The principal religious practices accompanying the unfolding of the various stages of life are baptism, First Communion, marriage, and the funeral.

In accordance with our extensive analysis, at life's beginning all have been "born" to social life through a decisive religious mediation: baptism. Just as it would be inconceivable to leave a newborn child without baptism, so it would be inconceivable to have a child baptized without a festive sharing in that event, in the company of family members and friends. No expense is spared for an event of such high significance. The sacrament of baptism and its festival reproduce the institution of "godparenthood," of which we have spoken, solidifying bonds of social solidarity and firmly establishing cultural integration.

At the age at which cultures classically celebrate their rites of initiation—the period of puberty—our popular culture avails itself of the First Communion (as well as, to a far lesser extent, "confirmation").

Conjugal life must also receive a religious seal, even though the religious meaning of the marriage bond, key to the alliances of kinship, is on the wane. With the secularization of the law and the separation of church and state in Latin American countries, civil marriage has acquired a growing importance, to the point, in certain cases, of a secular ritualization that is a counterpart of the religious rite—that is, a rite of the "civil religion" of modern citizenship. In the popular cultures, however, the main cause of the gradual abandonment of the sacrament of matrimony is not always civil marriage, but the practice of free unions, so widespread in certain urban popular groups. In the case of native American cultures or subcultures, it is the ancestral practices of union that are repeated, as in the case of Andean *servinakuy*.

The Latin American calendar is charged with "feast days," religious and secular. Just as the Day of the Immaculate One is celebrated throughout the continent on December 8, so another of the most intensively observed festivals is November 1, All Saints' Day, the fiesta commemorating the departed. During the days immediately preceding and following that date, time seems to stay its course; and when the day itself arrives, all rush to "remember their dead." Generally, just as the commemoration of the departed occupies a central place in popular devotion, so also does the ritual celebrated on the occasion of death. We may speak, then, of a common funeral pattern that becomes simplified as peoples are modernized.

At life's crowning moment—its ending in death—religion's bestowal of meaning is irreplaceable, precisely because faith gives meaning to life and thereby to death. However, we must be careful to note that the funeral ritual, the "wake"—the best-attended practice of popular religion—does not imply belief in an "afterlife." In studies that we have done, only about half of those interviewed believe in an "afterlife"; no one, however, seems to object to the wake, the final moment of "leave-taking" and a reaffirmation of the group's ties with life and life's constant dialectic of death/life. The wake is the most meaningful of popular religious rituals.

### Protection of Life: Evils, Rituals of Crisis and Healing

Devotion to the saints or to the Virgin in the subordinate cultures, in the majority of cases, is connected with the symbolical solution of relevant daily problems: work, health, affective and family relations, studies, and so forth. The devout faithful offer petitions bearing on the universal problems that the popular cultures must confront.

In families, we almost always find pictures and *santitos* ("dear sainties," as it were) of the Virgin, crucifixes, images, prints, and medals of family devotion. Numerous and manifold are the rituals of impetration, whether expressed in gesture (by crossing oneself, touching the images, placing children before the images at various shrines, and so on) or in prayers. Prayer is offered up with relative frequency; but it is especially at moments of anxiety or need that one has "a mass" offered, and on especially solemn occasions (the patronal feast, anniversary masses for the dead, masses for health) it is usual to call together members of the community who are regarded as the best *rezadores* ("prayers"), who pray like "little blind persons," and so on.

Women are generally more devout, and leave their houses to pray to the saints and to make promises. But depending on locality and region, men at times can be in the majority in the churches and on pilgrimages to the shrines. Promises and pilgrimages, votive offerings and prayers, massive pilgrimages and private petitions in church—all such things are the requests of a people who trust in God's goodwill to intervene by means of his intermediaries and grant "favors."

In an extensive study done in Peru (González 1987), the question was asked, "When do you most frequently seek out Christ and the saints?" Forty-seven percent replied, "When someone is ill"; 22%, "When the economic situation is hardest; 11%, "When our people are on strike, or claiming their lands"; and 14%, "Other." This coincides with what has been observed in other regions of the continent. The fact that the first thing mentioned is illness confirms the intimacy of the bond prevailing between the religious experience and vital needs. Indeed, the religion of the marginalized sectors is orientated to the immediate satisfaction of the needs most felt by persons. But while, on the one hand, this entails a certain pragmatism—understandably, given the wretched situations of deprivation in which these subjects eke out their existence—on the other, it should not be taken as the reflection of a materialistic spirit. We may assert that, while petitions, promises, prayers, requests for miracles, favors, and so on, are directly related to vital needs such as health, hunger, poverty, death, and housing, they also bear on satisfactions of a higher order in the scale of needs: interpersonal relationships, good luck, affectivity, moral condition, and the healing of the soul. Generally, what is besought of the divine powers is the protection of life: health, good fortune, deliverance from evils.

But popular faith accompanies not only the stages in the growth of life; in important segments of the population (and in the case of certain religious models), it also accompanies the moments of *crisis* in life. As Titiev says (1979), not only the "calendrical" rites but also the so-called "critical" rites must be considered. Wherever the meaning of life hangs in the balance, persons have recourse to God and the saints, with whom a kind of pact is struck, governed by a ritual exchange: the suppliant must fulfill his or her promise in exchange for the working of the miracle. In the face of a tragic, unexpected death, recourse is had to the saints and the souls of the departed. In the case of a serious illness, prayers are offered, a mass is said, or rituals of healing are performed. The precarious life of a little baby is protected by means of amulets, a blessing with the sign of the cross, or protective baptism; a situation of urgency and anxiety, material (unemployment, layoffs, and so forth) or moral (family conflicts, marital strife, alcoholism, drug addiction, and so forth), motivates promises, pilgrimages, and votive offerings. A dangerous or high-risk situation (threat of accident, assault, and so on) is conjured away by means of the sign of the cross, commendation of oneself to God, solicitation of protection, and the like.

Popular faith heals the integral (material as well as symbolical) crisis by the profound belief in the intervention of God. It is asked especially through *mediators*: the Virgin, the saints, on occasion certain angels, and, to a lesser extent, the souls of the departed, who thus rescue the suppliant from the "evil" situation. Depending on the type of mentality at work, this "evil" situation may be interpreted through recourse to causal categories of the religious field (extrasocial causes of a superstitious magical type) or to causal categories of the natural or social field (in descriptive or explanatory form).

The problem of health, for example, offers serious challenges to a culture that, precisely by reason of its life in conditions of misery, marginalization, and exploitation, has no secure access to modern institutionalized, specialized—but mercantilized—health practices. This is the case in the popular sectors, where exceedingly high rates of infant mortality constitute a particularly poignant indicator of the defenselessness felt by the population with regard to their newborn and nursing babies. It is not strange that various forms of baptismal or initiatory rituals should be celebrated, or that there should prevail, in the popular culture, a special sensitivity when it comes to protection from evil—"rites of protection against evil, blessings (including blessings with *agua de socorro*, water of succor), parish baptism accompanied by a spectrum of attitudes, and analogous ceremonies (blessings with water, rites of incorporation into associations), with positive and negative aspects" (Codina and Irarrázaval 1987:41). The "evil," in this case, is closely associated with the health of the baby, which is fragile, maintained in poverty, and needful of the protection offered by baptism.

Here, for example, no mean role is played by recourse to the old traditions and the ancestral wisdom: traditional medicine, natural healing, and, of course, devotional practices and promises accompanied by petitions for health, impetratory practices and attempts to obtain religious cures, and even rituals with the intervention of traditional religious agents, sorcerers, shamans, *yatiris*, mediums, *macumbeiros* (who preside at the rituals of Macumba), *bendecidoras* ("blessers"), diviners, *curanderos* ("healers"), *manosantas* (those of the "holy hand"), and so on. Incantations and conjurations abound in these rites of healing, often in the form of a counterwitchcraft, for the purpose of "extracting the evil" and making it possible for "good to enter." If the infirmity is attributed to witchcraft, the agent of popular religion must, by magical procedures, "divine" which person of the community has a quarrel with the victim and is the cause of the disease. The victim must perform rituals of "purification" in order to drive out the evil and denounce the culprit. If the suspect confesses, or is expelled, or is reconciled, the victim will probably recover. If the illness is attributed directly to the influences of evil spirits, recourse is had to exorcism (García-Ahumada 1981:77).

The origin of an illness can be natural and biological; but it can also be due to an *evil*. (In the study done in Santiago de Chile, 40.8% of those interviewed believe in curses, and 73% in the "evil eye.") Or the disease can be due to the intervention of the *spirits of evil*.[4] Whatever the origin of the disease, the problem is an alteration in the balance of life, which threatens to interrupt that life and throw it into disorder. In the face of this chaotic threat to the order of life, there arises a rampart of protection, coming to restore *nomos* (the symbolical and harmonious order of life)—the intervention of God through the intermediary of his *miraculous* mediators. The miracle is not merely some mysterious, arbitrary intervention of the power of God, but this intervention precisely in response to the petition of the popular subject. The petition must be made in conformity with the traditional dictates of impetratory ritual: the promise, the gift, the prayer, the blessing of the amulet, the sign of the cross, the laying on of hands, the cure.

In all locales, folk seek amulets, talismans, and blessings and perform rites and impetrations for the purpose of escaping "evils" generally connected with health. The *curanderos*, *manosantas*, *meicos* (for

---

4. About "evil eye" see Grebe et al. (1971), Plath (1981:33ff.), Read (1966:78), Vicuña Cifuentes (1947:109ff.).

*medicos*—here, the popular "physician"), *sanadores* ("healers")—however they be denominated—in whose function the female role comes very much to the fore, are charged with "crossing" (making the sign of the cross over, conjuring) the "evils" and restoring health to the victims. The popular practices in question are of a shamanic type, and are persecuted by official religion and culture, which label them "witchcraft" and "paganism"; hence the silence and mystery surrounding them. But for all their invisibility, they are at work. In certain cases, they are effective. In most cases, a medical physician is sought out; but if there are no results, or if the origin of the illness is seen as supernatural, then there is no hesitancy in consulting the agents of traditional medicine, or witchcraft with indigenous roots or spiritistic antecedents.

It is not characteristic of all of the population to have recourse to this kind of expression of religious magic. With better-qualified industrial workers or those holding better jobs, just as among youth or better-educated persons, we frequently observe a rationalization of beliefs, a fall-off in the rate of official religious practice, and the abandonment of practices and beliefs of religious magic.

Religious groups are not lacking whose Christian faith has undergone a certain "renewal"—groups of persons who sustain their Christian life through a fertile exchange with the agents of a renewed pastoral ministry on the part of the Church. The "base communities"—a new form of expression of Christianity in these popular sectors—would deserve an entire ad hoc consideration, and have been the object of a great deal of study, along with the important role they have played in recent decades in the elaboration and development of the liberating currents of Latin American pastoral theory and practice. For these groups, health is a social problem and ought to be faced in a coordinated manner. Base groups, polyclinics and popular infirmaries, are set up for action and education in the area of health and hygiene. Simultaneously, a "right to health care" is proclaimed, and the authorities are petitioned for the improvement of public systems in this area. Health is not viewed as a private matter, or a matter of individual illnesses. Instead, strategies of community health are adopted. Mental health and environmental hygiene also come in for attention. But for the popular subjects who participate in these groups, health also continues to be a matter of divine providence. To these persons, the utilization of modern medical technologies does not seem incompatible with prayer to God and the Virgin for their personal health and the collective health of their families and communities.

## Celebration of Life: Festival

Every city, and every village, celebrates a calendar thick with fiestas, each under the patronage of a saint or of some representation of the Virgin or Jesus Christ, all of these being regularly celebrated in festival and devotion. Barrios, associations, and labor unions have their fiestas, as well. As Octavio Paz puts it: "Our poverty can be measured by the number and prodigality of our popular festivals. Festivals are our only luxury. Rich countries have few: they have neither the time nor the mood for them."

Generally speaking, another unmistakable trait of popular religion is its festive character, although the type of religious festivity involved varies considerably from region to region and country to country. Addressing the difference in meaning and manifestation between the peasant religious festival, with its ecological and local rural sociocultural hues, and the urban popular festival—so much less expressive, and so brief in its duration—we must say that the social meaning, although not necessarily the religious one, varies enormously. The patronal feast is typical of the rural village, and is generally connected to the farm calendar (Rueda 1982). The collective celebration in honor of the patron saint of a given locality is an expression of the local spirit and the particularism that characterize country life. The fiesta is also a community event. It reinforces the community's traditional structure, conferring on the religious organization of the peasant associations and stewardships (lieutenants, stewards, foremen, etc.) its full meaning on the feast of the saint, while also emphasizing the self-affirmation of the community in the face of the clericalism of official religion. On the patronal feast, the members of each sociocultural community unit reinforce their identifying bonds with a lavish flow of song, food, drink, and dance, all in exuberant extravagance. The patronal fiesta fulfills an integrating function of the first order in the large city, where integration is lost—where there are no longer any local bonds like the ones that knit the small community together, where even the immediate neighborhood is composed of mutual strangers. Amidst the relative anonymity of the urban barrio, the patronal festival, or a fiesta celebrated on the occasion of a baptism, marriage, or wake, serves to break the monotony and briefly quell the anxiety of an urban routine overwhelmed with poverty. But it also affords an opportunity to rebuild the symbolical fabric of former social identities, now objectified once more through the devotion to this or that particular saint; thus, the festival fashions a symbol of collective identification, which it rebuilds by reestablishing the bonds of the primordial community.

Each of these stages of the progression and advance of life is an occasion for joy and festival. In the daily life of the people, then, religious ritual always takes on a sense of jubilation, out of gratitude to the Giver of existence and out of the sense of celebration of life that surrounds each advance in the personal and collective life course. The fiesta, like any popular ritual, is a condensation of out-of-the-ordinary rites, which transform daily living by symbolically introducing their subjects into a new world. Fiesta is a suspension of the "normal" parameters of ordinary space-time and an introduction into an extraordinary space-time (hence its extraordinary expansiveness, in shouts, music, and song and in the extraordinary consumption of drink, alcohol, and food, all present in such abundance). And a regeneration takes place from the subversion of the ordinary through the free expression of contradiction, discontinuity, the grotesque, and the spontaneous. Fiesta is a moment of reconstitution of meaning in a space of relative anomie: suddenly the modulations of the expressive and the bodily revitalize the affectivity dulled by everyday life. Fiesta is a moment of collective effervescence, in which the religious element, as collective reality, has its origin, as Durkheim says. Fiesta is ever a return to symbolism, to expressive corporality, to feeling, and to imagination. Its rules are different. A morale, a sociability, an economy, and a logic come into play that contradict the life of every day. Fiesta is a culture-impugning return to the formless, an immersion in the more vital and deep, in pure life. Through festival, the people deliver themselves from the norms and oppressions that have been imposed upon them: gods, principles, and laws are made a laughingstock. But the people do more in these expressions than deliver themselves from past and present. They also anticipate, as Duvignaud (1974) posits, the never-experienced. They challenge society, they call for change. This is why times of social change and revolution spark festival. Fissures in a changing civilization are just the thing when it comes to fiesta. In times of revolution, festival bursts forth more frequently. All revolution has something of the festival about it, and all festival something of the revolution.

Religious festival is, furthermore, an explosion of mysticism, of detachment, of sacrifice, of fantasizing the "festival of heaven," in which there are no rich or poor, tears or weeping. Popular festival is counterculture to modernity—a space of resistance to rationalistic, instrumental logic, a symbolical ambit profoundly free, regenerative, and delivering.

We can appreciate the medieval legacy of the popular religious festival of Latin Americans—that is, its overwhelming visual component, to which Huizinga has pointed. This spirit has been preserved, and enhanced in the cultural synthesis of the colonial baroque: "Everything anyone wants to express is gathered together in an optical image. All anyone can think of is visual representation ... Pictorial media, much more extensively developed than literary media, contribute to the predominance of this inclination" (Maldonado 1975:243). But the Latin American fiesta has its roots in pre-Columbian and African festive rituals as well, and full satisfaction comes not by way of ideas, but by way of the theatrical gestures and rituals of religious festival. Fiesta arises out of colonial popular festive syncretism, charged with the act of "setting the world on its ear," as when blacks paint themselves white, "devils" receive hymns of praise, and "Spaniards" are made to look foolish in the unbridled magic of carnival.

Among the principal tools of the first evangelization, in the framework of an oral culture, we find liturgy, festivals, and religious celebrations; we find rituals of passage, *autosacramentales*, and popular theater. The influence of popular traditions coming from without, to be fused with native popular traditions, cannot be denied. The vigorous carnival-spirited, picaresque Spanish medieval culture, with its deep religious sensibility, all set in the framework of an oral tradition, arrived with the commoners and soldiery of the Old World and spread through the farm cultures of the Ibero-American indigenous peasantry. Here it flowed together with pre-Columbian religious ritual's deep festive sense, with dance in all its rhythmic and ceremonial choreography, with percussion and wind instruments, with prayers in song and rhythmic recitations. In a word, where official liturgy yielded, the indigenous rhythm, baptized, acquired a space of its own.

In the city, festival becomes more distant, less expansive, more modest and brief. But it is not, for all that, less present. For city people, pilgrimages acquire a new, different meaning and become the occasion for a reencounter with the original festive sense by virtue of the massiveness of the collective presence. In the poor or marginal barrio, fiesta takes on the precise function of revitalizing a life that is typically so low-key and routine.

### Christianity as Nucleus of the Cultural *Pathos* of the Latin American People

The type of popular religion that we have reviewed presents itself, in all its facets, as a religion of life rather than a religion of ethics or reason. Popular religion is a religion of rite and myth, of dreams and sensitivity, of body and the quest for this-wordly well-being. But it is a religion that asserts itself in transcendence, and not in an aggregate of superstition and magic.

Rather than being a manner and spirit of acting—an ethos—popular religion is a manner of *feeling and expressing*. Popular religion is rite, then, and *pathos*. We may assert that popular religion is the core of the popular *pathos*. Popular religion is surely not a way of being and feeling, a desire and a culmination of that desire, in conformity with the formulae of rationalistic, Western canons. It is surely *another* way of feeling, thinking, and operating, alternative to an Enlightenment rationality and the kind of rationalized faith that is the byproduct of that rationality.[5]

But the thesis that popular religion is a form of cultic religion, diametrically opposed to an Enlightenment logos, fails to take in the phenomenon in all its aspects. Popular religion, too, is a kind of religious "word" pronounced upon life and history, even though it is not expressed in terms of a Western "logos." More than anything else, popular faith is a popular theodicy. It defends a God of life. It believes in the sure possibility of the passage from evil to good, from precariousness and desperation to well-being, from disease to health, from situations of less life to situations of more life, from less human situations to more human situations. To a large extent, popular religion, in its urban manifestation—transformed by capitalistic modernity—continues to be the vehicle of Weber's essential attributes of religion: it is an ethic of compensation, whose particular need is for deliverance from suffering (Weber 1964:394). Of course, this interpretation of popular religion as "compensation" could lead directly to the conclusion that its function is an alienating one—an altogether questionable conclusion, based on an abusive generalization that will be the object of our commentary in another part of this book. An empathetic interpretation of the "compensatory" significate and function of popular religion certainly leads us to conclusions of a different kind. In other words, we are dealing here with a vitalistic religion of deliverance through the mediation of a good God who assists, consoles, protects, and, of course, demands—always by means of particular signs and symbols, altogether concrete *mediations* proximate to the collective life of the people.

The popular faith that we have analyzed is not "alienating" in the

---

5. For a more specific analysis of this "different logic" we refer the reader to chaps. 9-11 below.

sense of being a "sigh of the oppressed creature" (Marx 1979) inhibiting all human action in the heteronomous hope of a "miraculous" intervention of God. The subject has to act, not just ask. The subject acts ritually in reference to the transcendent, but the action does not stop there. That ritual action is also accompanied by a social action bearing upon the "secular" ambit (for example, looking for work, or going to the doctor). But the subject trusts in the intervention of the transcendent powers because he or she knows that the foundation of life is beyond, and not in his or her own autonomous capability. We do not confront here an "Enlightenment" consciousness in the sense that the latter is correctly predicated of the bourgeois or the proletarian, each of whom claims and strives to conquer the world in his or her own way. Nor are we before a superstitious mentality whose conviction is in the immediate, mechanical result of its magical manipulation.

The popular faith that we have analyzed is nevertheless lacking in a historical sense—an analytical capacity with regard to the natural and social causes of the evils suffered by its subject and a more self-reflexive understanding of its actual capabilities and limitations as a lifegiving force at work in the individual, collective, and historical life of the people. In this sense, the "regenerative-liberative" potential of popular faith sees itself limited to the most immediate salvation from situations of collective anxiety and uncertainty, without necessarily entailing a historical project, except when this faith overflows into millennialism and is objectified in concrete religious movements. True, a certain kind of millennialism (as that of the "sects") can also host the seed of a "social strike" that exempts its adherents from a commitment to a world regarded as "sinful" and lost.

However, the regenerative and liberative potential of popular faith acts as a symbolical protection in the face of the adverse social conditions that invest the life of the marginalized popular sectors.

## Popular Religion as Counterculture

Popular religion such as it has been typologized in the foregoing pages is an ambit of symbolical-semiological condensation which, in the sphere of its relation with the transcendent, manifests a mentality that imbues and constitutes the popular cultures. Popular religion can be better understood as a counterculture to the "modernity" mentality propagated by the dominant culture of globalized capitalism. This alternative, "other" nature of popular religion is manifested—in explicit or underlying fashion—on a number of distinct thematic levels.

First: As we have seen, popular religion affirms *life*, in a socioeconomic and political context of death and violence that daily threaten the survival of the popular classes and groups and affect the whole of Latin American society. Under many aspects, popular culture itself is shot through with aggressive behaviors and manifestations of violence, emerging from its own relations (family, interpersonal, sexual, criminal) or from the general conditions of the social system (the violence of social factors, the economy, repression, terrorism, the drug traffic, and so on). Nonetheless, in its religious layers those behaviors that are orientated to a different "life," a life bound up with the transcendent—thereby expressing the most profound yearnings of the collective mentality (a nonsystematized utopian project)—surely assert a vital project of protection, survival, and affirmation and growth of life, all the way to its culmination in full, festive life, the "afterlife," the "glory of heaven," which for popular subjects is a life in God, with all suffering and all injustice on earth finally overcome. The studies show that, in the popular mentality, God's judgment upon the rich and upon wealth as it appears in the Gospels is internalized, and that "it is much more difficult for a rich person to enter into the reign of heaven than for a poor person" (see Matt. 19:23-26, Mark 10:23-27, Luke 18:24-27).

Second: Popular religion affirms *woman* and *the feminine* through the central position of the figure of the Virgin Mary. While the Marian symbology is no longer directly linked to nature as source of life, as it is in agrarian popular religion, it abides as a figure linked to the gestation, growth, and protection of life. In the figure of Mary, as we have seen, is concentrated the popular vision of the mother, who is so important in the constitution of the popular culture's network of family and social relations. But popular religion shows us that the mediatory agents associated with health are also preponderantly women: *curanderas* ("healers"), *bendicidoras* ("blessers"), *santiguadoras* (healers who make the sign of the cross over the sufferer while crossing the thumb and index finger), *parteras* ("midwives"), *curiosas* ("diligent ones"), *rezadores* ("prayers")—all in the feminine gender. This affirmation of woman and life stands over against the dominant culture, marked as it is, and has been for centuries, by the patriarchal models that are vectors of power and domination. While, in the popular culture, *machismo* is surely a prime cultural model, the centrality of the maternal and feminine in popular religion, as other data establish regarding collective representations, manifests a feminine counterpower—the maternal face of God—that insists on woman's equality and rights, at the very moment that this equality and these rights are so frankly trampled underfoot both by the dominant culture and by the models of a mentality of *macho* domination hosted by the popular culture itself.

Third: Popular religion affirms the feelings, affirms *pathos*, in the face of a dominant culture that is intellectualistic and moralistic. As we have said, rather than a popular ethic, what we see in the various popular religions are forms of manifestation of a *pathos*—that is, forms of incarnation of the passion of the popular individual that are not always consistent with his or her own reason. The importance of the saints for popular religion goes far beyond a mentality that, articulated by the "logic of the concrete," would be channeled, on the strength of a certain pragmatism, toward a semiology deprived of rational or abstract mediations. The value of the icon—the polychrome carving of the saints and virgins, or the plethora of plastic figures and ornaments (because it is the "little plaster saint" that counts)—lies precisely in the fact that the icon is a concrete symbol of a reality that mediates the transcendent, a symbol in terms of which, in sensible, corporeal fashion, one can pour out the mighty charge of feelings accumulated by the popular mystical experience in the course of a year, to be expressed on the precise date of the patronal feast. The actual life of the saint is not very important, nor are people even generally aware of the ethical dimension that, for official religion, is so decisive in the canonization process—the "exemplary biography" of the candidate for beatification. What is important is the icon and its capacity to catalyze feelings and desires in a precise time-space (the element of marvel in fiesta and ritual), together with its mediatory capacity as efficacious symbol of a transcendent action upon living persons: "that it be miraculous."

Fourth: Popular religion affirms the *vitalistic* in a world dominated by intellectualism. This *vitalism* is related to the conviction that life is sustained in vital sources that are beyond human beings' rationalistic grasp. These vital forces may have many names: God, Virgin, saints, Holy Spirit, spirit of good, healing power, blessed souls, and so on. True, an exact hierarchy is acknowledged in the pantheon: first place in the transcendent world is assigned to God, the Father and Creator of all things and every form of life. On occasion, depending on the sort of religious worldview at hand, these forces of good and of life are locked in a violent symbolic struggle with the forces of evil: spirits of evil, *males* (curses, spells), devils, satanic forces, and the like. But—except for certain religious currents, alien to the typical popular mentality, that are characterized by a belief in the omnipresent power of Satan and the empire of the forces of evil (proper to esoteric mystery sects of nonpopular origin)—for the popular mentality, trust in the power of a God who is good, superior, and transcendent (the Christian image of the Father) makes it possible to restore in the symbolical order a *nomos* in which life and good always triumph. To be sure, this theodicy stands at a good many removes from contemporary rationalistic, intellectualistic theology (Protestant or Catholic), but it may not be so distant from the mentality that dominated Catholicism from the sixteenth to the eighteenth centuries, when the witch hunt typified the dualism of the inquisitorial mentality (Kloppenburg 1977). For the dominant technological scientific mentality, this vitalism is obviously a threat to the dictates of "reason" and must be combated as a sign of the "archaism" that presents an obstacle to human progress.

Fifth: Popular religion affirms the *expressive*, the festive and carnivalesque, over against the formalism and rationalism of the dominant culture (attributes of the industrial culture). We are dealing with a vitalistic, collective religion, both from the viewpoint of its content (its semantics) and from the viewpoint of its ritual manifestation (its semiology). Popular ritual is expressive, emotive, iconic, and festive. In the act of visualizing religious experience and transforming it into the palpable, popular ritual intensifies and qualitatively enhances that experience.

As we have said, the popular expressions manifest a very profound vitality through their affectivity as well as through the expressive ritualism, iconic exteriorization, and devotional depth of the traditional practices. Thus they stand over against a more ethical, ascetical religion (whether of a monastic or a Calvinistic type), on the one hand; or a more mystical religion (proper to the experiential unicity of classical mysticism); or a more abstract and rationalized religion (rationalized, theologized faith, with the accent on the doctrinal). It also runs counter to the piety of the dominant groups and classes—the privileged strata of bureaucrats, intellectuals, and warriors, who either are indifferent to religion or focus on it as a source of divine legitimation of their own fortune in this world (Weber), and groups of the bourgeoisie, whose religion is interioristic, spiritualistic, disincarnate, and privatized.

Sixth: Finally, popular religion affirms the *transcendent* in the context of a dominant culture still very much imbued with a Cartesian and positivistic scientism, which tends to reject the symbolical dimension and thereby classifies the dimension of mystery as outside the contemporary human being's sociocultural reality. Neglect of the hidden dimensions of the reality of the cosmos—which astrophysicists are beginning to acknowledge on the basis of their most recent discoveries—does not affect popular culture and religion; it affects, rather, the parameters of judgment maintained by the dominant culture with regard to such "occult" dimensions. For that very reason, we may regard the theories concerning "secularization," in their classic version, as "ideology," basing our judgment on the popular religious phenomenon. These theories fail to take into account the metamorphosis of the religious element in its contact with modernity; instead, they contribute to the frivolous submersion of that immense underpart of our societies' religious iceberg, classifying it as "unreal"—praising to the skies the little visible part, that of cold, secularized instrumental rationalism apologetically defined as "reality" (single, visible, and empirically verifiable).

Popular culture, then, and its religious traits constitute a counter-culture to modernity. Popular culture is not properly postmodern (for that matter, "postmodernism" is not a very clear term, and the debate over it is still confused), but neither is it a premodern counter-culture. In a certain sense, this meaning-core of popular culture and religion both is modern and is not. It coexists with, and profits from, the modern, but it resists and criticizes the modern as well. Popular culture and religion is—to coin a neologism—"hemidernal" (semi-modern). It is the "hemidernal" character of popular culture and religion, which we shall analyze in more depth below, that conditions their ambivalent attitude: popular culture and religion are both anti- and promodernistic. They are antimodern when it comes to the alienating and dehumanizing component of modernity and its instrumental rationality, to their rationalization calculated to legitimate the various forms of domination and control, to their tendency to diminish life in a frantic race for immediate satisfaction through consumption and competition (while the maintenance of the balances of life in the micro- and macrodimension of the daily and of the concrete historical is consigned to oblivion). But in another sense, popular culture and its religion are not antimodern. They accept everything modernity has to offer in terms of an effective advance in living conditions and in opportunities for the satisfaction of the human person's authentic needs, as well as in terms of liberation from the alienating elements of a traditional culture immersed in the fear and uncertainty of a mentality closed off from the critical possibility of apprehending the world with other eyes than those that have provided it with the myths of submission. Per se, this *openness* on the part of popular culture to the positive face of modernity is but an enabling condition given in historical form—dependent both on the coordinates of time-space and on the collective actor and his and her sociocultural experience. In a Latin American society in the course of moderniza- tion, in the heat of its conflicts and contradictions, there is no longer a "traditional" popular religion per se, nor is it possible to speak of a "liberative" popular religion in the categories of an Enlightenment culture. There are only various "hemidernal" religious forms and models, each endowed with a greater or lesser humanizing potential depending on each sociocultural situation and historical conjuncture, as we shall see in the chapters to come.

## PART FOUR

# PLURALIZATION

*"You see, actually the religion thing is kind of relative. You have to be really careful, especially when it comes to religions. We say we're Catholics. There are people who mean something different, like a Sunday obligation . . . Somebody can go to church a couple of Sundays and that's it . . . Then they get called believers. They're not actually members of a parish. I used to go to the Protestant church fairly often. It's a tricky thing. There's a lot of faking . . . That's why I say, be careful. You have to know what religion's for in the first place and what it's about, and then decide yes or no. We believe in God, we tell him our faults. God for some people is the biggest thing there is, because you can't go anywhere . . . You say goodbye with faith: "God willing, I'll be all right."*

José, cobbler, 31

# Chapter 6

# Fragmentation of the Catholic Field

## Rural Popular Religion and the Church

The autochthonous native culture, the Iberian culture, and the contribution of the African cultures are the basic components of Latin America's *mestiza*, hybrid, character in culture and piety alike (Methol Ferré 1977). The historical traces of the triethnic composition of the Latin American peoples are most readily visible in traditional peasant culture and piety.

By the end of the last century, Latin American societies were determined in their social structure by economies focusing primarily on the export trade, so that agriculture had decisive weight in national life. Rural lifestyles and values were preponderant, and the peasantry composed the basic class of the people. Even suburban and urban-rim areas about 1900 offered an ambient in symbiosis with the life of the surrounding ranches and small farms. The people's religious expressions were still strongly marked by field and pasture and by the cycles of agricultural life, although there were already signs of a process of transition to the city way of life.

In the first half of the twentieth century, the peasantry were the subjects of a deep piety, whose colonial roots had not been substantially modified with the passage of time. In order to characterize the salient traits of these religious forms, we must take account of their diversity, which had been determined both historically and by the regional location and social position of the peasantry that reproduced this diversity.

For example, in certain Andean regions or on the Central American plateaus, indigenous roots are more accentuated, whether because evangelization was feeble, or because of the influence of the high pre-Columbian cultures, or because of the loyalty, almost in the form of resistance to anything else, of the native American and mestizo peasantry to their traditions.

On the other hand, regions are clearly distinguished where Hispanic or Lusitanian influences have been more strongly preserved in the mixed culture, in consequence of the fragility of local native cultures or an intensive *mestizaje,* or hybridization, arising on the pampas and in the farming valleys.

Finally, on the Atlantic coast of South America and in the Caribbean and the Antilles, we sense the unmistakable influence of the African culture of the populations transported there as slave labor.

Nevertheless, we may assert that the peasantry share a type of syncretic piety endowed with certain traits more or less common across the continent (Methol Ferré 1977; Marzal 1977, 1986). This syncretism, in a kind of variegated symbolical map, combines the elements of colonial Catholicism with native and African rites and beliefs (Marzal 1986). Under the appearance of a "Catholic" faith, certain beliefs, myths, legends, and rituals are retained from the pre-Christian religions. Forced to abandon their former religion, Indians and blacks nevertheless preserved, in a sort of symbolical resistance, some of the old beliefs that were most vital to them or especially meaningful in their lives. In traditional "popular Catholicism," the sacramental life, to be sure, is of decisive importance (baptism, Communion, marriage, blessings, and so on). But old elements abide, such as beliefs in magical powers, a sense of popular fiesta, a taste for the multicolored, showy, and noisy in dance and celebration, emphasis on the observance of the formalities of ritual, belief in intermediaries such as saints and departed souls, fear of the devil and evil spirits, recourse to witches, and the like. Meanwhile, the central element, without a doubt, is devotion to the Virgin, which comes from Spanish and Portuguese popular Catholicism—her shrines and pilgrimages, her altars, her feast days, novenas to her, the rosary, the Month of Mary, and so forth.

The social system of the *hacienda*—the ranch or large farm—reproducing, as it did, precapitalistic social relations in regions where farming was not influenced by the urbanizing penetration of capitalism until after the Second World War—constitutes a sociological matrix for the reproduction of this kind of traditional religious expression. Peasant piety is organized primarily around the veneration of the Virgin, the saints, the souls of the departed, and, in some cases, as in the mountain range of the Andean countries, around the baroque figure of Jesus Christ crucified. Peasant piety is structured from the domestic level (with the family chapel corner and its sacred images) to the local level (with the patron saint of the locality) to the regional level (with the regional shrine).

Recent studies on the meaning and social function of the traditional piety of the peasantry bring out the inner dialectic of this religiousness. On the one side, we have a piety of consolation and protection, which supplies the peasants with a world of signification in which they can endow their lives with meaning without calling the dominant order into question, thereby legitimating their position as oppressed class. At the same time, however, this alienating function of their quasi-magical and fatalistic piety must not always be understood negatively, inasmuch as, while it legitimizes the oligarchical domination, at times it is a symbolical recourse of which the peasant classes avail themselves in order to protest the conditions of misery and exploitation to which their employers subject them (Caravias 1978; Giménez 1978; Salinas 1984, 1991).

By the end of the nineteenth century and, more obviously from 1930 onward in the larger countries of the region, the capitalistic order and its logic of urbanization and industrialization were on the move. The response that the Church attempted to mount, beginning in 1850, in order to reproduce peasant piety, became more and more emphatic as time went by, with a view to heading off the loss of church influence among the classes in process of urbanization. In 1858, the Catholic Church launched its "Romanization" movement, whereby it attempted to mold the clergy and church structures on the "Roman" model, with its doctrinal, moral, and hierarchical rigor. This process culminated in the first synod of Latin American Bishops, held at Rome in 1899, in an age of great emphasis on the Immaculate Conception and the Sacred Heart. The effects of Romanization on popular religion were considerable. In many areas, popular religious manifestations were criticized as "pagan," and the key concern of the bishops and clergy was with the people's "religious ignorance." As Pedro Ribeiro de Oliveira puts it: "Romanization presents itself as a process of clerical repression of the people's Catholicism. But the latter has not, for all that, disappeared . . . It has survived, just out of the reach of clerical control" (Ribeiro 1979:72). The trait of "lay self-management" (Giménez 1978) attaching to the popular religious expressions seems more accentuated in regions further removed, whether for geographical or for cultural reasons, from the influence of the clergy. It is typical of the native American peasant religiousness of the Andean countries, or the piety of the mestizos and Ladinos of Mexico and Central America, or the piety developed in remote rural localities, accessible to the clergy only with difficulty and reached by them only a few times a year. The survival of this popular syncretism, especially among native populations, has led the clergy to sound warnings such as those of missionary Jacques Monast with regard to the Aymara in Bolivia (Monast 1969).

Along with institutional reinforcement—which meant the introduction of new religious orders and congregations from Europe, to the rhythm of an ever closer control over popular forms of piety, whose "excesses" and "superstitions" were regarded as a threat to the symbolical predominance of official Catholicism and must needs be "purified"—there was an effort to introduce certain new devotions. Some of these were fended off by the people, but others became fairly well accepted among the popular classes. These new devotions, introduced or created, tended to be urban and were usually centered on new urban shrines, which gained in popularity over the course of the years until 1890-1910.

The French influence on the Latin American elite was in evidence not only among native and mixed-blood intellectualism, so receptive to liberalism and positivism; the Catholic Creole elite, as well, underwent the influence of French piety. New religious congregations arriving in America propagated the devotion to the Sacred Heart and the practice of confession and Communion on First Fridays. Aristocratic and middle-class groups welcomed these devotions and sermon topics; not a few persons joined the Apostleship of Prayer and the associations of the adoration of the Blessed Sacrament. The Salesians strove to introduce the devotion to Mary, Help of Christians; the Redemptorists, the devotion to Our Lady of Perpetual Help; and so on. These new orientations, introduced and furthered by the clergy, began gradually to gain strength among a growing number of laity. Many individuals joined the Eucharistic Crusade, the Marian Congregation, the Vincentian Confederations, and the Daughters of Mary, among others. But these devotions and organizations had very little lay character and were far more dependent on the clergy, whereby they differed from the associations of traditional popular piety, whose lay leadership was very important. Little by little, the latter associations entered a decline, and the clergy succeeded in reorientating the various popular devotions.

But this attempt at revitalizing the piety of the masses, in the context of a situation in which the Church was losing ground against the explosive advance of the liberal states, did not succeed in reconnecting the clergy to the people. Traditional popular piety, generally, was reproduced statically, through the sacramentalism and ritualism of the clergy. The imposition of liberalism or anticlerical currents on official culture did not affect most of popular religion, which continued to gravitate toward monastery and parish churches and, especially, shrines. The Church sought to reorientate this devotion by organizing sacred festivals, official ceremonies of "canonical crowning" of images of the Virgin, and Eucharistic Congresses. But the formation of the clergy in a neoscholastic mentality that turned its back on reality and used a conceptualistic language alienated them from the mentality and piety of the popular masses. Thus the bond between clerical culture and popular culture that had prevailed in the colonial era was broken (Prien 1985:583).

Worthy of attention, however, is what occurred in pastoral practice in connection with certain urban shrines in the first decades of the twentieth century. Here, a popular devotion took hold that was rather striking and characteristic, since it incorporated the popular masses then being integrated into urban life. The Shrine of Saint Cajetan in Buenos Aires, the Shrine of Our Lady of Lourdes in Santiago de Chile, the Shrine of Our Lady of Pompeii in Quito are good examples of this phenomenon. These were surely successful experiments in terms of a reencounter between official pastoral ministry and the popular sense and its religious aspirations. Generally speaking, however, even independently of official pastoral strategies, popular devotion continued its course, and this under conditions of rapid urbanization. In the world of urban popular religion in Latin America, a plethora of devotions developed during the first half of the twentieth century. The various devotions, processions, and customs varied from one place to another, from one region to another, from one nation to another. By 1930, for example, we observe a great difference in the religious expressions of the three principal cities of the Peruvian Andean south, Arequipa, Puno, and Cuzco. In Arequipa, a colonial city, Spanish influence predominated; in Puno, the native American influence; and in Cuzco, a mixture (Klaiber 1987:302). The various manifestations of popular faith were regarded with varying degrees of benevolence, from the most acceptable to the most "pagan," criticized and repressed. On the one hand, devotions and processions organized spontaneously; on the other, the Church itself promoted and organized other manifestations. Thus, we may speak of devotions that, even up until today, are more "official," and others that are more "popular."

It must not be forgotten that, in parallel fashion, springing from the inventive capacities of the peasant sectors, various reactions have been mounted to the urbanizing process of the early part of our century. This resistance, which takes place via religious symbolism, has sometimes materialized in messianisms, as in the Brazilian northeast in the form of a movement of religious protest which we shall analyze at some length in chapter 8. At other times, armed uprisings and rebellions have occurred at the hands of the native peasantry, as in Peru toward the end of the nineteenth century and the beginning of the twentieth (Klaiber 1987:280). These movements were led by native Americans who professed Christianity and thus on various occasions accepted church mediation between their forces and the national army. As these movements were merely regional eruptions, they were ultimately defeated, and never threatened the oligarchical order of the time.

### The Church, the Emerging Working Class, and Its Religious Expressions

Toward the end of the past century and in the early decades of the one now nearing its close, in the majority of Latin American countries, industry began to spring up, and capitalistic relations of production began to spread. The process was part of a model of "development outwards," so that it was mainly a matter of industries bound up with the primary or infrastructural sector. Governments frequently granted to Anglo-Saxon investors carte blanche to exploit underground resources. This meant the proletarianization of huge contingents of peasants, joined by a certain number of European immigrants.

In general, the capitalists were not supervised by the state, and could arrange any labor agreements they liked, employing their own system of wages (in credit slips) and their own judicial systems and police. Working conditions in the mines and factories, on the plantations, on the railways, or in the ports were arduous. Those who attempted to organize unions were regarded, and dealt with, as enemies of society. In the case of large-scale strikes, capitalism could rely on the support of the government army.[1] The genesis of the working class, then, would be marked by exploitation, misery, an attempt to organize, and violent repression of worker protest. In some regions, as in the Peruvian mountains, there were native uprisings in that same period.

Living conditions became more intolerable as the peasantry abandoned the countryside and its opportunities for subsistence and sub-

---

1. Throughout that period, work stoppages increased in number, at times with quite tragic results, as with the famous Cananea (Sonora, Mexico, 1906) and Iquique (Chile, 1907) strikes.

mitted to the helpless conditions of the new urban life. The development of a proletarianized peasantry provoked the collapse of the edifice of meaning and symbolical representations of a traditional cast— and thereby of the religious forms included in this edifice.

The Church, for its part, despite its policy of institutional reassertion and restoration, in many cases saw itself overwhelmed where the readjustment of the economy or the processes of urbanization or of incipient industrialization squeezed large populations into small areas. The scarcity of apostolic and parish personnel impeded the Church's response to the avalanche of immigrants, from near and far, that was beginning to swell the city populations. The consequence was a transformation in traditional models of religious signification and expression on the part of these mostly Catholic masses. Although no "de-Christianization" occurred, the number of the "officially nonpracticing" grew considerably, and certain sectors of the working-class leadership underwent the spread of indifferentism—even, at times, of anticlericalism—although this did not necessarily mean the abandonment of their faith, which did tend to become privatized.

Generally, the Church's concern for the lower classes during the period of capitalistic penetration was either sporadic or heavily paternalistic. The Church's activity here was inspired, of course, by the Encyclical *Rerum Novarum* of 1891 and by the European social pastoral activity of the era. Indeed, faced with the consequences of the process of a savage capitalistic accumulation at the end of the nineteenth century and alarmed by the rise of laicism and socialistic currents, several countries, such as France, Italy, Belgium, and Spain, began to be concerned with the controversial "social question."

At the end of the 1800s and the beginning of the 1900s, more and more such initiatives were launched. In Brazil, Argentina, Uruguay, Mexico, Chile, Peru, Colombia, Ecuador, Costa Rica, and other countries, the Catholics of the time inaugurated a series of social works on behalf of workers. Catholic congresses were also held on the social question.

In Brazil, the social problem of the first magnitude was the emancipation of the slaves, racism, and the system of labor relations prevailing among the rural population. Neither the hierarchy nor the clergy usually had any awareness of the misery and exploitation that reigned in the countryside. Especially worthy of note are the initiatives of certain Catholics who, beginning in 1891, endeavored to reduce Catholic social principles to practice, founded the Federation of Christian Workers, and held Catholic congresses that dealt with the social question. Outstanding among these persons was industrialist

Carlos Alberto de Meneses, who founded Brazil's first Catholic industrial cooperative in 1896, and in 1902 sponsored the first Catholic congress on the social question, held in Pernambuco (Prien 1985:525).

In Argentina, the first "circles" of Catholic workers were founded in 1882. Between the First Congress of Argentinian Catholics (1884) and the Second (1907), the center of interest, which had originally been political or institutional, turned to the labor question. The episcopate itself saw to it that collections were taken up and works founded to palliate social evils, and in 1902 recommended that the creation of Workers' Circles be expanded.[2] In the same year, seeing that the mutual assistance afforded in the Circles was not enough, Father Grote founded the Christian Democratic League, with its union activities, for the purpose of raising social consciousness. In the same direction, in Montevideo in 1904, the Christian Democratic Union was founded, followed by a series of initiatives in search of a concretization of the social Catholicism that was doggedly working its way in, in the presence of great tension between conservative Catholics and liberal tendencies (Zubillaga and Cayota 1988).

In Mexico, the Church's activity in the social area was also considerable, although it was somewhat delayed by comparison with early worker organization by socialists and anarchists (which, for that matter, was the case in the rest of the continent as well). In 1872, the First Great Circle of Free Workers was born. In 1875 the employees' unions were founded, and in 1876 the First General Labor Congress was held. Only in 1896 was the Catholic League in place.

In 1907, the Workers' Circles joined together in the Catholic Workers' Union, with its mutual assistance program. Later, in 1911, that organization became the National Confederation of Catholic Workers' Circles. Amidst the vicissitudes and instability of the revolutionary period, the Federation of Catholic Labor Unions was founded in 1920, and the National Catholic Labor Confederation in 1922—workers' organizations set up in opposition to the revolutionary unionism of the World Labor House and the Regional Confederation of Mexican Workers. The Catholic Social Congresses of 1903, 1904, 1906, and 1909 coldly addressed the situation of the peasantry and the moral consequences of the exploitation of workers (family disintegration, alcoholism, incapacitation for work), but were more concerned with

---

2. In 1907, in Argentina, socialist and anarchist workers' associations counted 10,900 members, while membership in the Workers Circles totaled 19,132 (Farrel 1976:75).

works of charity and religious instruction than with the need for labor legislation.

In Colombia at the turn of the century, workers' circles, mutual assistance associations, student restaurants, and so on, appeared. The most noteworthy institution was the Workers' Circle Savings Bank, founded by Father Campoamor. In Peru in 1921, the first meeting was held for the treatment of social issues: the Interdiocesan Congress of Social Action in Cuzco, representing the entire Andean south. In Chile, beginning at the close of the nineteenth century, mutual societies, especially those of artisans, were organized under Catholic inspiration. Even the Labor Federation of Chile (Federación Obrera de Chile, FOCH) was born in 1909 under the influence of conservative Catholic sectors, but it very soon adopted a frankly socialistic orientation. In Central America, with the exception of Costa Rica, the social question did not figure among the doctrinal and pastoral priorities of the churches in this period. Official church activity was frankly paternalistic and scantily reformist.

What Prien concludes for Mexico could be generalized for all Catholic initiatives in the various countries: "Most of the hierarchy and clergy were unable to draw the necessary conclusions from the wretched situation of the proletariat and take a position unconditionally on the side of a people of the poor" (Prien 1985:709).

In Argentina, as early as 1908, an enlightened priest with a great social sense made a similar statement:

Our labor associations no longer have at their disposal the organized means to protect our workers from these dangers and afflictions. They are useful for material outreach and mutual assistance. They are useful for civilizing our workers and giving them religious culture. But nothing more. That is, they have no direct influence on a solution to the labor question. Not the slightest. ["Discurso de Clausura III Congreso Nacional de Católicos, Argentina," *Revista Católica de Buenos Aires* 8:1054; quoted in Farrel 1976:68]

Generally speaking, organizations taking their inspiration in socialism and anarchism, when they collide with the Church, which ultimately has seemed an ally of oligarchical power, naturally accuse Catholics of weakening the labor movement, defending capitalism, and being the enemies of workers' enlightenment in spreading religious dogmas to tame the masses. We need only glance at any labor periodical of the time to find a criticism of the Church to the effect that it was against workers' interests. It was not generally a matter of accusing the Church of being absent, although, on a number of occasions, pastoral and social attention to workers was indeed observed to be absent or precarious. It was a matter of the diffidence with which labor organizations looked upon the social works of the Church. This mistrust was indeed justified, in terms of the attitude of the vast majority of the clergy, who at this time were by and large the children of the oligarchy.

The Church's activity in the nascent labor world was not always scant; but wherever it was most intense, owing to its paternalistic and collaborationist orientation it understood Catholic workers' organizations more as a confessional defense against socialism and anarchism than as an autonomous expression of the genuine interests of the workers. There was no general distinction drawn between an attack on socialism and anarchism, with their irreligious spirit, and what was interpreted as the cause of the latter: modern rationalistic liberalism. Catholicism's anticommunism, which at times went in tandem with conservative propaganda, as in Colombia and Chile, and at other times with an "intransigent Catholicism" (Mallimaci 1988), as in Argentina, led to the maintenance by the Church and the Catholic elite of a mistrust of unionism and its development.

Indeed, the conservative Catholic mentality of the oligarchies, and even of the hierarchy of the Church, prevented a genuinely in-depth understanding of the changes under way among the working classes.[3] It cannot be denied that socialism and anarchism played a fundamental role in the origin of the labor movement on the continent. But the facile disqualification of every union initiative as "communist" and "atheist" by conservative Catholicism actually led to a repudiation of social Catholicism's own initiatives in that milieu. For example, Father Hurtado's encouragement of the union movement in the era of the 1920s and 1930s came up against the reticence, and sometimes opposition, of the conservative sector of the hierarchy itself. The same thing happened in the case of numerous attempts to generate a "Catho-

---

3. In Colombia, for example, conservative propaganda of the 1930s cited the atheism of the communists and appealed to the Catholicism of the conservatives in justification of their electoral politics: "Nor can one be communist and Catholic at the same time." In violation of the laws of the Republic, the communists had made a political weapon of the union, taking advantage, for this purpose, of the naiveté and ignorance of the people. "If you are a true Catholic, support the official ticket of the Directorio Conservador de Bogotá" (quoted in De Roux 1983:36-37).

lic unionism" in a number of countries. Thus, while socialistic and anarchistic ideologies, imported from Europe, with their anticlericalism and their attacks on religion, alienated the labor organizations of the popular masses, Christian social corporatism itself, its paternalism, and its preoccupation with law and order crippled organized action on the part of workers (Farrel 1976:76).

A large majority of historians of the Latin American labor movement, who are generally liberals or Marxists, have not studied the relation prevailing between the Church and the working class at the beginning of the century. Church history, in its turn, overconcerned with the lot of the institution itself, has neglected a study of the popular and working-class mentality in those years.

While the Church and the Catholic elite were surely not absent from the labor world, their initiatives were undertaken in a limited sphere of activity, and were adapted neither to the religious nor to the social needs of the mass of new proletariat. Furthermore, traditional parish ecclesiastical structure, in many places, proved inadequate when it came to facing the new challenges of the labor world. In many instances, pastoral neglect left a vacuum that was promptly filled by socialist and anarchist propaganda. The nascent working class took its distance from the Church. But the question to be asked is whether this distancing inevitably led to the atheism of the working masses of the time. We are inclined to think that this was not the case. What happened, rather, was that a combination of factors—pastoral neglect, church paternalism, harsh conditions of exploitation, effective propaganda by socialists and anarchists—besides providing an impulse for worker struggle and awareness, introduced anticlerical attitudes indeed but failed to touch the foundations of popular faith among the peasant masses in process of proletarianization.[4] So far, very few empirical studies have penetrated the mentality of the working-class masses of the era.

## From Social Christianity to Base Popular Christianity

The first social-Christian groups sprang up from the first decades of the century onward in various Latin American countries, within or in parallel with conservatively oriented groups and sometimes in open strife with them. By the 1930s, the trend was no longer marginal. By the 1940s and the postwar years, internal renewal in the Catholic

---

4. See Parker (1987, 1991b), Salinas (1980, 1984, 1987, 1991).

sphere would lead to the consolidation of a progressive pastoral model, in harmony with the modernizations being produced in the Latin American society of the time. The pastoral approach known as the New Christendom meant the transition from a strategy on the defensive against the urbanizing, industrializing world to a more aggressive mass pastoral ministry that attempted to regroup Catholic personnel for the "Christianization of the world." It would be the "liberalized" and "secularized" elite—middle-class sectors, business and professional people, intellectuals, union leaders, and youth—who would most enthusiastically welcome the models of Catholic renovation, whose inspiration would be in Maritain's "integral humanism." On the pastoral level, Catholic Action, in the footsteps of the Italian model, and the specialized movements (of the Jocist variety) that would follow the Belgian and French model, were to express this movement of renewal quite clearly in various countries of the continent. On the political level, this would be done by the groups inspired in social Christianity, now transformed into Christian Democratic political currents (Dussel 1972, Pike 1970, Maduro 1987).

In the postwar era up until the 1960s, the Christian social movement that promoted a modernization of Catholicism within the Church grew in depth and extent (Vallier 1971). A unique ensemble of figures in the pastoral renewal of the Latin American Church of the era is a sign of the times: Archbishop Manuel Larraín in Chile, first president of the Latin American Bishops Conference; Hélder Câmara, prophetic bishop of the Brazilian northeast, a principal champion of the renewal at Vatican Council II and later an outstanding protagonist of the project mounted at Medellín; Bishop Sanabria in Costa Rica; Bishop Ramón Bogarín in Paraguay; Cardinal Landázuri Ricketts in Peru; and so on. All of these took their inspiration in an antiliberal conception emphasizing involvement in the world, whose autonomy is recognized but which is seen as in need of being impregnated with Christian values. This conception promotes the common good as the prime finality of the state, social reforms on behalf of workers, labor-management harmony, the social function of private property, and the like.

In the majority of Latin American countries, Christian Democratic currents sprang up. They crystalized into powerful, influential political parties with opportunities for the exercise of power, sprang up mainly only in Chile, Venezuela, and some Central American countries. In numerous other countries, the fate of these trends was very diverse, and by the end of the 1960s they were swamped by new political and ecclesial actors representing an alternative on the popular left (Maduro 1987, Correa 1986). In general, in this stage of democratization of Latin American society, other parties that happened to be at hand, liberal or populist—linked to anticlerical tradition—captured the center space, and social-Christian groups either found themselves confined in advanced currents of conservatism or were reduced to small groups throwing little weight. By the 1950s, these parties had incorporated the developmentalist, technocratic, and modernizing theories of CEPAL into their ideological fund, and in the 1960s, on the strength of their reformist character, they became the preferred agents of the policies of the Alliance for Progress on the Latin American continent. What was being sought was a policy for the reform of the capitalistic structure, especially in its lagging agricultural sector, with a view to bringing it abreast of the times and thereby broadening its market and improving the status of peasant masses and urban settlers. The aim was also to provide an effective counter to the socialistic impulses and aspirations stirred by Fidel Castro's triumph in Cuba (1959). We have the most evident symbol of this fact in the alternative project, "Revolution in Liberty," of Frei's Christian Democratic government in Chile (1964-70).

Whereas, from a political viewpoint, these social Christian-renewal currents exerted an influence in popular sectors and in some cases gained massive support, of a clientelistic sort, for their ends. They had no very great influence on the piety of the masses, which reproduces itself in autonomous fashion. The expressions of pastoral renewal that now appeared, accentuated by the interior renewal of Catholicism at Vatican Council II (liturgical reforms, religious education, parish life, and so on), and the renewals in the thought and the doctrine of Christian humanism, found their main audience among the middle classes. Here it will be worth our while to refer to Iván Vallier's study on the "religious elite," which, precisely in the era in which developmentalism was in vogue and the *aggiornamento* launched by Vatican Council II was beginning to be applied on our continent, declared,

A wedge is being driven between Catholicism and the traditional order . . . This new Catholicism is the fulcrum for the lever between Latin America's past and its future. In more obvious terms, anyone wanting to contribute to the development of Latin America is going to have to bet on a dark horse, at least if things be considered in a perspective long-term. Instead of being content with simply asking for more capital and new tools, the need is to help the new Catholic elite to transform the Catholic system and thus make it possible for the "Catholic factor" and its cultural power to be applied to the whole task of social development. In a word, the religious reform is a requirement of the social reform. [Vallier 1971:189]

The "modernizing" vector of these renewals, by introducing a process of rationalization of the faith that was strongly critical of the more traditional expressions of popular faith, led the renewal to take its distance from the religious sense of the people. As we know, the first conciliar reform to take on an unprecedented dimension was the liturgical renewal. Here, the new priests, adopting a spirit favorable to "progress" and change in secular society, along with suppressing Latin, celebrating mass in vernacular languages, turning the altar to face the people, stimulating the participation of the faithful in the Eucharist, and introducing other reforms, now began to strip the churches of the images and religious adornment that, for popular religious sensibility, constituted basic iconic anchorages. Criticism of popular religious practices grew in intensity. Requests for a blessing of the palms were once more aggressively qualified as a "superstitious practice." Votive offerings and carnival festivals celebrated by the poor on their patron saint's day were once more disqualified as "pagan and vulgar practices." Many of the people's expressions were thus repressed and, while the renewal did introduce a needed reform into preconciliar official Catholicism, which had been too formal and rigoristic, it threatened to provoke a new breach between the clergy and popular religion.

In reaction to the church project of readjustment to the process of modernization and capitalistic urbanization, and as a result of the crisis of the developmentalistic model and the upsurge of the popular struggle in the 1960s, a minority current of "Christian revolutionaries" arose, at first identifying with guerrilla strategies and then organizing into the "Christians for Socialism" movement (Richard 1976, Silva Gotay 1983). Camilo Torres was the great symbol of this current. Imbued with the Marxist socialistic ideal of the Cuban Revolution, these new activists took a socialistic and anti-imperialistic approach. Not surprisingly, the Rockefeller Report (1968) and the Rand Commission (1969) promptly expressed North American consternation at this development in Latin American Catholicism. However, this current was still very distant from the popular classes. On the basis of an orthodox reading of Marxism and a theology of revolution, it criticized the traditional forms of religion among the people, regarding them as alienating and archaic.

The document of the National Secretariate of Christians for Socialism on popular religion presented at the National Meeting of November 1972 in Santiago de Chile proclaimed it to be of the utmost urgency to espouse the cause of Christians of the oppressed sectors and to become detached from judgments typical of the "enlightened, secularized" bourgeoisie to the effect that the religion of the people was pure superstition, pure magic. It was acknowledged that, in terms of the human underpinnings of a popular faith that had sprung up under the stress of limit situations, that faith was indeed a quest for salvation. It was a very human practice. When the help of the Blessed Virgin or the saints was besought, the document went on, that was an attempt to find refuge in a sibling community. But popular faith had a fatal flaw: it separated the believer from the people's struggle. This religious practice was incomplete, then—a "false liberation praxis, which turns its back on the consciousness and struggle of the oppressed. It is a false praxis, because it fails to break the chains that enslave the people . . . Instead of taking history into their own hands, [the people] trust in the miraculous." In the face of this situation, continues the text, there are only two alternatives: either to reject the religious element in order to devote oneself completely to the struggle, or to attempt to transform that religious practice. But a secularistic, enlightened, vanguardist mentality ultimately prevailed in the document, and an antipopular view of the religious phenomenon was advanced:

> The basis of religion is total submission to an alien power . . . The working people are directly subjected to the productive process and to capitalistic relations of production . . . The great and fundamental religious practice, then, is workers' participation in and incorporation into capitalistic society. Christianity has a religious face when it is positioned as part of this society . . . This is the sort of Christianity practiced by all of those who resist the attempt of working people and their vanguard to take power. By contrast, nonreligious Christianity, liberative Christianity, takes its place among the forces of the people, who are ever closer to taking power . . . Religion is subjection to an alien, alienating power; and revolution is the taking of power by the oppressed and by their own might in history. Therefore religion must be overcome by way of revolution . . . In the socialist society, religious practice will be left behind. [National Secretariate, Christians for Socialism, in Celam 1977:38-41]

The process of *aggiornamento* launched by Vatican Council II unfolded in Latin America in a convulsive age (Houtart and Pin 1965). The crisis had quite a pervasive influence on the Church, and was manifested in polarization, the crisis in priestly vocations, secularization, the politicization and radicalization of apostolic movements, and so on. The Medellín Bishops Conference echoed the "longing for liberation" that was springing up among the popular masses, and initiated a process of acknowledgment of certain values in popular piety. But only in the second half of the 1970s would a genuine transformation begin to take place in the Catholic field that would set the stage for a reencounter between a Church making an "option for the poor" and the concrete believing and oppressed people, with all of their longings for justice and their characteristic religious expressions. The Puebla Bishops Conference formulated this new reality in doctrinal terms. Key figures in this historic pilgrimage undertaken by a Church opting to become involved once more in Latin American society, on the basis of an option for the poor and their liberation, were Dom Hélder Câmara (Olinda and Recife, Brazil), Bishop Sergio Méndez Arceo (Cuernavaca, Mexico) and Archbishop Oscar Romero (El Salvador), Cardinals Paulo Evaristo Arns (São Paulo), Ivo Lorscheider (Fortaleza), Raúl Silva Henríquez (Santiago de Chile), Bishops Bambarén (Peru), Proaño (Riobamba, Ecuador), Enrique Alvear (Chile), and Enrique Angelleli (Argentina); and the "rosary of martyrs" who experienced and shared the anguishes and sufferings of the poor by giving their lives for them (Debesse 1991).

Faced in the 1970s with the new authoritarian regimes of the Southern Cone or with authoritarian oligarchical domination in Central America and the attempt of all of these regimes to reshape societies under the inspiration of the new model of transnational capitalistic domination, the churches, or, by default, groups of Christians, rose up as defenders of violated human rights and, on the strength of their institutional weight, became a space of relative safety around which destroyed, repressed, and atomized civil society began to regroup. While it is clear that, in various countries, certain sectors of the Church were seen to be committed to the military regimes and to offer legitimation to the antipopular practices of these regimes, it is no less certain that, in other cases, a goodly part of the Church showed itself to be forthrightly committed to the popular lot and suffered the repressive consequences of its commitment as well (Marins et al. 1978, Dussel 1980). Oscar Arnulfo Romero, El Salvador's archbishop and martyr, was fully a symbol of the Church that had made its "preferential option for the poor" and that, from a point of departure in grassroots or "base" (*de base*) groups, was attempting to organize the people and offer them support and encouragement in order that—with the tightening of bonds of solidarity—the popular sectors might gain their rights, develop survival strategies, and organize for the struggle for justice and liberation. On the pastoral level, the *base church communities (comunidades eclesiales de base)*, the delegates of the Word, or lay ministry, lay participation, the spirit of popular initiative in the community, and the building of the Church itself were fostered.[5]

Thus, a "new way of being Church" among the people bore fruit and yielded a synthesis; and out of the actual religious production and tradition of popular struggle, a liberative "popular Christianity" sprang up (Richard and Irarrázaval 1981). In order to resist the new forms of oppression and misery implanted by the capitalism of the 1970s and 1980s, instead of rejecting their religious traditions the people reformulated them, drawing new strength and symbolical motivation from them, both for their immediate survival and for their medium- and long-term sociopolitical struggle.

In the case of the Sandinista victory in Nicaragua in 1979, the festive character of popular religion fused with the carnival spirit of the triumph over Somoza's oppression. The popular festival of the Immaculate Conception, the most important popular religious celebration, had a new motif after the Sandinista victory. In novenas, in homes and neighborhoods, the fiesta reached its climax on the night of the feast, when crowds filled the streets and the fireworks and singing were punctuated by vociferous shouts of "Why such joy?" And the answer would ring out, "Mary's Conception!" And children would race from house to house to get their candy (Irarrázaval 1981). In Estelí, Monimbó, Granada, Somoto, and Managua, the traditional saints and patronal Marian feasts were now celebrated in thanksgiving for the gift of liberation from the Somoza tyranny. It is not strange that the religious field should have been transformed into an area of sharp ideological clash between the official Church and the church groupings that supported a Church of the poor favorable to the revolutionary process. And in between stood a people who had continued to express their traditional faith in giving thanks for the Sandinista triumph, and who now relied on that same faith to resist the violence of foreign intervention and counterrevolution, although frequently enough there was an uncritical attachment to the higher echelons of a church hierarchy accustomed to using religion for purposes of con-

---

5. See Boff (1981), Borrat (1982), Bruneau (1980), Cáceres et al. (1983), Castillo (1986), Deelen (1980), De Roux (1983), Gomes de Souza (1982, 1986), Gómez Moreira (1987), Gutiérrez (1979), Mesters (1975), Muñoz (1983), Perani (1981), Rolim (1980), Soneira and Lumerman (1986), and the collective works of Alvear et al. (1983), and SEDOC (1979).

servative ideology. The current process of democratization is opening a new page in the history of this complex, conflictive, and rending relation between official religion and popular religion in Nicaragua.

A new "base Christianity," then, is arising from the confluence, in the praxis of popular struggle, of a Church making an option for the poor and of the people with their social and religious traditions. A new sort of "experience of church" fosters and reproduces this new form of Christianity among the people. In the small base community, primary relations of siblingship and democracy predominate: the Church is close to the people (Parker 1987), the symbol of a God who accompanies the destiny of the poor, the symbol of the God of life, that defender of the oppressed in the face of the injustice of the system.

## Diversity of Contemporary Forms of Catholicism

Popular Catholicism's current panorama evinces the fact that, on the one hand, the reproduction of traditional forms of piety goes on, while at the same time new forms of popular Catholicism arise, ranging from a Christianity of liberation, to a Catholicism that uses the popular formula but secularizes its traditions internally, to religious asceticisms that legitimate projects of integration and social climbing. The popular religious field has exploded in quite a heterogeneous multiplicity of expressions, which can be studied and grasped in terms of *"religious models."*[6] It is a matter of meaning structures that lack defined empirical limitations but that, instead, are open to a typological understanding as consistent ensembles of meaning, each having a rather specific content in terms of its beliefs and rituals.

Certain common traits aside, it is impossible to reduce the various heterogeneous forms of religious expressions of the different popular groups comprehensively to a single category. "Popular Catholicism," as we have mentioned, has come to be synonymous with a religious expression homogeneously extended among the people—a traditional, rather magical form of piety. Thus, the concept is weakened as pertinent and univocal.

---

6. In research carried out in Santiago de Chile, we have been able to verify the existence of a spectrum of religious models under the common affirmation of a Catholic faith. These are believers who can be classified in accordance with certain religious worldviews having a kinship with specific views of culture and society. I have analyzed these models in depth in Parker 1986a.

## Various Models, Heterogeneous Representations

There is in the people an entire, inexhaustible wellspring of religious creativity, which of course is not immune from the various influences of both the structural and the historical conditionings of society as a whole. One of the key characteristics of the new influences on the religious expressions of the popular masses during recent decades proceeds not only from society as a whole but also from the process of change at work within the religious field itself. The renewal of the Catholic Church, whose unique landmark was Vatican Council II, and whose consequences for our continent are patent at the Medellín Conference, left its mark on an entire decade here, from 1968 to the Puebla Conference of 1979. Recent evolution in religious currents, both among the Protestant churches and in Latin American Catholicism, will not yield to analysis without there being taken into account what has occurred in the past two decades. At the same time, changing conditions in the social situation of the various classes and subordinate groups and their concrete and specific daily practices, of which we have already made mention, produce changes in the religious practices and representations of those same sectors.

An in-depth analysis of urban popular discourse with reference to the religious ambit reveals the existence of distinct religious models. It is a question of the combination of semantic categories that shape typical codes of consistent sets of religious meaning. Each such code is a model whose manifestation occurs in its vehicle of communication, which is the popular grammar, vocabulary, and ensemble of rites and gestures. We are dealing with religious production in a culture that does not systematically develop its cultural productions and that is in constant symbolical and practical transaction with the official religion of the churches.

We have not sufficient space here to analyze in depth the content, meaning, and functions of each of the models we mention. Suffice it to point out that the heterogeneity of codified religious representations seems to be greater in the urban popular milieu than in the rural. This phenomenon has led Manuel Marzal to speak of a *Catholic pluralism* (Marzal 1990) in the case of Peru. But while it is important to recognize that it is within the Catholic sphere itself that the variants multiply, popular religious pluralism obviously goes beyond the Catholic sphere.

There are models at hand whose origin is in a religious dissidence from Catholicism, the hegemonic religion in the religious field. We refer to certain formally Catholic models that are internally secularized and substantively skeptical and rationalistic, which call into question a series of traditional and official beliefs. Along with these, there are the models in more or less open breach with Catholicism: the popular sects and Protestant churches (especially popular Pentecostalism), or the syncretic cults, such as *umbanda, candomblé,* voodoo, and so on, which are present especially in urban popular milieus in countries where the strong influence of a population of African origin prevails. The relevance of these models is the object of our attention in the following chapter.

In the Catholic sphere, side by side with surviving models of a more traditional Catholicism that departs, on more than one point, from official orthodoxy and that Marzal—infelicitously, in my judgment—calls "cultural Catholicism," we find other models as well, in closer proximity to the official Catholicism of the postconciliar era. Among the popular religious models more akin to official postconciliar Catholicism, we may distinguish three vectors. One of these is the model that has rather thoroughly assimilated the pastoral renewal, but whose ethical content is still under the influence of a bourgois asceticism. Another is that of "charismatic Catholics," who in certain countries are also multiplying in popular milieus, in Peru with greater intensity than in Chile, for example (Marzal 1990, Sánchez 1990), somewhat as a response—in the form of a more popular adaptation, along the lines of Pentecostalism—to the changes taking place in the city and to the social pastoral approach of the renewal and its more ethics-oriented Christianity. And finally, there is an ethical and moral model of activist commitment centering on the value of justice and on love for neighbor.

As for the *Catholic religious models* that we have mentioned among the subordinate classes and groups, it is possible to establish a typology[7] that, in broad strokes, might be set forth in the following manner.

*Traditional Catholic type*: First there is the traditional believer, who, in the countryside or in the city, tends to reproduce, under the influence of a number of distinct factors, a popular Christianity of a

---

7. This typological synthesis simplifies the traits found in the religious models that we have developed in our earlier work on the basis of our research in Santiago de Chile (see no. 5 above). These models should be compared with what Marzal and other authors posit (Parker 1986a, chap. 7).

traditional cast, preserving much of the catechism of colonial Christianity. This Catholic typically believes in God, the Virgin, and the saints, is attached to certain sacramental practices, and, in particular, cultivates popular rituals and extraecclesial devotions such as votive promises, impetratory prayers, and pilgrimages to the shrines of saints and of the Virgin. In general this type of believer maintains a critical distance from the Church, viewing with mistrust its postconciliar renewal, which seems too enlightened and nonpopular.

*Rationalistic popular Catholic type*: We also find the formally Catholic believer who subscribes to the core of the traditional profession of faith, but who—under the influence of the urban ethos—tends to secularize various of the more typically popular beliefs of the religion of past generations. This Catholic believes in God and the Virgin, but only nominally in the saints, has no devotion to the souls of the departed, and practices no sacramental or devotional life. Believers of this type may be typified as "Catholics in their own particular way"—rather secularized, and nonpracticing. They, too, take a certain distance from the institutional Church. They conceive their religion as representing an overall life-meaning, but stripped of any soteriological signification.

*Renewed traditional popular Catholic type*: Next there is the believer who is incorporated into the more renewed pastoral practices of postconciliar Catholicism, and who participates more actively in parish and sacramental life, developing more of a sense of church membership. These are persons of the popular world who have undergone a much greater influence at the hands of the Church's renewed pastoral approach in these years. Thus, they tend to attach scant value to the more traditional practices of popular piety, placing the accent on the ethical sense of their piety rather than on ritualism.

*Renewed popular Catholic type*: Finally, certain believers have made a more decided commitment to an advanced current of church renewal, and generally pursue a line of social commitment in various popular organizations. These persons' faith is characterized by a more personal attachment to Jesus, and they understand their social and liberative commitment as a necessary expression of their piety, which in turn is of a more prophetical tenor. They are usually active members of church communities, sharing in the life of these communities in a perspective of a greater "commitment to the poor."

It would be rash to attempt to generalize this typology for all of the urban popular classes of Latin America. However, taking into account the ensemble of investigations carried out in cities of Argentina, Brazil, Mexico, Peru, and Chile,[8] we may conclude that this typology is not far removed from those to be observed in expressions of popular Catholicism in various places. And so we trust that our presentation of this panorama will be helpful as an indicator of pathways for future analysis. However, the study of pluralism within Catholicism, and especially within Latin American popular Catholicism, is a process that continues to stand in need of completion.

8. See, for Argentina, Büntig (1970, 1973a), Farrel and Lumerman (1979); for Brazil, Süess (1979), who reports a number of investigations; in Mexico, Martínez et al. (1979), Zenteno (1972, 1979); for Peru, Irarrázaval (1978), Kudo (1980); and for Chile, Bentué (1975).

# Chapter 7

# The Widening Spectrum

## New Urban Popular Religions

Over the course of the first half of the twentieth century—along with the appearance of fissures in the oligarchical order, an accelerated urbanization and modernization of the economy, and the beginnings of the developmental model based on substitutive industrialization—a breach in the symbolical monopoly of Catholicism over the popular classes as a whole came clearly into evidence on our continent. It was not only anarchism and socialism that challenged Catholic influence among the new working masses; in various countries the first Pentecostal groups and Afro-American syncretic cults began to spring up in urban popular milieus. These groups would follow a specific trajectory in each country, but the general course of their development was to be more or less the same across the continent.

### *Latin American Pentecostalism*

Throughout the nineteenth century Catholicism was absolutely in command. Liberalism and Protestantism were the persuasions of very small, elite groups. The Protestant churches were "transplants" (Lalive d'Epinay 1975), devoted to the reproduction of the faith of Anglo-Saxon immigrants. But between 1910 and 1940, the panorama changed drastically, with the appearance on the scene of Pentecostal revivalist movements among the popular classes. The new sects propagated their faith with an enthusiastic proselytism, winning adherents by the droves.

As we know, Pentecostalism constitutes one of the last religious "revival" movements originating in North American Methodism at

*141*

the beginning of the twentieth century. It has spread all across the globe. Pentecostalists' firm belief in the healing power of the Holy Spirit, their biblical fundamentalism, and their dualism lead them to spurn the "sinful world," and gather them into cults typified by a great ebullience. There they are inspired, fall into trances, and prophesy, receiving the gift of tongues and the power of divine healing, as well as all manner of other blessings from God.

By 1907, in some Latin American cities, similar processes were under way. In Belén, Brazil, Swedish laborers Berg and Vingren joined the Baptist community and preached the power of the Holy Spirit. When some members of the community, rapt in ecstasy, received the Holy Spirit, began to "speak in tongues," and fervently proclaimed their conversion, the Baptist ministers expelled them from the community (Rolim 1979). In this same era, in Valparaíso, Chile, on the occasion of sermons to Methodists by a minister named Hoover, conversions to the Holy Spirit and manifestations of glossolalia occurred. Conflict erupted, and the new little group was expelled from the Methodist Church. Using Troeltsch's terms (Troeltsch 1950), we may say that what we have here is a church expelling the *sectarian faction* that had developed in its midst.

In this fashion were born in Brazil the *Assemblies of God*, and in Chile the *Pentecostal Methodist Church*—two of the principal autochthonous Pentecostal churches of Latin America. The year was 1910. That same year, in São Paulo, Luigi Francescon, a United States citizen of Italian origin, founded the Christian Congregation of Brazil, a Pentecostal movement that rapidly spread throughout the working-class barrios of the metropolis and its neighboring towns and cities. In the 1930s, Brazilian Pentecostalists spread into the more industrial and urbanized zones of the country, such as Rio de Janeiro, São Paulo, and Porto Alegro. Other evangelical groups joined them and began to send missioners to the interior of the country and abroad. As a result, in the case of the Assemblies of God, 80% of the membership is concentrated in the popular settlements of the strategic centers of national development, where 93% of the population of the country lives.[1]

Although the growth of Protestantism was general in "Catholic" Latin America, in the case of Chile and Mexico the Pentecostalist phenomenon was similar to that of Brazil whereas, by contrast, the cases of Colombia, Peru, Ecuador, Bolivia, and Central America, while

---

1. Hollenweger (1976:122). See also a panoramic view by Monique de Saint Martin (1984) of the studies on Brazilian Pentecostalism.

bearing resemblances among themselves, were different: their particular characteristic is the belated growth of the Pentecostalists, occurring primarily in rural and native American zones. Chile is the country with the highest percentage of evangelicals among its population. Brazil is the country with the highest number of Protestants in Latin America. In both countries, as well as in the other countries of our region, it is most significant that the greater proportion of national Protestantism is Pentecostalist, and that this Pentecostalism—unlike Pentecostalism in the rest of the world—besides being preponderantly urban, is of a popular character.[2]

As Hollenweger says: "Certain indicators incline us to assume that the situation in Latin America is altogether distinct. Latin American Pentecostalist ministers not only are leaders of churches of the proletariat but are themselves the scions of that social stratum. The Pentecostalist preacher is different not only from his colleagues in the United States or Europe but from the ministers of the other Latin American Protestant churches as well" (Hollenweger 1976:463).

Pentecostalists number 50-70% of Brazilian Protestants, and 80-95% of the Protestants in Chile. In both cases, we must notice the huge sphere of influence acquired by these churches and congregations with their remarkable missionary zeal. Certain authors propose multiplying the number of active members by a factor of between two and five, given the number of sympathizers as compared with that of formally active members (Kloppenburg 1978).

It is generally possible to assert that this religious movement among the Latin American popular classes grows at the same rate as society develops, and experiences the tensions of explosive urban growth, industry, commerce, and the new technologies and mass communication media. This new form of popular religion springs up mainly in the cities, but is also a response on the part of the peasant sectors marginalized by the processes just named. As Carlos Rodrigues Brandão declares: "The proposition that today, throughout the continent, Pentecostalism offers subjects of the popular classes—whites, blacks, and native Americans—a remarkable sense of adaptation to the ways of the city and peripheral urban life, as well as to the very structure of social relations determined by the current logic of the orientation of the changes governed by capitalism, seems beyond all doubt" (Rodrigues Brandão 1987:81).

---

2. See Bastían (1986), Hollenweger (1976), Irarrázaval (1978), Kudo (1980), Lative d'Epinay (1968, 1975), Martinez (1989), Medellín (1985), Valderrey (1985), and Willems (1969).

Although the expansion of the Mexican Pentecostal churches also dates from 1910, it is not as surprising as it is in the Brazilian and Chilean cases. As for the Peruvian and the Colombian cases, they resemble the Mexican case. Although Mexican Pentecostal churches boast that they are "Mexican," they maintain quite close ties with Pentecostal churches in the United States. As a general rule, the churches of Brazil and Chile are far more autonomous, and their "national" character is more accentuated. What we have here is the fact that, among both the proletariat or marginalized subproletariat of the great urban centers and among the isolated native groups marginalized by the dominant culture, similar sociological conditions arise which predispose these groups to seek an otherworldly salvation that they find in the Pentecostal message of redemption and in fundamentalist Protestant sects. In this sense, urbanization acts as a conditioning factor, an enabling but insufficient condition that must be joined to an ensemble of other factors in order to come to crystalization in the rise or spread of this kind of Pentecostal popular religion. In both cases—that of the culturally isolated natives and that of the marginal urban groups—the capitalistic system acts as a kind of detonator in situations of exploitation and marginalization in which anguish and uncertainty wax apace. In these situations, Pentecostalism, with its message of religious revival, offers meaning and hope, sustaining the monotonous life of the victims of the system with affect, spirit, siblingship, and religious euphoria.

Rarely did the influence of the historical churches surpass that of foreign immigrants because they were not able to significantly influence the popular sectors. In the press and in society, what the Protestant churches were doing passed as respectable. Their preaching was actually rather anti-Catholic, and they proposed an Anglo-Saxon individualistic spirit. That spirit operated as a symbol of the progressive society and capitalistic advances of the metropolitan countries, from which the Protestant churches received all the support and splendor of a culture that the Creole regarded as superior but foreign—"gringo." Not surprisingly, then, the Protestant faith did not "catch on" among the Catholic masses, who were accustomed to a more collective way of life and to a traditional piety more ritual and symbolical than ascetical. The Pentecostal congregations, on the other hand, were composed of little communities in which the proletariat, or peasants undergoing urbanization, subjected as they were to every sort of misery and uncertainty, found a symbolic space of *salvation* from a world perceived as a threat: the world of sin.

Just as Pentecostalism in the black community of the United States became a new force for protest against racial segregation (Hollenweger 1976, Williams 1980), the Pentecostalism of the popular urban classes of Brazil, Mexico, and Chile was a symbolical weapon in the struggle against an oligarchical order. Its beginnings in the early decades of the twentieth century consisted in a certain kind of adaptation to changing conditions of popular city life, and presented certain traits of implicit protest against the conditions of wretchedness and oppression in which the new contingents of workers and subproletarians lived. The more powerful dynamics offered by the Pentecostal congregation to the worker who was obliged to emigrate to find work won out over the immobile, territorial pastoral approach of the traditional Catholic parish. Indeed, the vacuum left by the pastoral ministry of the Catholic Church (Kloppenburg 1978) was quickly filled by the Protestant churches.

The question of the social function of this new kind of popular religion recalls Weber's prediction of the process of routinization inevitably awaiting these charismatics, and the consequent institutionalization of the sect into a church. The initial quality of religious protest becomes lost, and accommodation to the world symbolically rejected as sinful sets in. The support of the state is sought in the face of both persecution by Catholicism and the skepticism of civil and political society itself, which in the early years did not take kindly to this Pentecostal movement that threatened the predominance of Catholicism among the people, that symbolically subverted the Protestant faith of the bourgeois strata, and that explicitly impugned the dominant culture. The process of the institutional accommodation of these churches means their legalization and officialization in the framework of a religious pluralism recognized by the constitutions of this century and in the framework of a nonpolitical position on the part of the churches. This apoliticalism can lead to extreme alienation, as in the case of Chile's main Pentecostal churches, which, rejecting their popular and national origin, became the loyal defenders and legitimators of Pinochet's military government. Thereby they discharge a supplementary political function, that of the religious legitimation of the nation and state, in circumstances in which the Catholic Church is taking its distance from the National Security state and criticizing its violations of human rights (Lagos 1983, 1988; Lagos and Chacón 1986).

The tendency of certain forms of Pentecostalism to take on an alienating function has been underscored by Lalive d'Epinay in his *El refugio de las masas* (1968). In the case of Brazil, Pentecostalism has also been the object of such an analysis, which, in terms of a comparison with the developmental process of the Catholic base church communities, concludes quite convincingly that the two religious postures diverge when it comes to alienation from or commitment to the world (Rolim 1980). While the experiment with religious renewal in the Catholic base community determines a progressive enhancement of social awareness, the Pentecostal alternative, operating on the basis of new converts' cycle of frustrations—caught as these persons are in the conflictive conditions of urbanization—encloses them in the mythic circle of a protective religion by offering them, on the level of religious magic, the opportunities that they fail to find in society. In reproducing an ideology of respect for theologically legitimated authority and a sense of "social strike" (abstention from social involvement as worldly and sinful), Pentecostalism fulfills the twofold function of legitimating the reproduction of the traditional structure internal to the congregation and legitimating the existing social order.

An extensive inquiry carried out in Concepción and Talcahuano, a highly urbanized and industrialized zone of Chile, toward the end of the 1960s (Lalive and Zylberberg 1973), reveals that it is indeed the members of the Pentecostal congregations, and Protestants generally, who, being in the majority among the subproletarian strata, show themselves more conservative in their social and political options. At the close of the 1980s, this conclusion is still valid for Brazilian Pentecostalists (Rolim 1989). However, while Pentecostal theology's dualism gravitates to abstention from sociopolitical involvement, in various cases participation in the religious sphere does not actually exempt the individual from holding a political opinion in favor of change. Tennekes has demonstrated that, while Chilean Pentecostals evince less interest in society than does the average person, they vote, on the average, just as does the mean of the rest of the population, and that a high percentage actually voted for Marxist groups (Tennekes 1985). Other Pentecostal churches in Chile, Cuba, or Brazil—such as "Brazil for Christ"—are proof that the dichotomy between the material and the spiritual, between the Church and the world, is not necessarily radical and exclusive, and that the material (social and political involvement) can assume an active role in Pentecostal theology; but these churches represent a minority (Damen 1986). Seen from the standpoint of its social functions and significations, however, in the framework of the marginalized popular cultures, Pentecostalism has liberative traits, and we shall evaluate these in chapter 9.

What has occurred in other countries, where Protestantism has grown much more swiftly from the 1950s onward, especially in the Andean and Central American countries, is largely to be explained by the fact that their processes of urbanization and modernization have come later. In penetrating lagging societies, the process of capitalistic modernization does so by dislocating traditional relations, and this generates social and cultural tensions, especially in the more traditional subcultures of predominantly native composition. The response to that new situation on the cultural and religious level is not without its conflicts, and the vacuum of traditional cultural guidelines is filled by various alternatives. Here, Pentecostalism makes a very assertive offer of salvation, joined to a charismatic element of attraction with which the traditional subculture feels an empathy. This conditioning factor would explain the Pentecostal boom and the success of certain other sectarian groups among indigenous populations living in rural regions removed from the urban centers. There has also been a popular urban growth in Protestantism, but the characteristic direction of the process has been rather in a different direction from that of the countries of earlier urbanization and industrialization.

Another important variable, however, when it comes to explaining the more recent upsurge of the popular Pentecostalisms in the Andean and Central American countries, emerges from the explicit policies of penetration on the part of Protestantism of North American origin into the erstwhile "virgin, reserved field" of Latin American Catholicism. Taking advantage of the negative evaluation, by the political ideology espoused by the North American administrations since the 1960s, of the renewal occurring in the Catholic sphere (Ezcurra 1982), missionary activity has been intense, even using sophisticated means of communication and religious penetration, permeating the field of religious demand with a gamut of "religious supply." For example, we have the "electronic churches," the televangelism of preachers such as Billy Graham, Jimmy Swaggart, Rex Humbard, the Linguistic Summer Institute in Bolivia and Ecuador, or the evangelical sects of Guatemala and other Latin American countries. Also to be included here is another type of sectarian expression, among which we find the Adventists, Mormons, and Jehovah's Witnesses, which groups more nearly resemble a church type, and the more fanatical associations, such as the Unification Church of Sun Myung Moon, the Children of God, Jim Jones, and others. Competition for the masses, then, especially the popular masses, has been very intense among these missionary religious groups, and they have maintained it with most remarkable energy and aggressiveness, which have won them the epithet, among others, of "religious arm" of the CIA—the instrument of penetration by North American imperialism in the region.

Without a doubt, these strategies of aggressive penetration by the new groups and evangelical and/or semi-Christian religious sects have discovered fertile soil, especially in popular sectors. One of the reasons for this is the crisis in the cultural frameworks of these popular sectors, a crisis rooted in the structural changes and the misery, repression, violence, and lack of social participation of the 1960s and 1970s. Another reason is that these new groups and religious sects are almost completely compatible with the people's type of religious quest according to the frameworks of the people's own symbolical culture—their style of thought and their syncretic religious practices and beliefs.

Furthermore, in a political context like that of Central America, interinstitutional tensions and competition for the control of civil society increase in tandem with the growth of authoritarian tendencies in the state questioned by the Catholic Church. The spread of Protestant popular religion, then, can be likewise interpreted as a fracturing of civil society "to the advantage of a client-patron relation between dissident religious society and the state, in the context of a crisis of the Central American social field" (Bastián 1990).

### New Afro-American Cults

It is especially in regions of Latin America where the colonial economy once made extensive use of slave labor that the culture and religion of the subordinate classes are steeped in cultural elements of African origin. No Latin American country, however, has been without a population of African origin, at least to some little degree. In the majority of cases, when slave labor was not employed in large-scale production, at least the use of female and male slaves for domestic service was the general rule among the great aristocratic families of the colonies. At any rate, the significant demographic, social, and cultural contribution of the so-called *negros*, "blacks"—a derogatory term, to the ears of the dominant culture—registers with greater intensity wherever the plantation economy and geographical and climatic conditions made possible the extensive use of a slave labor force transported under compulsion to the New World from the coasts of Africa (Verbeek 1976:9-40). Official culture, however, with its ethnocentric prioritization of the West, systematically tends to reproduce racial prejudices, to the point where, "in many countries and regions, the flesh-and-blood black had turned into smoke" (Triana 1987:3). The presence of the black in the various regions and countries of the continent is, of course, diversified.[3] In a number of regions there are enclaves of almost pure-blood blacks, many being the descendants of fugitive slaves who managed to maintain their freedom. In the Antilles, blacks make up the primary demographic element. In Mexico and Central America, the *garífunas* abound—a *mestizaje*, or miscegenation, of blacks and various native groups. Brazil's population includes a considerable proportion of blacks and mulattos. In countries like Colombia, Venezuela, and Panama, the black race is being gradually diluted by miscegenation. In countries such as Bolivia, Guatemala, Paraguay, Uruguay, Argentina, and Chile, the black population is of minimal importance, as contrasted with the predominance of other cultural influences (whether native or resulting from the swell of European immigrants in the nineteenth and twentieth centuries).

The relevance of piety in the traditional African spirit is well authenticated. Anthropologists tell us that Africans' "entire culture is, as it were, saturated with the religious element" (Arboleda 1986:15). Of course, as Afro-Americans' piety is their "characteristic seal," that religiousness is difficult for Christian missioners to understand when they compare it to their chauvinistic European ethics and piety.

Today, we observe elements of African origin in the popular religious expressions—including those of "popular Catholicism"—of nations such as Brazil, Haiti, Cuba, Puerto Rico, the Dominican Republic, Venezuela, Colombia, and Panama. In the Anglophone countries of the Caribbean, the Antilles, and South America, where we find a much higher proportion of black or mixed population, a similar phenomenon occurs, although here it is on the basis of a Protestant predominance. In many cases, the mythico-ritual, archaic African contribution gives rise to syncretic cults incorporating Ibero-Lusitanian Catholic traits and even indigenous components in a new synthesis. What we have then are complex religious systems. Many of the adepts of these systems insist that they are "good Catholics." Just as the majority of the Haitian people are baptized—indeed, they think that baptism is required in order to participate in voodoo, without any sense of contradiction—so too, Afro-Brazilians, and even populations without actual African blood in their veins, "frequent the sacraments and have Masses said in honor of their *orixás*, their spirits. Owing to official church disapproval, they conceal their adherence to these cults" (Süess 1979:93). Taking into consideration the slave origin of the black and mulatto population and the classist and racist

---

3. Bastide (1973, 1982), Depestre (1982), Dussel (1982), and Triana (1987).

prejudices of the dominant culture, it is not strange that, in general terms, this Latin American population should correspond to important segments of the rural or urban popular classes of these societies. Popular folklore and culture—in music, in language, in beliefs and ritual—by way of cultural contact (stimulated by racial integration in the case of mulattos), have received the influence of contributions of African origin.

African religions no longer survive as such in Latin America. But they subsist there in latent form, however distorted and impoverished, or have come to include Catholic, and even Protestant, religious expressions by reason of new conditions created by the process of a change from traditional society to the modern urban industrial society (Bastide 1982). Traits of these black religions become revitalized, and thus new Afro-American cults spring up that preserve atavistic elements, but in a wholly autochthonous and original synthesis.

The most interesting such creative expressions are Haitian voodoo, Cuban and Puerto Rican Santería, *candomblé* in the Brazilian northeast, the Rastafarians in Jamaica, Brazilian *umbanda*, the cult of María Lionza in Venezuela, and others. There is a widespread belief in a Supreme Being, the preexistent Creator, but this Being is accompanied by a countless pantheon of "spirits" (who receive various denominations—*loas*, *orixás*, and so on). These spirits, and very often the spirits of the dead, are regarded as the mediators through whom the will of the sacred powers is manifested. To these spirits—commonly called by the names of Catholic saints—one must offer sacrifices and public worship in order to obtain their pardon, forgiveness, and protection. Belief in spirits, deities, and saints—together with visions, trances, and possession, as well as ritual dances, life norms, congregations, and so on—produces a syncretic mixture of the African element with the Catholic and even the Protestant, to the accompaniment of spiritism, superstition, and magic.

Afro-American ritual hosts a considerable element of festival, as Duvignaud (1974) has observed. Duvignaud's thesis is that, in Brazilian *candomblé*, as in so many other instances of popular festive celebration, the goal is to multiply all possible emotions by the invention of imaginary figures. The hysteria, and even paranoia, for which Afro-American rituals are reproached are only perceptions, says Duvignaud; instead, at work is simply a different way of understanding what the "true" and the "false" are on the part of a culture whose conventions are not those of a formalized and rationalistic society such as the bourgeois. The actors in *candomblé* know what reason and good sense are; it is only that they suspend these when entering into their trances and possessions. Indeed, for our part, we think that the Afro-American cults are a different way of communicating with the outside world, a way having little connection with the means of communication proper to official culture's stereotyped manners of exteriorization.

The magical religious rituals of the Afro-American cults are inspired in the combined notes of attraction and repulsion attaching to "the Holy" (Rudolf Otto), so that we may assert that the predominant motivating sentiments are fear, on the one hand, and gratitude, on the other. The motivations in question are certainly of a practical order, of the *do ut des*, imprecatory type, intended to protect or rescue the actors from the evils caused by the spirits or by the dead, such as sicknesses or enmity. Hence, these expressions of piety are frequently compared to animistic cults, in which spirits dominate the forces of nature accepted by human beings without reaction. But in the spirit of the Afro-American, so open to gratitude, one must thank the spirits and the dead in order to guarantee the reproduction of harmony—harmony with nature and with the group, solidarity with the community and a contribution to its stability and identity. Not to thank the spirits is to sunder this harmony: that would be an evil thing, and would make a person liable to punishment (Hurbon 1972:147-58).

All of these things can be attributed to the covert survival of African religious traditions (such as the Bantu sacred dances or the rites of Dahomey and Benin)—for instance, in the black folklore arising on the American plantation. (An example would be the legend of "Pai João," who tricks his master. Through these traditional Afro-American elements, blacks assert their identity and mount their protest, through burlesque, against the dominator.) Likewise at work is a dialectical interaction with official religion and the dominant culture. At times greater plasticity is employed, with special recourse to certain mechanisms in which, in striking fashion, we observe what certain anthropologists dub "antagonistic acculturation" (Martín 1986:161). By this process, the dominated culture takes on the external aspects (the signifiers) of the dominant culture and religion, but not the ends or significates of these. For example, extensive use is made, in all Afro-American cults, of the saints and Catholic devotions—but within a context of signification and rite that conceals beliefs in African deities. Thus, Batala, or Shango, will be St. Barbara in Bahía and Cuba, and St. Ann in Haiti. Yemana is the Virgin Mary—Our Lady of the Immaculate Conception in Rio de Janeiro, Our Lady of the Rosary in

Bahia, and the Virgin of Regla in Cuba. Osun will be the Virgin Mary in Brazil, and Our Lady of Charity in Cobre, Cuba. Esu will be the devil in Brazil. And so on (Herskovits 1937).

The Afro-American cults are not exclusively urban, nor are they of twentieth-century origin. In a number of cases, however, certain cults correspond to cultural and religious forms having their origin in a response to the urbanization processes of Latin American capitalism. At all events, their rapid spread, in countries of black or mulatto influence, from 1930 onward can be understood only as a parallel to the growth in the rate of the sociocultural "urbanization" of vast masses of workers.

In Brazil, the expressions of Afro-Brazilian religion, especially *candomblé*, were already current amidst the popular classes by the end of the nineteenth century, and Afro-Kardecist syncretisms appeared frequently in various urban centers. As the twentieth century opened, in a number of popular barrios and *favelas* (slums) of Rio, São Paulo, and other cities various centers of *macumba* developed an Afro-American magical ritual in honor of a set of divinities, including indigenous ones, performed for the symbolical healing and cure of ailments. Their stimulating dramatic quality attracted a considerable number of persons, especially of black and mixed race. The practitioners of *macumba* believe in diabolical spirits (*exus*) and sacrifice animals in an atmosphere of popular language, drink, and what the dominant culture criticizes as "vulgar excesses."

Toward the beginning of the 1920s, Zelio Morales received a revelation enjoining upon him the special mission of founding a new religion, to be called *umbanda*. Thus, the first Umbandist center was founded in the Niteroi district of Rio de Janeiro. From there, from 1925 onward, *umbanda* rapidly spread through urban middle and popular sectors. The project consisted not in an extension of the African cults, but in a "de-Africanization" of the *macumba* element and in the abandonment of the Kardecists' static, insipid rituals through the establishment of a "national" religion, in which elements of Catholicism were incorporated. As for the origin and sociological significance of *umbanda*, Bastide (1982:69-70) states that the cult was the product of the proletarianization of blacks in the city, together with their social rejection by middle-class whites. This new spiritism has arisen out of the struggle between the petite bourgeoisie (Kardecism) and the nascent proletariat (with the growing empowerment of blacks) in the old religious perspective. Its recruitment among poor whites and workers of color is an expression of the multiracial formation of this new urban proletariat. For Brown (Brown et al. 1985:10ff.), on the other hand, *umbanda* reflects a kind of symbolical alliance between the urban middle and popular classes, generating a nationalistic ideology in the context of the rise of Vargas's populism (1930-45). It combines Catholic, African, and indigenous Brazilian symbols, thus assembling all of the ingredients of a Brazilian national identity, in Gilberto Freyre's sense.

We have a similar case in the cult of María Lionza in Venezuela. Although this cult is less extensive, its peculiar syncretism demonstrates that, here, too, we are dealing with the symbolizing of a national culture, in this case the Venezuelan, with all of its ingredients and even contradictions.[4]

In the case of Brazil, despite the strong pressures exerted on *umbanda* by the state and the Catholic Church, both of which saw a threat to their hegemony over the emerging urban classes, this new urban religion registered an astonishing growth from 1930 onward (Kloppenburg 1980).

The popular nature of the new cult is disputed by the religious expressions corresponding to the middle and upper classes—Catholicism, Protestantism, and spiritism. These groups reject *umbanda*'s fetishistic "distortions" and criticize it as being opposed to progress. The prejudice has spread, by way of the educational system and its secularizing ideology, that *umbanda* is a "religion of the ignorant." Threatened and isolated—in the religious field as well as by a consumer, secularist culture—the Umbandists, mainly of popular origin, seek symbolical refuge in their cults of possession. There they recover psychological balance and a collective identity—both of which are necessary if they are to confront their adverse conditions of misery, ostracism, and oppression. However, their resistance strategy operates only on the symbolical plane. They are the first to defend the prevailing constitutional order and to support political candidacies—without a party preference—with a view to winning favorable spaces for their reproduction as an urban popular religion of the oppressed.

In the processes of integration and negotiation, Umbandists employ the traditional mechanisms of paternalism that characterize Latin American culture. These mechanisms are broadly utilized in the *terreiros* (*umbanda* meeting places) in the relations between the *pai de santos* ("father of saints") and *mai de santos* ("mother of saints") and their proselytes. But the same mechanisms are utilized in the relations between each *terreiro* and the Umbandist Federation, as

---

4. Martín (1986), Pollak-Eltz (1974), and Sosa et al. (1973).

well as between the latter and the civil authorities.[5]

Since the 1950s, society has been more open to *umbanda*, and thousands of centers, along with various federations, have been legalized. Access to the media has been made more readily available: radio programs, *umbanda* periodicals, and various activities have established *umbanda* as a socially legitimated religious option in the context of the cities of south-central Brazil. *Umbanda* as an option in the religious field has continued its growth, and in the 1990s its cultural and even political importance cannot be ignored.

## Religious Pluralization in Its Sociological Context

We observe that the tendency to a pluralization of the Latin American religious field grows as we descend the social scale. We see that Latin America and the Caribbean can no longer be regarded as a homogeneous continent from the viewpoint of their religious identification. While it is true that Catholicism continues to be the religion of the majority, it is no less certain that new religious responses are growing among popular and middle-class groups—a movement accentuated and facilitated by the processes of capitalistic modernization themselves. These new alternatives, scattered along the spectrum of the field of religious symbolism, are, all of them, in varying degrees, modalities of dissidence from the Catholic field. What we find is either Protestantism—mainly Pentecostal, in popular and marginalized groups—or else the great variety of alternatives presented by the Afro-American Christian syncretic religions. Now, sociologically speaking, what factors would explain the fascination that these new religions hold for the urban popular masses? Obviously the answer cannot be a simple one. We must recognize the multidetermination and at the same time the relative autonomy, polyfunctionality, and semiotic specificity of religious phenomena (Parker 1986a) in Latin American social processes. However, here we must adopt once more a rather widespread thesis concerning the growth of the

---

5. However, it is not a matter of a simple manipulation of the Umbandist people by the parties—merely a "mass of [campaign] maneuvers." In Pechman's view (Seiblitz 1985), we are not dealing with an asymmetrical relationship in which the parties would be taking advantage of the Umbandists. "Actually, [the Umbandists] also take advantage of the situation. Thus, as religion serves politics, the latter serves religion as well, whether by assuring it an institutional space for its demands or by supporting particular individual political ambitions" (Seiblitz 1985:42).

Protestant denominations among us. The explanation to which we refer has its origin in studies done in the United States by Richard Niebuhr (Niebuhr 1954). This author asserts that at the origin of certain religious expressions is a situation of economic dispossession. Especially, religious organizations of the "sect" type (in the sociological sense), Niebuhr says, arise in consequence of the deprivation in which economically dominated groups find themselves.

The data and processes that we observe in the Latin American popular religious field indicate that Niebuhr's thesis ought to be accepted, subject to revisions that would strip it of the determinism that threatens it.

After all, as we have seen, Pentecostalism and the Afro-American cults arise and develop principally in marginalized popular sectors partially integrated into the labor market and having less resources and socioeconomic status. It is a question of sectors which, in many cities, shape the masses of subproletarians, the unemployed or underemployed of the informal market. Urban popular sectors on this point share a class situation similar to that of certain peasant groups, mainly of native Americans, among whom the Pentecostal cults have also tended to grow. These groups have comparatively little primary schooling, and their traditional popular traits are more developed, as Lalive has shown. Writing on the subject of the Chilean Pentecostalists, Lalive establishes that in the life of the Pentecostal social bonds tend to be reproduced community that, in turn, reproduce in the city the old bonds between owner and peasant on the traditional large farm or ranch (Lalive d'Epinay 1968). These groups, owing to their poorer training, generally constitute sectors that live in particularly miserable conditions, have fallen into vice, delinquency, or prostitution, and are scorned and persecuted by the police and the official culture. They find in the Pentecostal congregation or the Umbandist cult a space in which to repair their lives—in which to be reborn to a healthy life free of the vices and evils (evil spirits) that abound in the sinful city. Corresponding to a rejection of the world by the Pentecostal convert, who seeks "healing" from vices, sins, diseases, and ailments in this world, is a magical religious deliverance from the spirits of evil by means of the rituals and dances of the Afro-American cults. No very frank will to climb the social ladder is in evidence, although the observable consequence of participation in the cult is an elevation in social status. Rather we see a will to abandon a situation of marginality by distancing oneself from the official culture via a religious dissidence in the direction of non-Catholic vectors: Protestant, especially Pentecostalist, and those of the Afro-American cults. Here, religion performs a very clear function in the symbolical strategy of survival. Together with the greater importance of superstitious magical religious rituals of symbolical protection, this strategy contributes to the subjects' actual abandonment of their status of sociocultural marginalization, to their incorporation into an alternative society (the religious cult in question), and—along the path of symbolism, generally a real path—to their ascent in social status.

The Pentecostal and the Afro-American cults are surely very different from each other in their beliefs, doctrines, traditions, and liturgies But they share a common characteristic: the key role, in their worship, of bodily expression. We find in these cults a bodily, expressive, festive mediatory rituality of song and possession (by the Holy Spirit, or by the "spirits"), in which the sacred is embodied by means of rhythm and ecstasy in cathartic sessions that snatch the adept from the most outward demonstrations of sensibility into a mysterious trance. There he or she is charged with an attraction, and at the same time a terrified reverence, for these "powers" so vividly incarnate in the here and now of existence. Charismatic worship and Afro-spiritistic worship are therapy and at the same time a brazen unbosoming—a reconstitution of identity on the basis of an antidisciplinary codification of bodily expression—a restoration of vital energy amidst the daily suffocation of the wretched treadmill of city life on the fringes of the megalopolises. As we have stated apropos of the festive character of popular religion, charismatic worship and Afro-spiritistic worship afford a moment of reconstitution of meaning in a space of relative anomie, a moment of collective effervescence. It is the characteristic expressiveness of popular rituality that draws the practitioners of this worship away from the stifling Roman formalism of the Catholic liturgy and frequently places them as converts in the Pentecostal church or the *umbanda terreiro*.

Thus, it is among the most marginalized popular sectors that a sort of religious revitalization occurs, having its origin in an initial movement of religious dissidence from the original Catholicism. The growth in Protestantism, the sects, the Afro-American cults, and even the number of "religionless believers" in some urban locales could be due to this kind of process, originating rather in these groups' daily, concrete, differentiated *social practices than in the mechanical influences of processes of structural modernization.*

True, as Niebuhr declares, in less favored social sectors religious organizations of the "sect" type tend to be generated (in this case, Pentecostal and Afro-American cults). But this phenomenon does not always correspond to a situation of material deprivation. It must also be understood in the context of the quest for a symbolical "salvation" from, or "way out" of, a generalized situation of social and moral deprivation. When Pentecostalists leave church, they leave transformed—joyful, alleviated of their crushing burden, inspired with greater strength and will to bear up under daily life with its problems and its misery. Catholic liturgy and worship (and much more so, mainline Protestantism), due to the coldness and formalism of their expressions as well as to other factors, would not satisfy the need of the masses of the very poorest—who apply, instead, to the Pentecostal charismatic cults, in which, along with finding a space for their expressivity in terms of bodily symbolism, they discover a real community of affective and moral support that goes beyond doctrinal or theological considerations upon the meaning of God, life, and history.

The pluralization of the religious field, as we have analyzed it, has centered around the two great manifestations of "dissidence" from Catholicism among popular classes or groups: Pentecostalism and the Afro-American cults. But as we have seen, tendencies to the growth of religious alternatives are at hand also in other behaviors, and these phenomena deserve consideration as well, however summary.

We may state that the other alternatives in question assume various directions. When new sectarian groups or new cultural currents which preserve no continuity with Latin American Christian traditions penetrate the popular and native American cultures, they do so at the price of the destruction of autochthonous traditions, and the implantation of a sense of identity antagonistic to authentic popular feeling and thought.

1. In areas where formal schooling is more advanced, especially in some cities of certain relatively more "modernized" countries, the choice for believers grows, but with far more privatized religious options (in a general framework of Christian reference): we mean the "religionless believers," who, according to investigations, are indeed "believers, [but] in their own way."

2. The new pseudo-Christian religious movements, such as the Mormons, Jehovah's Witnesses, or Adventists, enjoy a certain capacity to penetrate into the popular groups, but the evidence appears to show that these movements take more solid root among certain middle-class groups, especially among impoverished middle-class sectors seeking an elevation in their status and an alternative integration into official society.

3. As for alternatives of a spiritistic or occultist order, including membership in spiritist societies—be these of a Kardecist type,

or be they sectarian groups characterized by a scientific and occultist syncretism (Kloppenburg 1980), such as the Church of
Scientology, the Rosicrucians, black magic, certain satanic cults
and others, or magico-divinatory alternatives, however "rationalized," such as astrology, palmistry, tarot, and I Ching, among
others—there is surely growth, but that growth is generally more
limited and is seen especially among nonpopular groups having
more formal schooling.

4. We generally observe as well the relative growth, if far less extensive, of other religions, such as Islam, Judaism, and Buddhism,
although this is a middle- and upper-class phenomenon.

5. The growth of religious alternatives is spurred by the proliferation of innumerable sects of a syncretic eastern variety, such as
Hare Krishna, the Divine Light Mission, the Baha'i faith, the
Children of God, the Unification Church (Moon), and other philo-
sophic spiritual alternatives such as anthroposophy, macrobio-
tics, theosophy, transcendental meditation, and others, which
take hold among better-instructed youth and which the popular
groups stubbornly resist.

6. Finally, the proportion of atheists is growing as well, including,
for our purposes, agnostics, unbelievers, and philosophical atheists. As we have said, atheism is not a popular phenomenon.
What we should notice here is that, generally speaking, atheism's
growth tendencies are not usually very sharp and that, where
they are, they spring from indifferentism and coincide with the
spread of a youth or student counterculture of resistance to the
dominant, hegemonically Catholic culture.

Clearly, these latter alternatives—the spiritistic currents, so powerful especially in Brazil, as well as the orientalist cults and univer-
salist religions of Asian origin that are spreading more or less rapidly
throughout the continent—reflect the growth of what has been called
the "seduction of the spirit" (Bingemer 1990:37ff.). The various centers, associations, courses, events, and initiatives—for example, yoga,
acupuncture, naturism, meditation, the astral map, and Taoism—
inspired by these "new age" currents seem to flourish preponderantly
in certain middle-class groups and among segments of the population, especially youth, having more formal schooling. According to a
survey conducted in Brazil (Gibson 1989), the various philosophies,
religions, and sciences of oriental inspiration could be ranged along a
spectrum from rational to irrational (following Weber and Berger)—
from the *Seicho-no-lê* movement with its powerful mysticism and

theodicy of self-transcendence, to the macrobiotic movement, which stands in continuity with the more radical rationalization of the Buddhist *karma-samsara* complex, to transcendental meditation, which is the most innovative theodicy and of the most rational type of the *karma-samsara* complex, and, finally, to the holistic movement, which is an intellectual and scientific movement of criticism of Western science in function of a rationalistic reading of the anthropocosmic unity inspired in the philosophy of Taoism.

We are dealing with the form acquired in Latin America by the alternative religious quests that betray a veiled criticism of the traditional historical churches. The historical churches are regarded as having lost their original initiatory and mysterious character, prescribing instead their character as institution, community, or ethical transformative agent. The phenomena here are similar to those observed in the highly developed countries, in which this "nebula of esoteric mysticism" represents an original production, maintaining no relation of continuity with the classic religions apart from certain borrowed elements but arising instead from a worldly mundane logic, adopting the individualistic values of postmodern culture and maintaining the paradigm of psychological interaction and relation rather than mysticism in a classic sense (Champion 1989). Here we have a penchant for therapies of a physical or psychological type, or else a quest for an alternative to the anxieties and tensions provoked by modern life. All of this is taken deft advantage of by manipulators "clothed in the sacred"—"masters" or mystagogues who seize on these affective deficiencies or this need for catharsis. Thus the religious field sees itself transformed into a "supermarket" of religious items, in which there is a solution suited to each taste and every existential situation: religions of spectacle, and religions that work with the body, with the psyche, or with the need for transcendence and for contact with the Holy, in some cases actually involving outright hoaxes and fraud. In other cases, we find authentic propositions of a spiritual alternative not in contradiction with the new paradigms of contemporary science, but nevertheless opposed to the scientistic rationality of modernity.

In sum, the representations of the religious field have repercussions on the cultural and sociopolitical field. While amidst the popular classes and groups we discover a growing religious pluralism, cultural pluralism is even more accentuated. Without ignoring certain basic traits common to the Latin American identity—for example, the preponderant and decisive influence of Christianity, in its most varied vectors—we are compelled to admit that Latin America is headed in the direction of an increasing religious and cultural pluralism. This is the great challenge to any "evangelization of culture," such as the contemporary Catholic Church proposes to undertake, which will profit nothing by ignoring the phenomenon in question and becoming alarmed at the advance of "secularism." It is also a serious challenge to any comprehensive view or project of Latin American integration. Any integrative model will have to renounce all efforts at homogenization or hegemony. Only an acknowledgment of religious otherness—the assumption of diversity—and renewed efforts of cooperation based on the recognition of each individual, family, local, regional, national, subregional, and continental identity will make it possible to rethink the tendencies to Latin American unity in a realistic way.

Latin American religious pluralization lies along the same vector as the processes observed in national identifications and international relations—processes with which that pluralization is intertwined. There are various levels of cooperation now, and the world is moving toward new cultural aggregates. The idea of nation, on one side, and of class identification, on the other, such as we have known them up until today, are changing. The old ethnic passions and nationalisms are restless again, just as new collective identifications are arising. The native American peoples are stirring from their slumber, and new social movements are springing up: human rights, consumer advocacy, ecology, women's movements, economies in solidarity, and so on. New claims are being mounted by the peoples, and with a passion: quality of life, rights of women and youth, integral health, peaceful coexistence, humane use of leisure time, and more.

## PART FIVE

# RESPONSE

*I would always ask God to give me strength . . . We were back together, and when the jeep stopped—Somoza's* Guardia—*we were plain scared . . . but the strength of faith . . . what a support it was! With faith, we prayed, we asked God . . . Other people used popular religion so Somoza would win. Some would ask for justice, others would ask for injustice. But that's where God takes sides. For justice. And just pure faith won't do it. You have to do both. Faith and action. We believe that God is walking with us, to the last moment, but you have to act, too. God doesn't work evil. A human person works evil. And another person has to take the evil away. Faith is shown by works . . . Faith helps a lot, but you have to act, to get the yoke off our necks.*

Young Nicaraguan peasant

# Chapter 8

# Popular Religion and Politics

From classical antiquity, the *polis* has been not only the focus of the influence of culture but also the center of the establishment of power in society. In pre-Columbian America, the city was also a center of political, social, cultural, and religious power. The great cultures of pre-Columbian America can even be identified with certain large cities.

The city has not always played such a role in the history of civilizations. But in the Ibero-Lusitanian conquest its role was preponderant. In the wars for independence, the Open Chapter Meetings of the capitals of the viceroyships and kingdoms were decisive for the proclamation of the cry of independence. While Latin American society, throughout the nineteenth century, was far more rural than urban, the city always discharged the role of political center of the nation. It was in the cities that the most important pages of the struggles between liberals and conservatives in nineteenth-century Latin America were written.

## Popular Religion and Politics in the Dependent City

It is not strange that the process of "urbanization," under way by the end of the nineteenth century in the majority of the countries of the continent, should have stirred political change that was sometimes convulsive rather than peaceful. The *polis*, in the Latin American mentality, especially in view of the macrocephalic centralization characterizing those countries, has been the symbol of dominant power—the physical space of central economic, cultural, and religious power, and the terrain on which social and political conflict is waged.

*163*

The political history of the early twentieth century in Latin America was marked by the rise of the middle classes and the proletariat, who challenged the power of the old dominant oligarchies. The political fabric of that era, up until World War II, was woven of restless battles for the democratization of society: revolutions, coups d'état, bloody strikes, and the impassioned reply of the oligarchies, little resigned to the loss of their power. In many countries, especially in Central America and the Caribbean, the support of open intervention on the part of the United States has been decisive. As a consequence of the oligarchical crisis and the rise of the new urban classes—the cycle launched by World War I and given an extra fillip by the crisis of 1929—the middle classes and nascent proletariat mobilized and made their demands, calling the established order into question. As we have seen in chapter 6, the Catholic Church, not always understanding and tolerant, regarded these movements with great mistrust, if not as a direct threat to its own survival.

From the battles for an antioligarchical democratization, of which we are speaking, to the struggles against the authoritarian regimes of South and Central America in the 1970s, to the current processes of democratization that, with various manifestations, characterize the sociopolitical scenario of the continent, the Latin American political panorama continues to be a wild one, and violence under its various manifestations (misery, repression, terrorism, drug traffic) is the daily bread of a people who seek in religion a symbolical "handle" by means of which to orientate themselves and endow their lives with consistency.

Studies abound on the role of the Church in the crisis of the oligarchical order—which, among other things, brought the Church into confrontation with the state. Ecclesiastical historiography and social science have also addressed the history of the Church in its proper social and political context, from the beginning of the century up to our own day (Alcalá 1984; De Roux 1981, 1983; Dussel 1972, 1983; Hoornaert et al. 1983; Pike 1970; Prien 1985).

The religious mentality of the masses in the critical periods of our present century has been studied, but these studies have not brought out its meaning in the broader sociocultural context of the social and religious evolution that drives and impels these masses to new religious responses. For example, there have been studies, in some depth, of the Brazilian messianic movements from 1870 to 1930, but not in terms of a comparison with other, somewhat analogous, phenomena, such as the participation of the *Cristero* masses in the Mexican Revolution or the function of popular religion in certain populist movements in Peru (APRA), Brazil (Varguism), and Argentina (Peronism). Little study has been done on the evolution of Christian social thought and its emergence in Christian-Democratic movements (Chile, Venezuela, Costa Rica), and how these groups interacted with the religious mentality of the people. Finally, studies of the participation of groups of Christians in revolutionary processes, as in Cuba, Chile, and Peru, or in various guerrilla movements have been conducted by way of an analysis of the function of their leaders, without taking much account of the popular mass and its religious forms or of how, if at all, they were influenced by those processes. The triumph of the Sandinista Revolution, in which Christians shared actively and massively, reopens the question of popular piety in political processes, whether the latter be populist, reformist, or revolutionary. Finally, studies have not set in relief the function of popular religions in a process of democratization such as that of Latin American society since the mid-1980s. In this chapter we shall broach certain approaches to this study, whose relevance and quantity of factual material would surely deserve another book.

## Abuses of Popular Religion

In the first place, let us observe that an extended analysis of church history in the present century justifies the assertion that the religious mentality of the masses has almost invariably been the object of a certain manipulation—intentional or unintentional—on the part of the Church hierarchy and conservative sectors, both of these being generally caught up in an antiliberal and antisecularist struggle or even committed to certain economic interests in an alliance against atheistic communism. This can explain so many "coronations" of the Blessed Virgin in various countries in the early decades of the twentieth century, just in periods that were critical for the Church and the current government, the latter being threatened by conjunctures in which the popular sectors were being won over to a political cause adverse to the status quo. The religious legitimation of oligarchical governments by an appeal to the religious sentiment of the popular masses has meant, on the part of the institutional Church, the organization of great pilgrimages, liturgies, and religious ceremonies in which the Virgin has been "crowned" and proclaimed "Queen and Patron" of the nation or in which the nation is "consecrated to the Sacred Heart of Jesus" (as in Ecuador, Colombia, Peru, and so on). In 1942, in the National Stadium, the Archbishop of Managua crowned the only daughter of dictator Somoza García as "Queen of the Army" with no less than the golden crown of Our Lady of the Purification. Attempts have also been made to promote great religious mass movements proclaiming the sovereignty of "Christ the King," precisely at moments when unionizing and other popular movements have powerfully mounted their claims and their social struggle in defense of their interests, which had been forgotten by the authoritarian and oligarchical governments. In Central America, as the Protestant penetration became more intense, liberal presidents made pacts with the Catholic Church and, in lavish ceremonies, consecrated Costa Rica to the "Sacred Heart of Jesus" (1953) and Honduras to the "Immaculate Heart of Mary" and the "Sacred Heart of Jesus" (1959). Similar events took place in Cuba, at the moment of the triumph of the revolution (1959). The Catholic Church had officially welcomed the rebels into Havana, but the government declared itself Marxist and took certain measures directly impinging upon the fortunes of the Church; whereupon, in 1960 and 1961, a number of massive religious processions were transformed into overt counterrevolutionary political ceremonies, and tensions were aggravated. In Nicaragua, history repeated itself from 1980 onward, but in this case the situation was substantially different. The Sandinista regime not only included notable Catholics in its ranks but had never adopted an antireligious policy; in fact, quite the contrary. In sum, religious legitimations have not been wanting in support of conservative tendencies, and the effort to mount such legitimations has always plied the enormous potentiality residing in the flawless religious attachment of the masses to their traditional devotions.

In other words, conservative sectors, in the ecclesial field as well as in the political—at least, very clearly, up until the 1960s—have sought to point the Catholicism of the masses in an antimodernist direction. The intent has been to oppose the modernizations heralded both by liberalism, at one extreme, and by Marxism, at the other. Popular religion, in many of its massive manifestations, has been the object of manipulation and has been commandeered for an endorsement, on the religious plane, of a politics favoring neither popular interests nor the ongoing process of capitalistic modernization.

We witnessed a qualitatively distinct process in the 1970s, under the National Security regimes, which invariably presented themselves as defenders of "Western Christian civilization" in an "all-out war against atheistic Communism." Nevertheless, the authoritarian bureaucratic regimes that held sway in Brazil, Argentina, Uruguay, Chile, Ecuador, Bolivia, and Paraguay were characterized by a sharing of power among three groups seemingly of contradictory interests: the military, the neoliberal technocratic group, and the ideologically integralist sectors. The result was the implantation of models of neoliberal development that were highly exclusive and concentrative, but objectively modernizing, as we have been able to appreciate in chapter 3. The relative "success" of these models was due to a policy of openness to foreign markets on the basis of a repressed, closely supervised, and atomized civil society. All of this was legitimated by a discourse that also appealed to the religious argument. Even in the case of General Pinochet, the prevailing ideology managed to establish a messianic vocation on the part of the dictator, who had come to "save Chile" from atheistic communism. Thus, the effort to manipulate signs and symbols with a high unifying religious content—such as official religious ceremonies (for example, on the feast day of the Virgin "Patron" of the nation), or the indiscriminate use of images whereby military chaplains were understood to be imparting a blessing to the military authorities, or the attempted manipulation of papal visits by these regimes—constituted an attempt to utilize the religious potential of the people in favor of these regimes. But the churches, except for the sole case of Argentina, more or less abandoned this policy that, among other things, utilized the popular Creole religions for ideological ends. The prophetic posture of the churches and their denunciations of the violation of human rights by the military dictatorships have led them into confrontation with these governments. In the majority of countries, the religious masses, defending the institutional Church against attacks by the military regimes, have taken their distance from the latter. The vacuum of religious legitimation of the nation and state left by the Catholic Church has at times been filled by integralist Catholic sectors, as well as by a countless series of Protestant churches committed to this supplementary role. In Central America, the boom of Protestantism and the sects since 1975 is heading in the same direction, and the case of General Ríos Montt in Guatemala, dictator and fervent Protestant minister, is only a particularly revealing symptom of the process that we are describing. In Chile, Pinochet's dictatorship was able to rely on the unconditional support of a majority of the Pentecostal churches, which thus contributed to the supplemental legitimation of the defense of right order and a threatened "Christian civilization."

However, not everything has been the object of an eviscerating manipulation of the original meaning of popular religion. If we center our attention on the meaning and function of the religious expressions in question from the standpoint of the popular actor, a closer examination of certain historical processes of the twentieth century confronts us with another panorama, which, without denying the manipulation, nuances it and evinces parallel, even contrary, processes.

Without pretending to undertake an exhaustive analysis here, let us assemble a number of landmarks of the relation between popular religion and popular processes in certain Latin American experiences. We shall center our analysis on what occurs with the actual religious mentality of the popular groups in each case, and not on developments and conflicts among institutions or with the dominant elite. Let us review very summarily certain significant cases and, on the basis of these cases, attempt to indicate lines of approach for further, more in-depth, investigations. The situations that we shall address are intended only as illustrations of a more complex, broader phenomenon, and are paradigmatic for an adequate study of the symbolical mentality of the popular masses in their confrontation with processes of urbanization and politicization in Latin America. With many of these situations, what we shall be dealing with is the popular confrontation with processes of secularization that evince an anticlerical or irreligious attitude.

### Brazilian Messianisms: Peasantry versus Corrupt City

Mario Vargas Llosa, in his novel, *La guerra del fin del mundo* ("The War of the End of the World"), has given us once more the peasant messianic epic of the Brazilian hinterland that Euclydes da Cunha's *Os Sertões* first revealed. From the close of the nineteenth century up until the middle 1930s, Brazil was the scene of a series of messianic movements[1]—the expression of one form of popular Catholicism in peasant sectors of the interior. Their context was that of precapitalistic social relations of a patriarchal type. Such relations would crystalize around a "blessed" one or "monk," or else a priest, who would be regarded as the reincarnation of a saint, or even of Christ. Favorite biblical themes centered on the exodus, a focus that legitimated religious protest against the established order and mobilized a quest for a "Promised Land." The hope of Jesus' return held a special meaning, in function of the eschatological judgment. In the expectation of that redemption, "holy cities" were founded, on the basis of an autarchical organization and a particular ideology. The character of the religious

---

1. Lanternari (1965), Pereira de Queiroz (1968), Schaden (1982).

protest, even without the explicit inclusion of political objectives, finally led to a confrontation with the political powers. The dispatch of troops of police and soldiers to destroy the "holy city" culminated in a bloody "holy war." We refer to well-known movements such as those of the *Canudos* ("Tricks," led by "Blesseds" João Maria and, later, José Maria), *Contestado* ("Disputed," headed by Antonio de Conselheiro), and *Juazeiro* (a buckthorn similar to Christ's-thorn), led by Father Cicero (Pereira de Queiroz 1968).

These were religiously inspired peasant revolts in the context of an agricultural crisis, where worsening living conditions, drought, and an ongoing armed struggle among landholders ("colonels") occasioned a constant state of social anxiety. It was the year of the creation of the Republic, 1889, following the long reign of Don Pedro II. The Brazilian economy had begun to undergo an evolution marked by the introduction of capitalistic forms of exploitation, by urbanization, and by a liberalization of the work force with the abolition of slavery. A lagging agricultural economy was in a state of transition to an agricultural capitalism, in zones of poor and very marginalized small farmers. The social and economic vulnerability of these persons was very great, and the hope of a change to be wrought by their own efforts was replaced by the messianic expectation of changes of an eschatological tenor, woven on the basis of legends that had a deep impact on the masses and stimulated their fervor and eager mobilization.

These movements' criticism of the Republic, seen as the source of all evils—a lay state that secularized society—and their demands for the restoration of the monarchy, seen as the expression of an authority in conformity with the beneficent will of God, concealed their latent meaning. Indeed, we may observe by way of hypothesis that we are dealing with a case in which peasant masses see themselves threatened by a society caught up in the process of urbanizing and secularizing transformations—a society which therefore tends to refunctionalize its traditions, beliefs, rites, and religious organizations, assimilating these to its deepest cultural identity. What we have is a reinterpretation, in terms of a messianic ethics, of certain aspects of traditional Catholicism, transformed into the expectation of an imminent eschatological salvation concretized in a hope of salvation from the misery, evils, and vices of the Republican city. The alternative project, then—in protest against a forced integration into forms of capitalistic modernization and urbanization—consisted in a symbolical, and at the same time real, refuge in a "holy city" built on values of siblingship and weaving new social relations. This flight and resistance, including armed resistance, to federal troops manifest an opposition to the new order that prevailing power sought to impose. What is worthy of note, from the standpoint of latent meaning, is that this program, while conceived in terms of a monarchist, traditionalist politics, was not restorative or anchored in the past; it was planned as an urbanizing process, but one built entirely on the basis of a messianic religion that questioned the new Republican and bourgeois hegemony that sought to impose itself on the people.

One finds a series of messianic expressions in various eras and regions of Latin America. Those we single out for mention seem to be clearer examples of a symbolical and real resistance—of a religious character—that was a response to the processes of transformation in capitalism at the end of the nineteenth century, processes that were already accelerating a capitalistic urbanization and modernization, thereby threatening with disintegration the traditional rural world and the ethos of the culture and piety of the peasant masses.

The towering importance attaching to this peasant movement, in which it is so easy to see an explicit protest against capitalistic urbanization with its sequel of misery and corruption, is matched by that of the urban messianisms in Brazil, which have been studied by Gerbert (Prien 1985:813-14). The popular messianic religious movement of Zarur, a former radio announcer, is particularly exemplary here. Interpreting the message and person of Jesus in a spiritistic sense, with the war cry "Jesus is here!" this preacher roused the hopes of the dispossessed urban masses. This movement developed in the 1970s. Yokaanam, the "new Christ of Rio de Janeiro," mingled Catholicism, spiritism, and Freemasonry, and led his community of followers from Rio de Janeiro to found a "New Jerusalem" forty kilometers outside Brasilia. In the same period, in the northeast, an Adventist messianic movement founded a "heavenly regime." These messianisms did not include the exodus motif. On the contrary, their beliefs and rites stood at a point halfway, as it were, between the *macumbeiro*, with his magical powers, and the "miraculous messiah." According to Gerbert, these beliefs and rites represented a "struggle against social afflictions, or against the moral corruption of the great modern city."

## Popular Religion in the Mexican Revolution

It would not be to our purpose here to rehearse the history of the Mexican Revolution (Silva Herzog 1964). We only intend to set in relief its liberal-revolutionary and populist ideological inspiration (which it combined with a heavy dose of anticlericalism). We must not credit, however, the apologetical histories that see in that revolution only irreligious and deeply anti-Catholic positions. We must distinguish the various periods, processes, and jumbled political alliances of what was the first great social and political revolution of this century in Latin America. From the viewpoint of our study, it is important to emphasize that not all of the phases of the Mexican Revolution, nor all of the groups committed to it, were so virulently anticlerical and "friar-eating."

As we know, the great mythic leader of the revolution was Francisco Ignacio Madero. In the popular mentality, Madero's military uprising against dictator Porfirio Díaz was a symbol of Mexican national identity. And the religious sense of the people, especially their devotion to Our Lady of Guadalupe, was intrinsically bound up with this identity (Wolf 1979). The Mexican people transformed Madero into a myth and, as happens with any myth, invested it with a religious symbolism. Madero not only was the "apostle," the "redeemer" (as, after his death, he would be the "martyr"), but besides, could surely count on the unfailing support of God and the Virgin of Guadalupe. As a Mexican refrain of the time expressed it:

> Levantemos el grito!
> Viva Dios, es lo primero,
> La Virgen de Guadalupe,
> Y Don Francisco I. Madero!

> (All together, now!
> Long live God, first, then
> Our Lady of Guadalupe,
> And Don Francisco I. Madero!)

The mythified figure of Madero represents a form through which the religious mentality of the people combines their longings for justice and democracy with the symbolical protective function of the Virgin. Thus, religious faith offers a symbolical reinforcement that, to an extent, departs from the mythic legend of the origins of the Virgin of Guadalupe and impels its subjects toward a mobilizing utopia. The consolatory dream of a better future, in which all injustice and the sufferings of this life will be abolished, welds a profane political meaning (Madero as leader and personification of democracy) with a religious, eschatological meaning (the Virgin of Guadalupe, Mother of the poor and oppressed Indians, birth-giver of a new world, a world of siblings before the same Father).

Given the support—direct or indirect—that the Church had offered *caudillo* Huerta, the revolt of Carranza and the constitutionalists was very anticlerical. The constitutionalist generals, along with their scant appreciation for the clergy, had no respect for the faith. By contrast, the more popular leaders of the revolution, Zapata and Villa, were not anticlerical, as has been unjustly asserted. Their "other revolution," on the contrary, showed itself much more respectful of the religious sentiment of the people.

As Meyer says (1975), the Zapatistas respected the churches and made sure that field chaplains would accompany their troops. In 1915, Zapata entered Mexico City carrying the standard of Our Lady of Guadalupe and reopened the churches, which saluted him with the pealing of bells. Villa and Carranza did accuse each other of anticlericalism. Actually, Villa's anticlericalism was dictated by certain excesses on the part of his lieutenants. When Villa broke with Carranza and retook Morelia and Guadalajara, he ordered all of the churches reopened and the priests released. As is known, Villa had a subordinate of his who had murdered a priest summarily executed.

Prien concludes: "It was a tragedy for the revolution that Zapata was assassinated in 1919, and that his movement, so intimately bound up with popular Catholicism, was not definitively integrated into the revolution" (Prien 1985:913).

It is worthy of note that precisely the revolutionary movements enjoying greater popular participation and orientation—those of Zapata and Villa, which were composed mainly of poor peasants and a certain number of proletarians—maintained a religious attitude of greater respect for the Church and grafted themselves onto the religion of the masses, thereby paving the way for the practical confluence of the latent protest of popular religion with the social struggle against the landholding and urban bourgeois oligarchy. In the case of Carranza, Obregón, and Calles—all of them bourgeois directors of the revolution—their anticlericalism not only attacked the ecclesiastical institution but was profoundly disqualifying of and antagonistic to the religious sentiment of the popular masses. The resistance of the popular masses to antichurch policies, of which Villa's and Zapata's insurgents had taken advantage, by 1919 determined a change in Carranza's policy toward the Church. Going so far as to modify the antichurch Constitution of 1917, Carranza authorized the great manifestation in Mexico City on October 17, 1919, in celebration of the Coronation of the Virgin of Guadalupe.

Obregón's and Calles's identification of the revolution and the state, their social Darwinist, Masonic, and socialist—but anti-Bolshevik—inspiration, collided with Mexican social Catholicism, its growing influence among the working and peasant masses, and its project of a "Christian democracy" that antedated the invention of the concept.

The unrestricted application of the Constitution of 1917 and the repression ordered by Calles against the Church unleashed a tide of Catholic protest and radicalized the bishops—who up to this point had still been willing to negotiate—in more rigid positions, culminating in their promulgation of the interdict, which became effective July 31, 1926. The law that threatened the Church with death became a tool for that Church to preach resistance to oppression.

But what sparked the Cristero revolt (August 1926 to May 1929), Meyer tells us, was not the summons of the Church, but a hitherto unrecognized element "of which no one appeared to have thought and which all had at least underestimated: the attitude of the Christian people."

Those masses, composed mainly of peasants—among whom were veterans of the armies of Villa and Zapata—maintaining some of their ideals of agrarian reform, did battle with a government they regarded as criminal for having attempted violently to wrest from the people their dearest religious sentiments. They struggled against President Calles, whom they identified with Herod, as warriors of Christ the King: they believed Mexico to be allied with God by a pact that had been sealed by the apparition of the Virgin of Guadalupe and by the proclamation of God's Son as King of their land (Prien 1985).

The mestizo peasants transformed into Cristero warriors rose up holding in their hands the symbol of the Virgin of Guadalupe (identified with Tonantzin), spiritual symbol of colonial rebellion and of the struggles for Mexican independence and national identity. And so Lafaye can say, in the conclusion of his imposing work on Mexican national consciousness: "Beginning with the Independence, the image of Guadalupe, from her principal function of protector against epidemics, turns into a 'goddess of victory' and liberty" (Lafaye 1973).

## Popular Religion and Populist Regimes

Logically enough, many analysts interpret the relations between certain regimes and populist currents as standing in contradiction to the interests of the Church. In the case of the Vargas regime in Brazil, however, not only was there no major confrontation but the Brazilian Catholic Church actually allied itself implicitly with the state in the persecution of certain cults and religions, such as *umbanda* and *macumba*. In the case of Peronism, on the other hand, while there were no major problems between the regime and the Church at first, a radical confrontation eventually emerged. With APRA, in Peru, especially in the 1920s and 1930s—when APRA represented a revolutionary populist vector locked in combat with imperialism and the Creole oligarchy—there were indeed confrontations, but not so much in an irreligious spirit on the part of Aprismo: rather, a certain anticlericalism was included in the connatural ideological expression of those who were battling the domination of the popular masses by an oligarchical religious ideology.

What we would like to bring out here is that there has not always been a solid line of confrontation with the Catholic Church in the history of the Latin American populisms. On occasion, there have been situations of coexistence, and even mutual collaboration. We ought to discard the reductionistic focus which, in function of its peculiar ideological options, conceives Latin American populism as the sworn enemy of religion and the Church. The reality is actually more complex, and requires a finer analysis. Too little studied, if it has been studied at all, is the relation between the political projects of the Latin American populist movements and the popular religion of the masses—especially the popular religion of urban popular classes in process of modernization and industrialization.

What first strikes the eye is that, in the three populist movements that we have cited (with the purpose of introducing an analysis of the phenomenon), there is no explicit declaration, on the religious plane, of an irreligious or atheistic attitude. Rather, what we see are national projects endeavoring to reassert certain consensus values and projecting policies of social reform calculated to engage the masses, especially the urban masses. These are nationalist reform projects that attempt to mobilize the masses, but on the basis of the state, under clientelistic and paternalistic modalities, organizing the workers, but under the tutelage of the directive organs of the state or the movement. And the important thing is that they are not movements with a definite ideological profile: a great diversity of expression and ideological current is possible within them. They are movements reflecting a multiclass, antioligarchical, and nationalist alliance, but an alliance whose "popular" content is often more rhetorical and romantic than actual. However, these movements express the dispossessed classes' aspirations for reform and justice, and therefore these regimes or movements can count on a broad base of popular support.

One of the most significant elements in the relation among these populist movements, from the standpoint that interests us, is that they manage to dovetail—in rather peculiar fashion, not exempt from manipulatory maneuvers—secular aspirations for justice and the religious feeling of the popular masses. Populist movements respond to the need the masses have for myth if they are to be mobilized for integration into a state that is in full process of modernization and industrialization.

Latin American populisms cannot be adequately explained without taking into account their use of "popular" symbols. These symbols incarnate a whole energy and a project precisely where political ideology seems too "diffuse" in the eyes of the masses as a whole. Here the caudillist leadership is a factor par excellence of bonding between the movement and the mass. Bypassing the mediations of a rationally structured discourse, Haya de la Torre, Perón, or Vargas appeal to the deeper, symbolical sense that is so much a part of the religious forms of the Latin American people. The leader is transformed into a kind of secular messiah, come to redeem the masses from the misery and afflictions of this life. A highly illustrative example is to be found in Imelda Vega-Centeno's profound study on popular Aprismo as a kind of popular religion (Vega-Centeno 1991).

In the case of Argentina, it is the charismatic figure of Perón that stirs the allegiance of the working classes. A scholar of the relationship between Peronism and Christian religion concludes: "The activity of the Peronist government promoted the dignity and well-being of the workers, providing them with an organization that enabled them to be the principal protagonists of the Argentinian political process, on the basis of a stamp that was not only national and independent of Marxist ideology but also explicitly Christian" (Farrel 1976:102).

During the first years of General Perón's government, public religious ceremonies were held by the state, religious education was reestablished in the schools, and the "justicialist" doctrine, founded on Christian ethics and doctrine, was propagated—a heavy blow to the laicism that had been the order of the day in Argentine political life since the dawn of the century. Cardinal Caggiano himself, addressing a large Jocist seminar in 1954 and referring to the fruits of Peronism among the working masses, declared:

> [The working masses] have begun, once more, lovingly to hoist their Argentine flag, and have become convinced that it is possible to be an advocate of labor and labor organizations

without being socialist and without being communist—and, I must add, without renouncing their religious traditions and sentiments . . .

Meanwhile, it is an undeniable fact that the name of God, pronounced with frequency by higher governmental authority and by the Chief of the Revolution, has exerted an influence evident to all. [Quoted in Farrel 1976:102]

At the International Eucharistic Congress of 1934—an entire symbol in itself—some 60% of the inhabitants of that urban enclave of laicism that was Buenos Aires received the Eucharist.

All critical considerations aside as to the political significance of the first Peronist government and its tragic end—with the oligarchy and the Church at odds for various reasons owing to anticlerical blunders—it remains a fact that in this "third position" (*justicialism* as the alternative to capitalism and communism), messianic flavors were simmering. On one occasion, General Perón would say:

When I think that we have been the first to proclaim to human beings this [justicialist] solution and as I realize that we have been the first to apply it, I cannot but confirm my faith in the high destinies that God has willed to assign to our native land. And my soul trembles with emotion to think that the day cannot be far off when, in order to glimpse some star in the night, humanity will have to fix its eyes on the flag of the Argentines. [Quoted in Magnet 1953:57]

But while every populist movement requires a mystique, which uses or abuses the religious depths of the popular masses, in the case of Peronism this mystique was reinforced by the mythic symbol incarnate in the person of Eva Perón. "Evita," as the people affectionately called her, represented the aspirations for justice that stirred so widely in the lagging popular classes. Defender of the "cabecitas negras" (the mestizo poor), activist in the cause of feminism, ally and protector of the union movement, Eva Perón waged a fierce struggle with the dominating oligarchy.

In her fiery, revolutionary discourse, she proclaimed that the deep inspiration of her sentiment for justice was love, not hate. Her funeral was the grandest popular manifestation of its time. Eva Perón has come to be a revolutionary mythic symbol, raised aloft by the dispossessed sectors of Peronism and venerated to our very day, in the field of the people's religious symbolism, in the same category as so many official saints of broad and widespread popular devotion (Carutti and Martínez 1974).

In the confluence of political and religious sentiments provoked by the Peronist phenomenon, it is scarcely strange that the plane of faith, in the religious syncretism of the Argentinian poor classes of today, should continue to be integrated with the political plane in terms of leaders now virtually canonized by popular devotion. It is not strange that the Argentinian people, a profoundly believing people, should have so anxiously awaited Perón's return. Proof of this syncretic congruence of messianic and political hope was a 1973 plaque of gratitude inscribed to the deceased Correa, the object of one of Argentina's favorite popular devotions. It read:

Thank you for giving us back General Perón, the father of the poor.

A comparative study by Büntig of various social strata establishes that, mainly around 1972, among a marginal population of Buenos Aires (those of Villa del Parque), where the vast majority of Catholics were loyal to Perón, the "good Catholic" was identified as "someone who fights for the good of the country"—all ritualism and moralism aside—and the "good priest" as the one who had elected to serve the poor (Büntig 1973a). Here we see that, at the beginning of the 1970s, the majority option of the urban popular classes, unlike that of the more traditionalist peasantry or of the upper or middle classes, was for Peronism, and that these urban classes reconciled their political option with a renewed popular Catholicism.

In the case of Brazil, no consideration of the relationship between religion and politics among the popular classes must be allowed to gloss over the complex, and at times contradictory, bond between the Afro-Brazilian religions and the populism of Getulio Vargas. During the 1930s and 1940s, as we have seen, the number and the activity of the *macumba* and *umbanda terreiros* grew among the urban popular classes. Here were popular religions, feared and despised by the higher classes and the official Church, in search of social legitimation. During all of that period, the Afro-Brazilian congregations and cults were alienated, persecuted, and subjected to extortion by the police. The difference between the protective treatment accorded middle-class Kardecist spiritism and the discrimination practiced against *macumba* and *umbanda* (the latter being at that time a small religion on the rise) rather clearly evinces the symbolical threat seen in these popular religions by an oligarchical order identified with Catholicism.

Under the Vargas government (1930-45), populism gradually acquired a corporative and authoritarian accent, and in 1937 the New State was founded, which took as its model the Italian Fascist state. Police persecution of Afro-Brazilian religions in this era was justified by the argument that they were linked with the subversives. According to this argument, Obúm—a Yoruba warrior divinity, identified with Saint George, astride a white horse and wearing a great red cape—symbolized the "Red Knight of Hope." Although this alleged link has not been elucidated, it is true that certain Afro-Brazilian centers maintained close relations with the schismatic Brazilian Catholic Church, of a nationalist and socialist orientation (Brown et al. 1985:14-15).

Currently, along with other sectors of the population, the Umbandists seem to have forgotten the repressive nature of the Vargas regime. The police are blamed, or governments antedating the persecutions, while the figure of Vargas is idealized as a protector of the cults. Up until the military coup of 1964, many *umbanda* centers displayed photographs of Vargas side by side with representations of *umbanda* spirits. Indeed, many Umbandists were convinced that Vargas himself frequented their places of worship.

From 1945 onward, along with the enormous spread of *umbanda* in urban popular sectors, the political system was democratized, and the urban popular masses began to be ardently wooed by candidates and parties on all political levels. Impelled by the need for social legitimation, the leaders of the Umbanda Federations sought to move into politics by establishing alliances with elected officials and by embarking on political careers themselves. The objective of these alliances was the defense of *umbanda* as a valid expression in the religious, political, and social field; thus, their orientation was pragmatic and instrumental, deprived of any cut-and-dried ideological loyalties. In the Brazilian political history of recent decades, the Umbandist masses have become something of a fought-over political clientele. However, Umbandists were in agreement with the politicians who courted their vote when it came to two principal causes: nationalism and the defense of religious liberties. Nationalism—so important in the cultural meaning of *umbanda*, as we have said—was also identified with populism, and was utilized as a political tool to win the support of the urban masses. Furthermore, nationalist sentiments offered an ideal opportunity to unify the various social and political interests represented in *umbanda*, thereby masking that religion's internal tensions. In this case, then, a twin manipulation was at work, occasioning on the political level the emergence of "modernist" nationalist sentiments that, on the one hand, favored capitalistic development and, on the other, in the religious field, legitimated the expansion of new urban popular religions.

In the case of APRA in Peru, which has been extensively studied by Imelda Vega, the relation between religion and politics exhibits no clearer frontiers than it did with Peronism. The entire history of APRA is shot through with religious components—and their messianic hues—and the polemics that this question entailed.

Víctor Raúl Haya de la Torre, a member of the University Reform generation, led the May 1923 popular youth protests against the attempt of Leguía's dictatorship to take political advantage of the consecration of the country to the Sacred Heart of Jesus. The manifestation was violently repressed, and many of the leaders deported, including Haya de la Torre himself. The oligarchy—allied with the conservative Catholicism of the era—accused the Aprista leader of atheism, irreligion, even the diabolical.

But the accusations were far more a matter of bogies and political maneuvering on the part of the civil dictatorship and its ally, the institutional Church, against a serious political competitor. Indeed, it seems that the APRA of this era (1920-30) was no more anticlerical than the majority of the intellectual and independent sectors (Vega-Centeno 1985, 1991).

Actually, Haya de la Torre was a relativist who simply had no hesitation in appealing to the religious feeling of the masses, even quoting passages from the Bible and having recourse to the sphere of the religious (Christian, Andean, or other). His personality, which looms over the politics of Peru in our century, has also become a symbol, systematically fueled by the quasi-religious mystique of the party and the cult that surrounded its leader. The most important leaders of the APRA of the time—even enlightened intellectuals—referred to their caudillo in religious figures, such as "the redeemer of the country and Indo-America," or "the new Moses," or "the prophet who guides his people."

The charism of "Master" Haya de la Torre (risen, after his death, in the Aprista people) summoned his followers to a conversion, understood as the "awakening" of youth to an American Indian anti-imperialist politics and a "new political creed"—a "creed of justice, nobility, and wisdom" (Haya de la Torre), a creed standing in opposition to the "foreignizing," materialistic Marxist alternative. Aprismo's "mystique is political; but, being religious as well, it leads Christianity to its realization" (Vega-Centeno 1991:150).

Thus, the religious component of the populist project here under analysis takes on forms and structures of meaning and symbol that are characteristic of popular religion. APRA's discourse and political practice, in its capacity as a connotatively religious symbolism, bestowed a second meaning on the religious sense peculiar to the Christian, Andean, or magical popular masses. The Aprista discourse assumed a religious signification already at work among the people and applied it to the new object of a political project. "It unifies the Aprista mass in a medium of the sacred (the Party, the Casa del Pueblo, Villa Mercedes, Trujillo). It gives them a share in a luminous sphere (illumination by *el Jefe*, the Chief who is Light); it calls them (vocation) to build a history (salvation history), to make history by celebrating siblingship and the utopia (liturgy, meetings, colloquies, 'brotherhood days')" (Vega-Centeno 1986). In this fashion, Aprista popular symbolism reinforced the specifically religious sense of the popular milieu; and so that symbolism was able to reproduce itself along the characteristic symbolical channels of the religious field, by complementing these explicitly religious beliefs and rites of the Peruvian people, this faith that goes in quest of an otherworldly salvation, with a motive for the struggle within history.

This example once more confirms our thesis that the political behavior of the dominated and believing popular classes of our continent is not divorced from their religious convictions. The populist project, anticlerical as it may appear, while introducing a political logic, does not bring a secularization of the religious life of the masses, its base of support and mobilization. For its part, that project enables the popular classes and groups, while preserving their religious beliefs and practices, to achieve integration into modernization processes whose impulse is in the populist movements. The populist movement itself is a sort of compromise between, on the one hand, values and attitudes that seek to introduce modernizing reforms, but in a line of continuity with openness to innovations in the capitalist system, and, on the other, an ensemble of ideological practices and representations that reproduce traditional relationships such as caudillismo, paternalism, and messianism.

## Popular Religion and Recent Revolutionary Processes

The evolution at work in the Catholic Church registered a sharply accelerating curve in the 1960s, when Vatican Council II began to have its effects in our region. Manifold factors were at work here, such as progressive currents in European Catholicism, the development-alistic "spirit" of those years, and the new Latin American scenario produced by the triumph of the Cuban revolution in 1959. Long before Medellín, which finally issued an invitation to the task of "liberation," Catholicism had felt the impact of the option made by Colombian priest Camilo Torres, who died fighting as a guerrilla. It was a season of death for certain sacerdotal victims of repression. Other priests, including two bishops, were under arrest. And priests began to organize to denounce the injustices of capitalism and issue a call to the liberation struggle (Houtart 1979). In 1967, the Movement of Golconda Priests was born, in Colombia; in 1968, the Movement of Priests for the Third World, in Argentina; in 1968, the Youth Church, in Chile; in 1970, ONIS, in Peru; among other suchlike phenomena. All of this culminated in the foundation, in Chile, of the movement Christians for Socialism in 1971, which openly sided with the socialist regime of Salvador Allende.

It need not surprise us, then, that, in recent historical evolution, wherever the churches have taken a sharp, decisive turn in favor of the popular sectors and have supported a restructuring of the popular movements, new religious expressions have arisen, more ethically orientated than before, making possible the convergence of a prophetic sense with a revolutionary spirit. The Cuban Revolution is the counterexample. There, the regime's Marxist ideological definition has led it to confrontation with the Church, and to the development of an atheistic propaganda among the masses (Dewart 1963, Meyer 1989:245ff.). But even here, popular religion—despite official secularist influences—seems to be enjoying a revival, or at least to be mounting an underground resistance (Pereira 1986).

The incorporation of growing contingents of Christians into popular parties and movements—generally of Marxist inspiration or influenced by laicist traditions—beginning late in the 1960s, in Chile, Peru, Brazil, Central America, and, on a lesser scale, in many other countries, indicates a course along which popular grassroots Christianity is gaining strength, on the one hand, while, on the other, popular political parties are abandoning their irreligious ideology, so that it becomes feasible for them to support a people of believers without assaulting their religious faith.[2] The triumph of the Sandinista Revolution, in which, for the first time, Christians shared actively and massively in a process having these characteristics, provides a fresh perspective on the question of popular piety

---

2. See Instituto Histórico Centroamericano (1979), IEPALA (1982), DEI (1980), Correa (1986), Carrión (1986), Richard and Meléndez (1982).

and its function in social and political processes in Latin America.

From one point of view, the secularization processes generated by capitalistic urbanization can be understood as the result of a change in the relationship with nature in the face of the advance of the sciences and technology and their diffusion in mass society. But from the viewpoint of the political field as well, a secularizing logic is introduced when the "powers that be" no longer find legitimation in terms of religion, as has occurred in Western modernity. Early in the 1970s, the processes of secularization were generally interpreted as representing an inevitable phenomenon in Latin America. True, the boom of the popular movements directed by an "enlightened" vanguard, and the advent of socialist or populist regimes at the beginning of the 1970s, went hand in hand with the growth of secularizing tendencies, especially in the intellectual field. The culture of the elite—groups of clerics and intellectuals—proclaimed revolution as a task to be performed, and lashed out venomously against any form of "popular piety," pronouncing it to be riddled with anachronistic superstitious elements and other profoundly alienating factors.

The culture of the elite criticized the ideology of pacification at all costs, with its appeal to a "commandment of love" that prohibited all violence. The paralyzing effect of so much ecclesial rhetoric in this direction was pointed out. By contrast with the enlistment, in Europe, of all ambits of human life in the secularizing process, in Latin America, it was said, it was the revolutionary ethos being created that embraced the totality of life and activity. That ethos could not renounce the religious element, however, as we see from the christological framework of the mythic figures of Che Guevara or Camilo Torres in revolutionary iconography and song.

As we have seen, politicization processes on our continent did not move exclusively in a revolutionary direction, nor, frequently, did they even manage to impose a rationalistic, secularizing logic on the religious traditions most deeply rooted in the people. The example of the populist regimes and movements indicates that political processes can move in tandem with a reinforcement of mythic messianic traditions, or can generate space for the rebirth, in the city, of syncretic religious forms with overtones of religious magic, as in the Afro-Brazilian cults. Messianic hopes can be raised by certain revolutionary processes either in the form of protest (the Cristero case) or in the form of support (the case of Nicaragua), precisely because the rationalistic discourse characteristic of the enlightened strata of the leading groups fails to penetrate the collective awareness of the people except as the expression of certain deeply felt values and aspirations in no way opposed to the mystical and symbolical sense of the masses. It would be superfluous to insist on the mobilizing potential investing communicational codes that appeal to the human being's symbolical dimension, as a factor of mobilization for any political project hoping to enlist the popular masses, whether to manipulate them with a view to various interests or to represent them legitimately.

## Popular Religion and Redemocratization

When President-elect Tancredo Neves of Brazil fell gravely ill in 1985, the people responded with a massive prayer movement for his health. Tancredo had won the first democratic presidential election to be held after twenty years of military government. Thousands of masses and prayer ceremonies were celebrated. Catholics, Protestants, spiritists, Umbandists, Jews—all demonstrated an unwonted piety that surprised even their own leaders. The moribund president incarnated the democratic aspirations of the Brazilian people, and that people did not hesitate to appeal to its faith to ask for his health (Rodrigues Brandão 1988).

When Aprista candidate Alan García was elected president of Peru shortly after the death of the "Master," he could count on the broad support of the lagging urban and peasant masses, who, from the midst of their Andean-Christian religious syncretism, saw no obstacle in supporting his actions and projects as the continuer—with his own, perhaps vicarious, charism—of the "redemptive" work of Haya de la Torre. But on a soil as religious as the Peruvian, it is not strange that, just as Aprismo includes an implicit religion that dovetails with popular Christianity, so the Shining Path, as well, contains a latent messianism, although in this case that messianism is sharpened to maximal radicality (Ansión 1990). The messianism of the Path, in a certain sense, is a political and religious millennialism, exhibiting all of the characteristics of fanaticism.

There are two sides to the coin of popular religion, then, in its political functions. While it can merge more or less consistently with modernization processes, it can also constitute a symbolical counterforce, opposing modernity in the latter's dehumanizing element. This "countermodernity resource" (Balandier) in the Latin American popular cultures favors democratic change, but can also be the object of manipulation, or can shut itself up in rigid sectarian, messianic, esoteric, and/or magical alternatives that prevent its advance along the path of democracy and a greater social justice. The case of the Shining Path is pathetic in this respect.

In Chile, the firm position of the Church on the human rights issue generated a space for the rearticulation of civil society (Parker 1990), along with the progressive emergence of a movement of protest against the dictatorship as the Church called for democratization. Political activity was forbidden, and the parties proscribed; thus, a will to opposition, partly out of sincere conviction, partly out of the unintentional need to find a symbolical language to manifest a protest, developed very close bonds with religious language and practices. This process both converted the erstwhile "secularized" activists of the left and revitalized signs and symbols of the religious traditions of the people.

The traditional popular pilgrimages to the cemeteries on All Saints Day, for example, were transformed into a public protest when, in the General Cemetery of Santiago, a hundred headstones were discovered reading "N.N."—marking the graves of persons who had been "disappeared" and murdered by the Secret Police. Thus, nonviolent protest and religious protest were combined on numberless occasions: campaigns of fasting and prayer for the "disappeared," "Defense of Life" campaigns, nonviolent meetings to protest torture, religious funerals for the victims of repression, killed under various circumstances, the Way of the Cross celebrated by the Popular Christian Communities, and a plethora of other manifestations. And in community life, even the smallest signs—the reading of a passage from the Gospel, for example—took on the character of "subversion" of the dominant order. Gradually a popular cult to the new martyrs of the Christian people developed: Juan Alsina, André Jarlan, and other priests who had died at the hands of the military.

Struggles for democratization are developing in all of the countries of Latin America. As in Paraguay with the papal visit of 1988, so also in Haiti, occurrences have reinforced democratizing tendencies. In the case of regimes with laicist traditions, as in Mexico and Uruguay, anticlerical attitudes are on the wane. Relations between Mexico and the Vatican have improved to the point where diplomatic ties have been reestablished. In Uruguay in 1990, as President Lacalle took office, consolidating a process of democratization, the ecumenical ceremony celebrated on March 1 of that year is worthy of note. Lacalle himself has declared: "At one time, on behalf of a misunderstood laicism, hospitals were taken from the Sisters of Charity, crosses were removed from cemeteries, crosses from the hospital—a Jacobin stage that I believe, fortunately, to have come to a close" (Lacalle 1990:2). In the case of Haiti, the fact that Aristide, a priest and a partisan of the theology of liberation, was elected to the presidency was no coincidence. In a culture steeped in a sense of religion—synthesized by the Afro-American element—just as Duvalier had availed himself of the *Patronato* to impose his will on the Catholic Church, so also the role that fell to voodoo leaders in the overthrow of "Baby Doc" was not inconsiderable. And although the Aristide government was subsequently overthrown, it is interesting to note that it was a "Creole" Catholic priest, very sensitive to the religious expressions of the Haitians, who attempted to head a unified political and religious process.

In Central America, especially in El Salvador, as well as in Colombia and other regions, the Church has played the role of mediator in social conflicts by directing its action toward negotiation and pacification. The recent intervention of a hierarchical authority as mediator between the drug traffickers and the Colombian government, winning the surrender of Pablo Escobar Gaviria, shows that the Church can play a key role in a conflict even as criminal and violent as that generated by the drug traffic. Popular religion continues on its way in dynamic interaction with official religion, with the churches, but preserving a goodly part of its socioreligious autonomy. There have been attempts at an instrumentalization of the religious sentiment of the masses for political purposes, but no one need fear another situation like the one that arose in Havana, Cuba, in 1959, in which a desperate appeal was made to the Christian people to embrace an attitude wholly opposed to processes of change (even granting the complexity that those processes were eventually to acquire).

In Nicaragua, pressure from the conservative wing of the hierarchy has clearly striven to utilize the faith of the people on behalf of the most extreme positions. It has not completely succeeded. Rather, the role of the Church as mediator has fostered an understanding between Sandinism and President Violeta Chamorro.

In El Salvador, where the war lasted more than twelve years, the mediating efforts of the Church were constantly sabotaged by the intransigence of the hard-line wing of the military and extreme right. In the recent elections voters shunned the polls in large numbers, assaults and murders are still committed by the death squads, and now there is election fraud to boot. Popular religion in El Salvador plays a central role in the survival, or symbolical manifestation, of rebellion. A recent report from San Salvador announced:

For March 24, the Eleventh Anniversary of the Martyrdom of Archbishop Romero, the Communities and Parishes are preparing for a Novena of Reflection on Archbishop Romero's life. The Novena will conclude on the 24th itself, with a pilgrimage to the center of San Salvador, with the participation of the whole people.

The popular impact of recent papal visits to Latin America, with its overflow crowds, reflects the fact that the simple people see in the Pope a figure with charisma—invested with religious symbolical power—who, in mythic and in real fashion, incarnates their aspirations for peace and justice. And this is more significant than all of the critical analyses we read concerning the political meaning of such visits. It is significant because it reveals a characteristic element of the mentality of our people, who receive the Holy Father as a leader of theirs after the fall of the great popular or populist leaders—"Daddy" Cárdenas, Getulio, Perón, Haya de la Torre—a huge resulting vacuum in popular legitimation when it comes to so many authoritarian regimes (Gomes de Souza 1982:184-85), and so much popular disenchantment with the parties and traditional liberal democratic politics (translated into support for presidential candidates outside the party system: Collor de Melo, Fujimori, and, in a certain sense, Menem). The impact on these visits on the democratization processes is difficult to evaluate with precision. However, they seem to have been the occasion of great gatherings of persons, through which, along with manifesting their faith, the people have expressed their yearnings for a peaceful and democratic coexistence in justice and solidarity. The various peoples have recovered their energies and their will to struggle, and this has fostered a climate of mobilization and understanding that has contributed to democratic solutions.

### Concrete Historical Dynamics: Adaptation and Resistance of the Popular Religions

In a historical view, one perceives that, in any society in which the official culture characterizing the dominant elite develops, a popular culture tends to be formed that is not the simple reproduction of official popularized forms. The popular culture that materializes has a relative consistency of its own, and develops a worldview in implicit opposition to official conceptions of the world (Gramsci 1954, Portelli 1974). In the religious field, this same dialectic between the productions of official and popular meanings is to be observed, although it does not occur in reflex fashion. Whenever an official, institutional religion is maintained, functioning as the guardian of orthodoxy in belief and ritual, there arise and develop, in a spontaneous process and by way of a response, religious forms that respond to the needs, hopes, and yearnings of the masses that are left unsatisfied by the official religion (Lanternari 1982:36).

In any study of the complex, multifaceted dynamics of the religious field (Maduro 1978), we ought to strive after a more systematic discovery of the conditions under which a cultural encounter or historical process. This is particularly true when there is a threat of domination by one of the sides over the other, as with the conquest of America. This is also true today given the process of urbanization and secularization imposed by official society, or the convulsed social and political life of our continent in this century—issues in reactions on the part of the masses, under the form either of active rebellion or of passive response through the process of syncretizations of beliefs, rites, and customs (Herskovits 1937:541).

The most noteworthy fact in our case is that a goodly proportion of the new forms of popular religious expression that we have analyzed have to a certain extent been the product of overt or covert resistance, by way of syncretization, to changing conditions provoked by the urbanization process and by the turbulent, unstable Latin American social and political life of the twentieth century. It would seem that the cultures' tenacity in defense of their values, ideals, and interests can lead them, as we have seen, either to reactivate religious traditions or to develop new and original responses (González 1985). Popular originality and creativity, conditioned by the type of popular subject at hand and the degree of freedom allowed by the structural and conjunctural context, will be a decisive factor in the generation of new religious expressions that have widened the spectrum of alternatives available to the subordinate classes.

Latin America's social and political history during the present century has been marked by constant conflict. The political fabric is woven of convulsive battles for democratization, from emerging groups' fights with the domination of the traditional oligarchy at the beginning of the century to the democratization processes of today that, in their various manifestations, characterize this continent's sociopolitical scenario.

The response of the popular classes in each nation's critical periods of history have in some cases had a decisive effect on the restructuring of their religious energies and beliefs. With the establishment of the Republic and the bourgeois order in Brazil from 1870 to 1930, the peasantry's response was produced under the form of religious messianisms. The Cristeros' rebellion against Calles's revolutionary government in Mexico (1926-29), with its messianic embellishments (Meyer 1975), like other messianic expressions in various eras, reveals a religiously inspired protest, a protest mounted by peasant masses defending their traditional piety and *pathos* in the face of the political and social processes of capitalistic transformation under way, with their urbanizing and modern, but destabilizing, impacts.

The case of the urban messianisms in Brazil, which have been little studied, is instructive, inasmuch as it shows us a type of response having many analogies with those underlying the formation of popular Pentecostalism and the new Afro-American syncretic cults. The absence of "exodus" themes in the urban messianisms of Brazil results in an oscillation of their project between *macumbeirismo* and the "magical messiah" (Prien 1985:813-15).

Many nationalist, reformist, or populist expressions characterizing so much of the political history of many Latin American countries have been regarded as anticlerical, with a resulting neglect of any study of their bond with the religion of the popular masses who have made up these movements' base of support. Apart from predictable attempts at an instrumentalization of religious motives for electoral ends in order to win sympathy and political legitimacy—in the case of the Mexican Revolution, for example, or in the cases of APRA in Peru, Varguism in Brazil, or Peronism in Argentina—we readily discern points of contact between, on the one hand, the project and ideology proposed and, on the other, the piety of the popular masses who have supported those projects.[3]

The common characteristic in these movements, despite the notable political and historical differences in each of them, is that they are able—not without contradictions—to be the vehicle for merging the aspirations for justice of the popular classes with their religious feeling. In the Mexican case, we think of the respectful attitude maintained toward religion by the most popular caudillos of the revolution, Villa and Zapata. As for Vargas, he never directly attacked Catholicism, but rather allied himself to it in his project. In the case of APRA, a nebulous, syncretic ideology appealed to native American roots and to religion in order to hoist its antioligarchical and Latin-

---

3. See, for the Mexican case, Prien (1985) and Rutherford (1971); for case of APRA, Vega-Centeno (1985, 1986); for the case of Peronism, Carutti and Martínez (1974) and Farrel (1976); for the case of Vargas and *umbanda*, Brown et al. (1985).

Americanist banners. Coming to Peronism, let us recall its history, in which it sought to combine "justicialism" with the social ideals of Christianity. We are dealing with movements that have been interpreted by official religion as a threat, whereas they actually respond to the need for the myths that the masses require in order to be mobilized in their process of integration into a state in full process of modernization and industrialization. We are dealing with movements incarnating a pent-up "popular" energy and ill-defined nationalism, and the pseudoreligious symbolisms of these movements fuel the popular perception that they carry no contradiction of their traditions and most deeply felt faith. Bypassing the mediations of a rationally structured discourse, populism, through its hazy ideology, appeals to the popular sense of religious symbolism. The leader (Madero, Haya de la Torre, Perón) is transformed into a kind of secular messiah, come to redeem the masses from the miseries and afflictions of this life. In the Argentinian case, Evita Perón becomes the symbol of a revolutionary mystique, and is practically canonized by the people after her tragic death, in the same way that so many other leaders are who enflesh the Latin American people's deep aspirations for justice, such as Archbishop Oscar Romero, who rises up from El Salvador as a new "saint," not a canonized one but a popular one.

Urbanization entails an ongoing integration of the masses, including the "informal" or "marginalized" masses, into the spheres of power of society as a whole, and thereby brings with it a relative politicization of life. But the ambit of the representations into which political opinion is condensed is a sphere of reality, among others, that exists within the popular synthetic mentality. We are in a period in which we witness the "end of the ideologies," and the Latin American popular masses seem disappointed in politics and its traditional styles of action. While there are situations in which overpoliticization leads to the abandonment of religious faith, as occurs with activists committed in more totalitarian fashion to a political "cause," in the vast majority of cases this does not happen with the popular masses. Instead, the religious sphere tends to be articulated in parallel with the political sphere, and the spheres coexist, even under logical contradictions—logical in the light of Cartesian "rationality" but do not necessarily affect the religious sense. We shall analyze this manner of constitution of the representational processes in the popular style of thinking in the following chapters.

As a corollary of what we have asserted, the secularization process in Latin America cannot be explained as a result of the processes of politicization, as certain authors posited in the 1970s. In his search

for the specificity of the process on our continent, Míguez Bonino con-
cluded that the process of universal secularization was, in our countries, far more deeply scored by the political dimension than it was by
technology. Hence the need to search for categories of interpretation
that will be different from those of the North Atlantic world. "The
interaction of this process with popular piety manifests its own dynamics and characters" (Míguez Bonino 1974:440).

In any case, this interpretation has been out of place. After all, as
we have seen, even in the Latin American political field there is room
for a revitalization of the religious element, just as there is on the
basis of the new communications technologies. Certain processes of
politicization have at times even given rise to a new currency of messianic and mythic phenomena, or else of new ethico-prophetical expressions, in the piety of the popular masses.

# Chapter 9

# Opium, or Popular Religious Resistance to a Modernizing Capitalism?

The question of the alienating character of religion, in particular the religion of the people, has been at the center of the theoretical discussion underlying, in goodly measure, critical interpretations of religion. The classic definition of religion as the "opium of the people" remains as a background that no one can afford to neglect in a sociological analysis of popular religion (Marx 1979). We refer not only to the classic, familiar Marxian thesis but to Weber as well, who, in analyzing popular piety, shows how the latter serves to tame the dominated and legitimate the dominating powers.[1] On an underdeveloped and, in its majority, Christian continent such as Latin America, however, religion subsists, and is even being revitalized, as significant meaning among the popular masses. The function of protest against oppression that religion has performed in many processes of popular struggle and resistance challenges the sociologist to reconsider the problem.

The subject kindles lively polemics and debates, whose ideological and political connotations are unquestionable. Until recently, a goodly proportion of Latin American intellectuals—children of enlightened modernity—saw in the religion of the people pure prejudices, superstitions, and atavisms: "illusory" components of an alienating consciousness, all needing to be defeated by rational criticism. Most recently, certain currents of theology and pastoral theory are attempting to rediscover, in traditional popular religion, the "soul of the people"—the deeper Latin American identity, regarded as opposed to liberal, Marxist secularism. This perspective is counterbalanced by

---

1. See Weber (1964, 1:379ff.; vol. 2, chaps. 7, 9).

that of a liberation current that seeks to discern the germs of liberation in a religion of the oppressed that is a protest of the dominant
culture.

As we have said, the religious element is a component of culture,
and culture must be understood as a historical phenomenon. This
means that the significates and functions of the religious element are
relative to the specific eras and situations of the social actors who
produce and reproduce this set of codified meanings. Our hypothesis,
on this point, is that the people, qua historico-social actors, collec-
tively produce their representations and practices of religious symbolism through a process in which is evinced, in differentiated fashion in function of their relative position in the class structure and the
religious field, the dominated and, at the same time, relatively autonomous character of these representations and practices. Through
the process of a production of meaning—a process both conditioned
and conditioning—the various subordinate fractions and classes express, in some of their multiform religious manifestations, a *symbolical
protest*. This protest is not always overt, and only in some cases, in
function of historical and structural circumstances, does it come to be
operative in the constitution of an authentic class consciousness among
the proletarian and subproletarian masses. Our complementary thesis maintains that the alienating elements of popular religion, when
present, are never alienating by *essence*, but only by their concrete,
socially and historically situated *existence*.

### Religion as Resignation in the Face of Oppression: An Incomplete View

In the quest for the satisfaction of their basic needs, popular
human beings are subjected to their situation as a dominated class.
The daily life of the working classes, like that of the mass of underemployed and unemployed and their families, unfolds, in the underdeveloped and dependent countries, under the sign of exploitation and misery. Capitalistic society denies them their legitimate
rights, and deprives them of opportunities for work and well-being. Thus, no alternative remains to the popular individual but to
have recourse to a series of "survival strategies." It is precisely in
this context that—as a general rule—popular religion takes on its
full meaning as a parallel and complementary form of "symbolical
survival strategy."

According to a more or less current interpretation,[2] then, religion constitutes a sort of supplementary symbolical means in the popular classes' daily struggle for subsistence. Animism and magic are simply the mechanisms of an attempt to control and regulate the ambient milieu in terms of a religious pragmatism. The endemic situation of social insecurity and chronic dependency in which popular individuals find themselves trapped is thus alleviated by recourse to symbolic instances within their grasp, a recourse offered by beliefs in the miraculous powers of God, the Virgin, the saints, and the *animas benditas*, the "blessed souls." Piety in the popular milieu assumes the character of a supernatural power of aid to the displaced poor, bestowing benefits that society denies them, or else consoling them in their frustration.

Religion, we hear, acts as a factor of adaptation to domination by reinforcing the fatalism of the "culture of poverty."[3] The culture of poverty is supposed to be characterized by its internal disintegration and by a constant frustration (not always openly expressed)—a situation arousing general feelings of impotence, helplessness, and despair and provoking resigned, fatalistic responses. In the measure that the religion of these subjects contributes to their power to imagine idealistic solutions, of an individual, symbolical kind (such as making a promise to a saint in order to solve a concrete problem), which inhibit autonomous, organized behaviors, in that same measure, it is said, religion reinforces the fatalism of a hope for an unreal, ahistorical solution to concrete, historical social problems. According to this interpretation, popular religion constitutes an important component in popular resignation and alienation (Marzal 1970), which is another

---

2. Interpretation systematized by A. Bentué in an interesting study on popular religion in Santiago de Chile. See Bentué (1972, 1976).

3. The theory of the "culture of poverty," developed by anthropologist Oscar Lewis in the 1960s (Lewis 1961, 1969, 1988) on the basis of his studies of the Mexicans and Puerto Ricans, is also shared by the developmentalistic theoreticians of "popular advancement" (DESAL 1969, Veckemans 1969), in the sense of emphasizing the internal disintegration and atomization of the marginal groups, in which feelings of powerlessness, helplessness, dependency, inferiority, and resignation predominate. The Latin American social psychologists adopt the same idea in developing their psychosocial portrait of the "fatalistic character" of the Latin American (Martín Baró 1987). Recent sociopsychological approaches insist on this erroneous generalization, alleging that the main response of the marginalized to frustration is expressed not in violent behaviors, but in attitudes of resignation and conformism that lead to political indifferentism, self-aggression, presentism, and despair (Martínez et al. 1990). We believe we present abundant arguments in this book to refute the bases on which this picture of Latin American popular culture has been built.

way of presenting the old Marxian thesis—of Feuerbachian inspiration—(Marx and Engels 1972, Marx 1979; Wackenheim 1973) according to which religion alienates persons by subjecting them to a heteronomous dependency on a world of illusions, which inhibits them from taking their destiny in hand as praxis, as revolutionary and critical practice, and prevents their discovery that the vale of tears and the kingdom of heaven are caught up in one and the same dialectic of history.

Under certain aspects, and for only one segment of the population, this analysis is correct. However, the recent historical experience of the popular classes as we have analyzed it, and certain studies in particular,[4] indicate how erroneous it is to attempt to generalize this type of interpretation across the board.

## Magical Religious Traditionalism and the Reproduction of Life

Even in the case of the most traditional expressions—those seemingly more orientated toward magic and superstition—it is possible to discover, depending on one's interpretative standpoint, elements of a rationality proper to those sectors of the population that must confront the problem of subsistence on an everyday basis. In the case of the popular sectors sunk in conditions of extreme poverty, traditional religion—whether under the form of popular Catholicism, abstentionist Pentecostalism, the Afro-American cults, superstitious spiritisms, or, finally, the ensemble of rituals and devotions of a traditional cast, such as pilgrimages, impetratory votive offerings to the saints, devotions and prayers, or rituals of possession by spirits (rituals of healing)—has an objective social signification indicative of a "symbolical efficacy" when it comes to solving the more problematic questions with which the poor are confronted in their daily life.

## Traditional Popular Catholicism and the Protective Souls of the Departed

Let us now see what occurs, in the kind of popular religion that we are analyzing, in the face of the problem of hunger. In the first place, we shall have to single out certain characteristic elements that typify

---

4. See Giménez (1978), Irrarázaval (1978), Kudo (1980), Parker (1986a), Salinas (1991).

this kind of popular belief, which is that of a certain number of emigrants to the cities (between one-fourth and one-third, according to our studies), but which is one of a number of typical religious models.[5]

There are a number of typical traits attaching to certain expressions of popular religion that, in general terms, we may classify under what has been dubbed the "popular Catholicism" of a traditional type, prevailing especially in cities:

1. The beliefs in question are inherited as part of a family tradition—a tradition accepted without question, and not as mere lore but, rather, in a vital sense.
2. Such persons believe in God, the Virgin, the saints, the *animitas* (literally, "little souls," from *anima*, departed "soul"), and the miraculous powers of all of these. Their beliefs are part of the popular *common sense* of a traditional cast.
3. These persons do not believe in, or at least have doubts about, any life after death, thereby taking their distance from the official Christian belief in the resurrection of the dead.
4. They do not comply with official religious practices (they do not go to mass), but they do regularly carry out popular religious practices (they make "gifts"—impetratory votive offerings—to the Virgin).

These beliefs and practices call for a brief commentary. One is struck by the popular belief in the *animitas* coupled with a doubt of or disbelief in the resurrection. Are we dealing with a contradiction in the popular mentality?

The *animita* acquires material form in a little shrine, generally standing along the roadside and erected in memory of someone who has died a tragic death. People make pilgrimages to this "sanctuary" to pray, to make votive offerings, and to offer worship to the *animita* whose supernatural power they acknowledge.

In these countries, belief in the existence of the souls of the departed represents a pole of cultural religion standing in opposition to *official* religious meaning. This belief and its network of connected practices are not regarded by the Church as an expression of authentic Catholic practice. Rather, such practices are looked upon as the expression of a deviant religious behavior. This belief represents one of the key nuclei structuring the *traditional popular religious sense*

---

5. See chap. 6, pp. 138-139 above.

of the Latin American subordinate classes.[6] In many countries, recourse is usually had to the *animas benditas*, "blessed souls," with a homologous ritual of votive promise, but with a slightly different meaning of the word *anima*, (departed) "soul." The cases of the deceased Correa in Argentina, Sarita Colonia in Peru, and Dr. Hernández in Venezuela are much closer to the meaning of *animita* in Chilean popular culture.

The *animita* is a kind of *popular saint*. Unlike the canonized saint of official religious belief, this is the soul of some person, generally anonymous (and in no sense held up as an example of moral virtue or mysticism), who has died an unjust death, tragic or heroic. The soul (*animita*) of this person, mythified in the popular consciousness as a martyr purified by blood, traditionally has an ambivalent destiny: either it goes to heaven without passing through purgatory or it roams betwixt heaven and earth until it has accomplished its task of making those "pay" who have done it some evil during its earthly life. One of the most widespread beliefs attaching to this devotion is that the soul of the departed one does not "rest in peace," and that it manifests its restlessness by plaguing the lives of the living ("The *animas* are suffering," goes the popular saying). One of the *core* elements of this belief is the notion that departed souls are *miraculous* and benefactors of human beings, since they are exempt from sin (Navarro et al. 1975) and thus in greater proximity to the beneficent powers of Divine Providence. Thus, the *anima* has the property of a sacred being: it is venerated, and its beneficent potentiality is valued, while its virtual maleficent qualities are feared and one seeks to conjure them away. While we find the cult of the *animas* or souls preponderantly in rural milieus, the worship of the *animitas* is urban. In the popular outlying districts of the metropolises as well, generally along highways or railroad tracks, at crossroads, on street corners, on sidewalks, or in well-frequented public places, one sees niches, with the unfailing crucifix, where the folk of the place venerate a miraculous *animita*. Adorned with flowers and burning lamps, they are the object of devotion in the form of prayers, promises, votive offerings, and other forms of impetration in exchange for some material or moral requital.

To be sure, this is a form of worship of the dead (and not a manifestation of animism like that underlying the Afro-American cults, as some authors mistakenly declare); but it is conceived and practiced under a *popular* formula, according to which the notion of the *anima*

6. Bentué (1972:145ff., 170, 174), CISOR (1970:216ff.), ICODES (1970:79ff.), Vásquez de Acuña (1956), Zuluaga (n.d.:109-12).

does not fully coincide, in its life beyond the grave, with the official religious concept of the resurrected soul and body, exulting in God. The *anima* of the subject, regarded by the people as a kind of innocent, anonymous *martyr*, comes to form part of that undifferentiated, omnipresent world of the kingdom of the dead, which at every instant intervenes once more in the daily life of the traditional universe of representation of the world. Thus, the properties of the departed soul, in popular belief, make it to be a sort of religious object, situated on a level only slightly below God.

Latent in this popular belief is an element of symbolical subversion of that official orthodoxy that lays down that any "saint" (of exemplary life) only acts vicariously, in the name of and by virtue of the almighty power of God. However, it is not that God's primacy is questioned in this understanding of the departed soul as a mediating being. It is only that the popular subject in need of some concrete benefit (health, luck in love, luck in finding work or money for food, moral strength for righting a faulty life, and the like) has recourse to a semiotic object, the *anima*, that has the faculty of extranatural intervention in life. The subject attempts to control his or her chancy life symbolically, thanks to a pact established with the object—the departed soul: he or she makes that soul a promise entailing some type of effort and sacrifice, mystically shouldered and borne by the person making the offering (lighting candles to it, bringing it flowers or a votive offering, good behavior, not drinking again, and so on), in exchange for some recompense: obtaining the desired boon.

Like any magical ritual, the promise made to the *anima* or departed soul—analogous to the ritual of promise or gift to the saints and/or the Virgin Mary so proper to traditional popular religion—after the fashion of any instrument of scientific technology,[7] is con-

---

7. According to anthropologists, magic and science have an unmistakable kinship. Frazer (1969) has called magic the "science of the primitives"; for Lévi-Strauss (1962), it is the "science of the concrete." Being a form of alternative "technology," magic seeks its efficacy by means of a manipulation of the environment via standardized procedures and formulae. As for the distinction between religion and magic, this has been one of the problems most intensely investigated by the studios of the Western religions. Prescinding from the variety of responses to the question, the most adequate element in these responses, and indeed their common element, is that the authors understand magic and religion as ranged along a continuum, where either expression represents an extreme among manners of behavior bearing on the supernatural (Benedict 1952). Weber asserts that the separation between religion and magic "is not genuinely achieved anywhere, since 'religious' ritual almost always contains magical ingredients" (Weber 1964:345).

ceived as endowed with its efficacy in function of the conformation of the procedure to the letter of its formulas and the scrupulous observance of its routines down to the last detail. If the prescriptions of the ritual are followed step by step, then the favor is sure to be granted. One must observe, however, that, in the processual morphology of the rite under analysis here, unlike the mechanical procedure underlying the classic theory of sympathetic magic (which operates by simple homeopathy or contiguity), the intervention of *faith*, on the one hand, and the *sacrificial* sense of the rite, on the other, distinguish it from that magical routine and assimilate it to the religious sense of sacrifice and supplication, of whose results the ritual is a necessary but not sufficient condition, since these results depend, besides, on the supplicant's spiritual state with regard to God and, ultimately, on God's will. The last phase of the semiotico-contractual structure with the object-*animita* is thanksgiving: at times a plaque will be engraved, at other times the act of thanksgiving will be effected by the fulfillment of new promises. At all events, the basic semiotic structure of the promise to the departed soul presents itself as nearer to magical ritual than to the sacramental ritual proper to an official religion of salvation in intellectualistic terms (Weber 1964, Mauss 1980), but removed from the classic schema of superstitiously orientated magic, since its petition and ritual are not necessarily conceived as exercising a mechanical coercion on the *anima*. Let us qualify it, then, as a ritual of *religious magic*.

## Syncretism and Magical Religious Ritual

Now, how are we to explain the paradox of a belief in the *animitas* and the doubt or unbelief in the resurrection of the dead? Are we dealing with a contradiction in the popular mentality?

The typical believer, in this case, denies a belief in life after death (or has doubts), but manifests a firm conviction as to the *animitas* and their miraculous power. This seeming paradox could be explained by the *syncretism* of these two beliefs. (We refer to syncretism at greater depth in chapter 10; for the moment, our analysis will be simply a descriptive one.) The discourse that we are analyzing calls itself *Catholic*, and therefore includes a traditional dualistic thought; but it incorporates a belief in spirits (a surviving element of the pre-Columbian native religions), with a reformulation of this latter belief. The soul of the deceased is thought of as dwelling in the corpse or in the places frequented by this deceased person in his or her life. It is not a belief in a personal *resurrection*, but a belief in a vague survival of the dead. It is a belief that could be a popular deformation of the traditional official belief in the "souls in purgatory." There does not seem to be any clear sense of Christian salvation here, and yet we are many removes from primitive animism.

The peculiar combination of beliefs at hand may point to a worldview according to which the sacred cosmos, inhabited by spirits and souls, is a sort of "symbolical protective umbrella" extended over the living and shielding them from the adversities of this life—a kind of *sacred canopy* (Berger 1969) that makes it possible to relegitimate a *nomos* capable of structuring the meaning of life.

Consistently with this conclusion, we must call attention to the central character of the votive *gift* as a ritual of communication with the supernatural. The context here is that of an extraecclesial ritual involving a supplication and ritual sacrifice addressed to the Virgin, the saints, or the *animitas* and orientated to a search for rescue, in concrete life, from any evil, or succor in any need ("I ask health, that we won't be without it," "that we may have something to eat for the morrow," "that Juanito will find work," and so on). Through the investigations that we have ourselves carried out, we have found that the ritual of promise supposes a kind of *do ut des* contract: "I ask of you and I offer in return." This "offering in return" can be some sacrifice, lighting a candle, a particular attitude, a votive offering. The ritual must be performed strictly, since otherwise the miracle is not expected to occur. This permits us to assert that the symbolical efficacy of this popular ritual follows the mimetic logic of all magical ritual, but that, as we shall see in the next chapter, we are not dealing with a "magical" ritual in a classic, pejorative sense.

Our interest in this model of popular religion is a pragmatic interest in the origin of the religious sense. The magical religious orientation recommends an assiduous, constant ritual exchange with the sacred beings, but especially with those "proved" to be miraculous (the Virgin, the saints, the miraculous *animitas*). All of this so that the supplicant, or someone dear to him or her, "may do well, and live long years on earth" (Weber 1964:328). The "gift" is more useful than prayer to God or Christ: it is tried and true, while one's ability to influence the will of God the Father or the Lord is uncertain. One is more devout, the more effective the ritual-symbolism contract has turned out: miracles have been worked.

### Some Sociological Considerations

On the basis of certain investigations that, as it happens, we have conducted in popular sectors, we can assert that this type of religious expression—significant in very broad sectors, but not among the majority—has a very characteristic sociological ambit.

The subjects reproducing this type of belief and practice are folk who live in the world of urban settlers displaced from the countryside, especially women and subproletarians with less formal education and more heavily influenced by peasant culture. They are less completely integrated into the industrialized urban world. The acute conditions of misery and exploitation to which they are subjected and the impossibility of solving their problems through employment in the formal system of the economy lead them to embark upon a series of behaviors that, via the reinforcement of bonds of solidarity, generate relations and practices orientated to survival ("survival strategies"). Their life is under the daily stress of having to ensure their daily bread. Generally, the popular sectors are regarded with contempt by official culture, so that they have to suffer not only hunger but persecution and police repression. In these convulsed historical situations, the systematic violation of human rights and other political violence affect primarily the popular classes, aggravating their already wretched situation. Hunger, cold, a lack of even minimal resources, a life marked by pain, suffering, and violence, as we have seen, lower the threshold of *uncertainty*. All of this frames a certain "falling back on oneself" and on the nucleus of the family.

In general, this soil of incertitude gives rise to a religious sense characterized by a strong sense of dependency. The subject seems not to be in control of his or her own destiny, but rather to be at the mercy of an uncertain fate. The longing for *tranquility* calls for an "order" in which harmony will reign. We mean a certain primordial, cosmic harmony, upon which one ultimately depends, and with which one must strike a relation through supernatural mediators. Inasmuch as one depends on extreme conditions, there is a certain *fatalism* here, but not one calling for an absolute resignation, seeing that it does not prevent concrete initiatives on the part of displaced peasants with a view to solving their problems. The gift to the Virgin does not replace but complements direct action undertaken for the purpose of obtaining a piece of bread for the children. Ritual—with a certain magical content—offers a meaning, withdraws its subject from anxiety, alleviates tensions, and makes it possible to face uncertainty in this life by reinforcing and revitalizing the subject in his or her quest for concrete solutions to the immediate problem of hunger.

The quest is not for a compensatory boon in the next life, but for a direct relation with the supernatural powers (God, the Virgin, the departed souls) for the purpose of making life more bearable *in this world*. Here religion fulfills an altogether precise social function, by assisting the simple reproduction of *life*. But this does not necessarily mean a submission to the prevailing social order, although in many cases fatalism translates also into a legitimation, in the social ambit, of the subjection of the urban poor to the dominant classes.

In chapter 5, we have analyzed the importance of rites of crisis in the popular religion that accompanies the life of its subjects. There we speak of the importance of the petition for health, and we know that, in the popular mentality, bodily health is intimately bound up with moral and spiritual health: the view maintained by that mentality is, in this sense, integral. The great call for "healing" in the Pentecostal and Afro-American cults takes place in the same logic. The various healing rituals in the syncretisms of the native American and the Catholic of the Andes and Central America, the importance of rituals such as faith healing or cures for the healing of "evils," the "evil eye," "spooks," or evil "winds," have no other function than to guarantee the individual and social reproduction of life. Early in 1991, when a cholera epidemic scourged Peru and from there spread to neighboring countries, the activity of popular healers notably increased. In the decisive days of the epidemic, television news brought us dramatic images of healers engaged in a spiritual battle (in this case, a fruitless one) with the "evil" of cholera in the context of a public-health system in which there is one physician for every 30,000 inhabitants when in the United States there are seventy times that proportion.[8]

In the Latin American Pentecostalisms, their exultant, charismatic, and festive celebration does not represent, any more than does the type of piety that we have just analyzed, a form of avoidance of the problems posed by daily living. Rather, that celebration is another way of solving them. The Pentecostalist's emphasis on the health of the body and on individual and community life evinces a concern for concrete, material problems. "We must not forget that Pentecostalism

---

8. In Chile, a country whose public health system is acknowledged to be a good one, there are 8 physicians for every 10,000 inhabitants, while in England there are 14, and in the United States, 23. In Chile, there are 33 hospital beds per 10,000 inhabitants, while in England there are 77, and in the United States, 58.

has made important gains in the battle against alcoholism, drug addiction, and domestic violence. Its determination and ability to find a solution for these problems that weigh down the life of the lower strata of society bestow on Pentecostalism a credible, undeniable liberative dimension for the dispossessed of society" (Damen 1986:49).

Three great social functions are performed by religious beliefs in this case: a consolatory symbolical compensation, for one; a form of occult, silent symbolical resistance, for another; and third, a "more" of meaning to a life lived under constant threat.

The supernatural powers and faith in their efficacy give the displaced settler the peace of mind that comes with the conviction that he or she will never lack the necessities of life. As we see, religion—faith in God, the Virgin, and the *animas*—is a guarantee of symbolical protection. They are always there to succor their clients, and either to supply settlers with the objects and goods denied them by the dominant society or else to console them in their frustration (Bentué 1975). Life can be very harsh and afflicting, but it will never be despairing, thanks to faith. That it may be thus, the popular believer knows that his or her abstract, intellectual belief is not enough: the ritual of the "gift," imprecation or impetration, prayers (for example, novenas), pilgrimages, ritual healing, and so on, are the sacrificial rites—ambiguously present, with their burden of effort and pain, and their festive, joyful face—that are necessary in order to guarantee the efficacy of supernatural intervention. It is not enough to believe; one must "live the faith," the people say, and living the faith is the practical conjugation of the faith in a particular popular ritual not necessarily tied to institutionally oriented official religious practices. Therefore a Catholic can go to mass on Sunday, and the next day ask a Protestant minister to bless a dying baby; or make a pilgrimage to the Virgin in the morning, and in the afternoon attend an *umbanda* meeting.

On the other hand, this type of belief reproduces a *traditional* code, which silently resists, if at times precariously, the cultural invasion of a consumer society and its mercantile logic. ("You don't have to pay to go to Church," is the way one popular subject put it.) The healer, the *rezador* (the "pray-er"), also receives money for services rendered, but the price is a good deal lower than the cost of professionalized modern medicine. The additional advantage to the poor of this alternative health service is its greater accessibility. While a trip to the local polyclinic or hospital means a long series of bureaucratic steps, the neighborhood faith healer is always available in an emergency.

Aversion to religious change or "renewal" must not always be interpreted as pure negative conservatism. It also represents its subject's will to reject certain values in the dominant culture and thus to preserve certain autonomous traits in the usages, beliefs, and customs of the people. It functions as a "latent symbolical protest"—if an ambiguous one, since it can be the object of manipulation by various ideological orientations to "protest" antagonistic concrete projects. Fatalism can be transformed into religious alienation at the service of a conservative project or, on the contrary, can be open to a more liberative religious awareness.

Finally, we must point out that this kind of belief, in a context of popular religion, is the basis of a cultural *meaning* endowed with profound content. In the basic contradiction implied by the problem of hunger, as we said, *life* and *death* are at stake. Hunger is slow death; nourishment is the recovery of life, biological and integral. Illness is a manifestation of death; healing is the reestablishment of full life. Traditional popular religion—as a symbolical mechanism contributing to the people's ability to bear up under uncertainty, without presenting any obstacles to concrete efforts to reach immediate, comprehensive solutions—takes sides with *life*.

The problem of hunger and health is the problem of the *reproduction of life*. Popular Catholicism, and the various expressions of popular religion generally, have a function here and a particular meaning: that of fostering the sense of life and contributing to the disappearance of the sense of death. Popular faith enables its subjects to recover the dignity that has been expropriated by hunger and sickness. Traditional popular faith is a kind of "symbolical survival strategy" (Parker 1986c): a struggle against death through a symbolical nourishment of material and practical survival strategies. Traditional popular faith is nourishment that affords life and help in the confrontation with the traumatic experience of the hunger of the poor. That is, sociologically it is a religio-cultural model contributing to the reproduction of the life and very culture of the subordinate classes through resistance to the contradictions of the modernizing structure of underdeveloped capitalism. But at the same time, the macrosocial logic of this same traditional popular faith makes possible an "adaptation" (however antagonistic) to the system and to the subjection of the popular groups to the dominant social relations of production.

Popular religion, in its various manifestations, contributes to the reproduction of life, to protection from the perils that beset life's path, but also to the endowment of life with a fuller meaning through a restoration of value. Religion, in this sense, is not only consolation and survival strategy—it is also a wellspring of life, in which the poor and indigent recover their dignity and come to identify themselves once more as human beings, as "children of God," as "Christians." By means of popular beliefs and rituals, the human being is saved from being "lost" in the midst of misery, vices, dehumanization, and disfigurement, and recovers his or her human dignity, gains personal meaning once more, and recovers a personal and social vocation. Hauled down to a depersonalizing alienation and threatened with destruction, in their primary cultural identification, by misery and social oppression, popular subjects receive from popular religion a new dignity by means of their reconnection, their religation, with God—the link that reestablishes a religious, cultural, and social identification—and through their community rituals they find their bonds of identity and solidarity with their community and their people reinvigorated. This is how the function of renewal and regeneration proper to sacrificial rituals, with the various historical manifestations of their mythologies, symbologies, and hierophanies (Eliade 1975), is manifested in the popular cultures of contemporary Latin American capitalism.

### Plural Functions: Religion Not an Insuperable Obstacle to Modernization

If popular religion is not an opium of the people, as Marxist theory has proclaimed it is, and if in popular religion there is a "germ of protest," then to what point would this protest represented by popular religion not be merely a kind of refuge of tradition, a refractory counterculture to modernity? Might popular religion not be simply the survival of a religion that sees itself threatened by the modernizations of contemporary capitalism, the spirit of a world whose existence is already undermined, the soul of a world whose hour is now past, a symbolical referent forming an obstacle to progress and thus to the advance of history?

At least in the historical experience of the contemporary West, that would seem to be the panorama. Here is a piety that, for a good long time now, has ceased to instill life into the symbolical field of society, and that fails to die through the simple inertia that customs imprint on it in the cultural dynamics of history. True, in the West, the reality falling under the concept of popular religion seems to limit itself progressively.

Popular religion will be no more than a residual religion, temporarily escaping the victorious march of modernization and not yet succeedingly eliminated by the conciliar reforms, the innovations of every denomination, or the militant orthodoxies, clerical or not. There remain, here and there, local cults, processions a little strange, from which tourist agencies have not yet derived all of their profit, rather esoteric or marginal blessings, pilgrimages not yet commandeered by religious professionals, dubious cures and apparitions that spontaneously attract faithful. In any case, what strikes one is, generally, their low social visibility. [Delooz 1988]

In previous chapters we have analyzed the various modular types of religious representations, both for Catholicism and for the other—Pentecostal, Afro-American, or sectarian—expressions among the people.

Generalizing, we may assert that the more traditional religious models perform their various functions at different levels within their respective situations, on the margin of the process of dominant capitalistic production—among subproletarians and impoverished and overexploited masses. On the one hand—evincing the accuracy of what we have already said—they serve as a symbolical protective shield against adversity in labor instability, exploitation, and misery. On the other hand, the fact that they reproduce traditional codes in the context of a modern society has the function *ad intra* of reproducing a basic collective identity in the face of the invasion of the dominant culture. Hence the fact that this type of piety can also be regarded as a form of *passive resistance*, on the symbolical level, to the official modernizing culture. However—in a seeming contradiction—these kinds of models of popular religion in their operation *ad extra* (toward the reproduction of the reigning order) also function as factors of resignation and alienation, and thus favor comprehensive fatalism vis-à-vis the dominant project of a capitalistic modernization that, as we have stated in chapter 2, generates an uneven development and a segmented, polarized social structure.

Traditional religion, at the heart of popular culture, turns, as we have seen, on an axis of representation in which the actor is heteronomous. God and the agents of God intervene providentially wherever daily life presents the urgency of this intervention. The supernatural powers are the guarantee of the efficacy (symbolical, and even real) of the reproductive processes and of survival in misery and oppression. The particular rituals of imprecation, pilgrimage, and supplication utilized center on objectives related to the satisfaction of unsatisfied basic needs.

Church renewal, however, especially in Catholicism, has determined in recent decades the emergence of types of popular Catholicism that do not oppose the processes of modernization but that, either in the same direction or as a critical model, accompany the processes of "rationalization" relative to urban and postindustrial life. We see models of Catholic expression that emphatically contradict, on the basis of empirical evidence, Weber's theses associating Protestantism with the modern "spirit" of capitalism, as well as his corollary thesis of Catholicism as an obstacle to the processes of modernization. These theses, as we have shown in chapter 3, were widely accepted by Creole sociology in its developmentalistic or dependentist currents.

The models of popular religion of which we are now speaking are striking for their abandonment of magical religious content and its replacement with greater ethical content (models that reformulate, and at times reject, popular traditions). As we have shown in another work (Parker 1986a), these models become part of two alternative projects. Some develop as the more individualistic model of faith—the "rationalistic" type and/or the "renewed traditional" type fit in here (Parker 1986a:325-30, 352-58)—reinforcing an ascetical spirit orientated to the social promotion of the individual, and corresponding rather closely to certain segments of proletarians or subproletarians who have received a more extensive basic education. Others develop as the social-ethics model—"renewed popular" type (Parker 1986a:331-42)—accompanying a class consciousness in those sectors of the industrial or administrative proletariat that, through the intermediary of labor organizations and the struggle to organize, have arrived at a critical view of capitalistic society and seek its transformation, and have incorporated themselves (not necessarily altogether publicly) into the renewal process of a Church that makes a "preferential option for the poor."

For the type of Catholicism that legitimates and reinforces a spirit of integration into official and modernizing capitalism—a model fairly similar on many points to the one that can be observed in numerous groups of French "practicing Catholic" proletarians (Michelat and Simon 1978)—the central problem in terms of which the representations and practices of religious symbolism dovetail with the social project is the evaluation of the social status of the individual. A determination to climb the social ladder implies the assignment of value to those institutions and symbols that denote precisely a higher socio-cultural status. The Catholic Church would thus appear as invested with a higher symbolical status, which is consciously sought by subjects attempting to improve their lot, and participation in the official community and its religious practice would be the logical consequence of the materialization of a step in that social trajectory. Thus, far from being an obstacle to "modernization" (understood as greater access to society and greater integration into the social structure), the "religious practice" of these popular Catholics would actually function as a symbolical mechanism contributing to the movement of social betterment by strengthening aspirations for social status and ascent. To what extent does this movement reinforce individualism and tend to relegate to a secondary condition any practices and manifestations of a popular mentality of solidarity? This question cannot be answered in absolute terms. But it may be supposed that the sense of belonging to the Catholic religion would be associated, in this case, with a sense of identification with the "middle classes"—would be an indicator of the social and symbolical place still held by the Catholic Church, despite the fact that, admittedly, recent decades have witnessed a huge diminution in the distance separating that church from the Latin American popular classes, especially the urban classes. The Church's institutions, its parishes, its churches and chapels, its agents, in this case would not be projecting an image of a poor and servant church, but would be reproducing the image of a preconciliar Church, the hegemonic institution, the unifying and agglutinative symbol of the "Catholic nation," and thereby the triumphalist sign of symbolical and social status.

For the base-renewal type of popular Catholicism, incorporation into the movement of church renewal under the impulse of the ecclesiastical institution since the Council and the official church meetings of Medellín and Puebla has meant the step from a traditional type of Catholicism to a more rationalized, ethically oriented Catholicism. In one of the most important studies conducted on the base church communities in Brazil, F. C. Rolim (1980) has been able to determine that the type of practices being performed by the faithful before joining the base communities has focused on traditional devotions—devotion to the saints (67%)—and they were not very "practicing," since they had low regular attendance at official practices (the Mass), whereas joining the base community has determined a decrease in that type of practice and an increase in nonsacramental practices, reflection on social practice with the help of the Bible (83%), and an increase in official practice (67%).

The source of current membership in the base church communities is fundamentally in traditional popular Catholicism, much as this may be painful for many pastoral agents and missionaries of a "renewal" orientation, themselves of extrapopular origin, to acknowledge.

Actually, not only have religious practices changed; popular beliefs as a whole have themselves been modified. In this case, the ethico-utopian vector of Christianity merges consistently, in solidarity, with a class consciousness which, in its quest for justice, reinterprets the Christian values of the reign of God and of salvation in function of the historical transformation of society. The influence of the religious agents of the base church communities, which in Latin America have made an "option for the poor," in this type of renewed popular religion is indubitable. However, we must forthrightly admit the cultural difference between the religious agent and the member of the base church community, a difference registered in language and in analytical and expressive capacity. In studies that we have done, "renewed" popular Catholics are orientated by the semantic category "justice" as the category that articulates their social worldview. They do not tend to cite the semantic category "liberation"—the corresponding key category in advanced Catholic theology and in the ecclesial language of a popular pastoral ministry.

But it cannot be ignored that the base community experiment and pastoral activity in a milieu of the popular groups constitute a new kind of synthesis between renewed official religion and popular culture and its religious forms. In general we are dealing with Catholics, mostly employed laborers but also subproletarians, who, while they are Christians, are also politically aware, and who organize to fight for the defense of their violated rights. In this context, we can appreciate the unprecedented dovetailing of popular religion's protest potential with the prophetical and liberative vector of official Christianity.

The social commitment maintained by this type of popular Catholic, with its ethical orientation, with its definition in terms of a more analytical and historical rationality, accepts, and acts as the vehicle of, a set of modernizing values and "logics," and popular Catholics making this commitment are certainly far more deeply inserted into the urban-postindustrial-technotronic world than are their homonyms of a traditional religious type. By their critical and analytical sense, however, their reading of the social appeals no longer to religious categories, but to structural categories, resulting in a sharp criticism of the processes of capitalistic modernization. By virtue of their insertion into the processes of church renewal, which are forms of modernization within the religious field, these subjects are at once children of modernity and its detractors. In no case do their alternative projects constitute a traditionalist reaction and a nostalgia for the past.

## A Protest Factor Dependent on the Historical Conjuncture

Our observations on the diversity and complexity of daily religious productions among the people indicate that the functions of symbolical protest maintained by popular religion are situated at varying depths, and that often the conjuncture at hand has an influence only on the form of their manifestation. If the Latin American Christian people, under the oppression of Somoza, Pinochet, Stroessner, or Duvalier, for example, have protested their situation and have defended life in the face of the violation of human rights (Smith 1982:283-355, Parker 1991b), appealing to their religious faith for the legitimation of their movement, this fact can be seen as a form of contemporary updating of the potential for protest lying within popular religion.

We have seen, in this chapter and especially in earlier chapters, a variety of forms of manifestation of a symbolical protest latent in popular religion. Various ritual and representational expressions are indeed forms through which the "underdogs," the oppressed, take their distance from the dominant culture, establishing a principle of otherness and identity. Harking back to a declaration by Gramsci (1954:215), we may assert that many popular religious expressions contain an implicit conception of the world (this conception itself being frequently mechanical, objective) that is opposed to the "official" conceptions of the world—except that this principle must be nuanced in the light of a historical and structural contextualization for each particular case.

Frequently, symbolical protest is manifested in "underground" fashion. The popular subject, weighed down by a series of traumatic experiences of humiliation and oppression, protests in silence, without allowing the protest to reach the ears of the dominators lest reprisals and annihilation ensue. For this reason, the popular subject seems deprived of speech. These persons are speechless not because they are mute, but because they have been silenced.

We are dealing with a protest that enables its subjects to survive by reconstructing a world of meaning—by way of a vital attitude, difficult to reduce to rationalistic schemas, that endows the popular culture with a collective identity. It is the people's way of defending themselves on the symbolical plane in the face of the rending, destructive oppression to which they are subjected on the material plane. Obviously, this form of latent protest serves the immediate interests of the dominant. But that should not make us forget that it is the "sigh of the oppressed creature" and a "protest against real misery" (Marx). It will be the historical praxis and influence of a critical culture—mediated by organic intellectuals (Gramsci), whether clergy and laity—that will render this protest overt and conscious. In this fashion, popular religion becomes liberative popular Christianity, as we see in the recent historical experience of Latin America.

As we can appreciate, there is a latent protest function in many of the manifestations of Latin American popular religions, but not in all of them, and not always manifest in the same historical periods and eras.

The religion of the subordinate classes, depending on its articulation with other sociocultural representations and corresponding to each class situation, has a variety of social functions. These present themselves now exclusively, now in parallel, and can even coexist in contradiction within the popular culture. They are a factor of alienation, a factor of popular identity, of symbolical indictment of official culture and religion, and, finally, of ethical reinforcement for a project of social ascent or for a project of social transformation. Popular religion may or may not be any of these, depending on the social and historical situation.

Viewed in the abstract and on the basis of classic interpretative frameworks, the religion of the people can be regarded, in some cases, as the mere reproduction of elements of official religion and the dominant culture. The popular actors could be seen as discharging a passive role, as simple "consumers" or "users" of a religious production developed beyond their reach and without their participation.[9] On

---

9. As we shall see in our analysis in chap. 10, Bourdieu's theory of the religious field, while pertinent in many respects, is inadequate in its analysis of the religious "consumption" of the popular masses. See Bourdieu 1971.

the other hand, if we look attentively and from the standpoint of the popular classes, the popular subject's religious self-production represents a way of recovering meaning and dignity in the face of the adverse, harsh conditions of a life lived in misery and oppression, a life that otherwise is a piece of absurdity. It is precisely this autonomous religious production which, on the basis of the network of practices of daily life and collective life, tends to resist—objectively—the negative consequences of capitalistic modernization, but which, under many aspects, is a way of incorporating oneself (not without contradiction) into the process of modernization that is under way and that influences as well, dialectically, popular religious production itself.

In the light of what we have now seen, the pluralization of the Catholic sphere, the rise of new popular religions, and the various forms of relations between religion and popular politics can all be reinterpreted as products, by syncretization, of open or covert resistance to the changing conditions provoked by the process of urbanization and by the agitated, unstable Latin American social and political life of the twentieth century. It would seem to be the case that the tenacity of the cultures in defense of their values, ideals, and interests can lead these cultures, as we have seen, either to a reactualization of religious traditions or to a development of new and original responses (González 1985). Popular originality and creativity, conditioned by the type of popular subject at hand and by the degree of freedom permitted by the structural and conjunctural context, will constitute a decisive factor in the generation of new religious expressions broadening the spectrum of alternatives available to the subordinate classes.

## Popular Creativity in Terms of Religious Symbolism

As we examine the manifold, complex manifestations of the religious expressions of the Latin American people, we observe a panorama that only under certain aspects maintains a formal similarity with what has occurred in the case of the religious expressions of the European or North American popular classes. A secularizing impact has been produced in religious beliefs, but this does not manage to eliminate the religious sense. There is a process of rationalization (to use Weberian terminology), but without secularism. Ethical and prophetical aspects are emphasized, and magical and mythic traits are transcended, but in comprehensive terms, the religious sense does not disappear: rather it is transformed, and can even be seen to be revitalized. Faith is not privatized, and the field of religious symbolism is not secularized in the direction of nonbelief and atheism. Popular faith continues to reproduce itself, mainly in the family and local ambit, but tends to be privatized only among a minority. It has various significations and performs various functions, it bestows a meaning on life in the painful conditions of misery and exploitation in which the popular masses of the continent live, it serves as a symbol of identity on various levels, and it enables its subjects to mount a cultural resistance under frankly "popular" codes and symbols, in a cultural and religious language and grammar very different from those of official religion and the dominant culture. While in some cases it legitimates social alienation, in others it offers meaning and stimulates not only a symbolical resistance but even, on occasion, a commitment to real liberation.

The Church has accepted certain popular devotions of popular mythologic origin. This is the case with the majority of devotions to apparitions of the Virgin, as well as with certain devotions to Our Lord, of remote colonial origin, whose veneration has regional or national breadth in Latin America: Our Lady of Guadalupe, of the Apparition, of Caacupé, of Copacabana, of Chiquinquirá, of Charity, of Cobre, of La Tirana, the Lord of Miracles, Our Lord of Chalma, and so on with so many devotions and shrines that dot the continent. But popular religious creativity is also expressed in certain popular devotions generated and reproduced extraecclesially, although the Church has subsequently sought to control and make use of their development.

> Replacement and reinterpretation of beliefs taken from the dominant culture by the dominated culture are, in the last analysis, simply attempts to rescue the latter. The devotion to Tonantzin endured for centuries under cover of a shrine of the Virgin Mary. Together with the staying power of the shrines and the revitalization of mythic images in a new religious context, we observe the creative activity of the collective memory. [Lafaye 1973:421]

This is the case with the well-known cults of the deceased Correa (in Argentina), of Dr. Hernández and María Lionza (in Venezuela), or of Father Cicero (in the northeast of Brazil), as well as with less familiar, less widespread devotions, such as that to the Child Fidencio (in Mexico), Sarita Colonia and Víctor Apaza (in Peru), and Romualdito Ibáñez (in Chile), or, finally, with so many devotions to the departed "souls" throughout the religious folklore of these countries. However, the creative potentiality latent in expressions of popular religion is clearly present not only in the fact that there are a multitude of "saints" venerated by the people but not having the slightest connection with the list of saints officially canonized by the church institution, but also in the constant generation of new popular devotions adapted to the changing circumstances of popular life in the large city—circumstances subject to the rhythms of life of mass society and to the influence of the mass communications media.

One could speculate on the authentic character of "protest" attaching to the manifold, heterogeneous manifestations of popular religion. What is certain is that no one can deny the fact of popular creativity, or the fact that magic, symbolism, and religious fervor are at work in the popular mentality of Latin Americans.

A debate is in progress over whether the various religious manifestations among the people—especially the more traditional ones, where magical and "superstitious" traits abound—are merely utilitarian and pragmatic. Weber had declared that the more a culture is inclined toward the peasant element and toward the traditional, the more withdrawn popular piety is from any ethical rationalization, and the more it becomes ritualistic and pragmatic. However, even in the case of a maximal expression of utilitarian magic, the problem of meaning—the ways of "salvation" as substantive demands of the masses—is present. In the context of the popular religions of Latin America—although, in their traditional or typically syncretic expressions, ritualism and the instrumentality of religious magic abound—rites are never deprived of a comprehensive representation (or theodicy) of the supernatural forces and their relationship with the life and death of individuals and social groups. This theodicy—not always rationally and systematically developed by the masses, but always systematically expressed and formalized by their religious leaders, be they shamans, mediums, priests, or ministers—poses the question of what things "mean."

> It verifies why and whither, it seeks to understand whence they have come and to what end they tend. The response that it gives to all of these questions can seem inappropriate and absurd. But what is important here is not so much the answer as the question

itself. When human beings begin to be concerned with their acts, they have taken a decisive new step. They have entered upon a new way, which will finally lead them very far from their unconscious, intuitive life. [Cassirer 1964:32]

On the other hand, we must recognize that not everything obeys symbolical strategies of survival, ritualisms of pragmatic magic, mechanisms of a religious legitimation of social domination, and unconditional submission to heteronomous powers. Not all things in the religion of the people are so readily the objects of manipulation as symbolical tools by religious and even political authorities.

In the subsoil of the popular edifice of religious symbolism—an edifice of many mirrors—awaiting an appropriate moment to intervene, lie the hopes, fervors, and religious energies of the masses. They take the form of messianism, propheticism and millennialism and its chiliastic raptures; magic and its mystery secrets, with their symbolical efficacy and power; the popular religious festival and multitudes of rites and pilgrimages, with their transgression of established normativity; and turbulent sessions of possession, trance, glossolalia, and collective exaltation. All of these phenomena are manifestations of religious counterforces which, displayed in all of their magnitude, represent a subversive threat to a symbolical status quo settled upon impeccable, unquestionable representations. We are dealing with enormous energies, shut up as if behind dams, ready to rush forth in torrents of positivity if well channeled. It is this fund of autonomy in the popular symbolism and mentality that, lying latent, manifests itself at times as implicit protest, at other times as symbolical resistance, at still other moments as organized struggle against the system. Like any other energy reserve when released, the religious energies of the people are subject to an ambiguous (and at times contradictory) destiny: well employed, they can be the source of inestimable human progress; overflowing spontaneously and explosively, they can unleash fanaticisms, with fatal, devastating consequences. From the contemporary updatings of the *Inkarri* myth to the messianism of the Shining Path, a gamut of manifestations is observable. These range, as we have seen, from the messianisms of the Brazilian hinterland at the close of the last century and the beginning of the twentieth, to the Cristero revolt against Calles's government in Mexico, to the Christian presence in political military organizations in Guatemala and El Salvador and Sandinista popular Christianity. All of these expressions of popular religion, in our recent past as in the present, stand in testament to the fact that mystical and revolutionary ardor does not always sleep. They stand as a warning to the (religious or civil) leaders of the people to see to it that this creative and liberative potential of popular faith be put into action as such, and not metamorphosed into its ever-present, latent, destructive antithesis.

## PART SIX

# ALTERNATIVE

*I am ashamed, dear Peter Egidius, to be sending to you, after nearly a year, this little book about the Republic of Utopia, which I doubt not you expected a month and a half ago, since you knew that, in writing it, I need carry out no effort of invention, nor mull anything touching its structure, but merely limit myself to narrating what, along with you, I have heard Raphael recount.*

Thomas More

# Chapter 10

# An Alternative to the Modernizing Paradigm

Contemporary society is moving over the uncertain terrain of change. At issue is no longer simply the modernization of industrial capitalism. We have remarked that we are living at the moment of a turning point in history, and that a new age is about to dawn. Out of our postindustrial society, a critique of urban industrial society is arising. In the countries of the Third World, subject as they are to such profound mutations—less perceptible, in a way, but manifestly different from what is occurring in developed areas—the complexity and rate of change are accelerating, aggravated by the growth of inequalities and misery and the lowering of the thresholds of incertitude.

## Evolutionary Crossroads

The time of this "evolutionary crossroads" is stimulating the emergence of new paradigms not only for understanding the change under way but, at the same time, for proposing a direction for its course. The surprising results of the "conquests" of science and technology since Einstein, far from making the terrain upon which humanity walks more reliable, not only answers some questions and sheds some light but leaves huge sets of questions and problems, and tremendous zones of darkness. Currently, for example, the astrophysicists' cosmos is in perpetual change, and from one day to the next any new theory can come into question.

In the human sciences, questions are being framed in new ways. Just as a new awareness concerning human rights forces a restatement of the paradigm of instrumental rationality (Magendzo 1991), the methodology proper to sociology comes into question, and no longer

*219*

in mere terms of a critique of empiricism or positivism (Adorno et al. 1973), but in terms of a questioning precisely of the scientific paradigm (cf. Kuhn 1971) that underlies sociology, which pares reality down in such a way as to get a regular, logical social world out of it, stripping the human "object" of its own consistency, real, relative, multifaceted, complex, heterogeneous, constantly in process and dynamism. Today we observe theoretical and conceptual approaches that, from points of departure on different horizons, go in quest of a new rationality, one which will be "capable of understanding and integrating in a new manner the varied facets that join together in the way of being human within the historical experience" (Salvat 1991).[1]

In another ambit, the patriarchal culture, with its concentration on subjection to power and reason, is denounced. We now acknowledge and defend the feminine dimensions of a common life based on the principle of bonding and solidarity rather than on hierarchization and domination (Eisler 1987). A new biological conception based on the principle of the *biology of love*, which rejects the idea that it is aggression, hatred, confrontation, and competition that have given rise to the human, is being founded (Maturana and Varela 1980) together with a new, holistic metaphysics and anthropology replacing those sprung from the Cartesian view of science and the world ever since the Renaissance (Berman 1981); and finally, the modern ecological conception, according to which it is no longer meaningful to speak of a domain of nature as if nature belonged *to* human beings—as if human beings were extraneous to it. What is more, a development that ignores the planetary era must be brought under control, in function of a conception of the human being as an integral part of nature itself (Morin 1990).

In a framework of crisis, in the face of various dangers to the Western developed world, Harvey Cox (1973) has called for a search after other alternatives. The threat of the extinction of the human species by the ecological disaster around us, the exhaustion of renewable resources, the poisoning of the earth's atmosphere and waters are aggravated by the homogenization of the system and its gradual worldwide intradependency. Survival depends upon the preservation of different options and the maintenance of diversity. For Cox, the market has failed humanity because it has failed so far—and thus has

---

1. As to the development of an alternative paradigm by certain Western social scientists, we might mention here, among others, the contributions of Fritjof Capra, *El Punto Crucial*; K. O. Apel, *Estudios Éticos*; Jürgen Habermas, *Escritos políticos* and *El discurso filosófico de la modernidad*; and A. Heller, *Crítica de la Ilustración*.

forfeited its opportunity—to furnish the values that the developed world needs in order to extricate itself from its morass. Citing the ecologists in their studies on the cultures that have managed to remain ecologically stable and prosperous, that author concludes that what has most given them cohesion has been religion, not the market. "Although they have markets, ecologically sound societies do not define the value of life in terms of producing, consuming, and accumulating." And he adds, proposing a solution geared to the conditions of developed North American society:

> We must begin our search for a new value system at that point in our own Western history before our religion was perverted by the worship of acquisitiveness, competition, and performance. This means retracing our steps and extricating what we can of the Christianity that informed Western culture before the rise of mercantilism, capitalism, or industrialization. [Cox 1973:86]

The persistence, renewal, and transformation of religious expressions in the various popular groups and classes on the Latin American continent are a patent phenomenon. Contrary to what Cox suggests for the developed world—where, according to his own words, "religion does not have the hold it had on people before the market began to dominate" (Cox 1973:87)—we must plumb the depths of this persistence of the popular religions on an underdeveloped continent where the market reigns, and reigns ever more powerfully and independently. What is certain is that, given the subordinate classes' structural heterogeneity and conditions of insertion into society as a whole, there is a partial marginalization of the market, or even an integration of the same into the informal market of Latin American capitalism. As we have asserted, the situation is tending to intensify. After all, our popular subjects weave daily and concrete practices in partial independence of mercantile logic: such practices structure a whole whose relations feature solidarity and cooperation, not competition or subjection to the logic of accumulation—which partly explains the persistence of the religious *pathos.*

But even apart from the field of structural practices and factors favoring the reproduction of religious meaning, there is a popular rationality that is different from the Western one, in which religious faith lives, lodges, and finds nourishment. Religion, as a determining factor in the shaping of the cultural patterns orientating the said practices, reproduces itself on the strength of a quality proper to and characteristic of the collective mentality of the people. We refer to what we call the *syncretism of the popular mentality*—extending the term, as we shall see, beyond its strictly religious signification. The collective thought of the people thus constitutes a concrete form of manifestation of a new, emerging paradigm. This paradigm is a subordinate, underground one, developing and feeding in the interstices of underdeveloped modernity. It is a nonsystematic paradigm, unavailable to rationalistic systematizations and standing at the antipodes of the paradigms of the Western science and philosophy that manifest themselves in the dominant culture.

This proper rationality of popular culture encloses, in germ, an alternative to the enlightened paradigm that founds and orientates contemporary modernization. Naturally, official culture legitimates its domination by labeling as "traditional" and "premodern" this popular form of representing oneself and acting in the world. But if by "modern" we understand what develops "in today's manner," then we are faced with a different type of modern thought, a different rational foundation unfolding in the various popular religions and subcultures, which is modern in the Latin American way of being modern. It is a paradigm that we may dub *hemidernal* (see chap. 5): it is neither entirely modern, nor premodern, nor, of course, postmodern. In Latin America, we have no need of retreating to precapitalistic, premodern society in order to bump up against those alternatives of common life that Cox is seeking.

It is not a question of a simple persistence of residues of magical rituals and ancestral myths in the collective consciousness—which indeed subsist with great vitality.[2] If it were only the survival of premodern beliefs and practices—tagged as "irrational" by the modernizing enlightened mentality—that we had to deal with, then, with the passage of time, the advance of progress, formal education, and the influence of a modern *ethos*, this "alternative paradigm" would be condemned to disappearance. As in Cox's proposal, we, too, should have to go back to a preindustrial, precapitalistic, traditional Latin America: the America of the colonial baroque, or even of the pre-Columbian cultures. Fortunately, however, there is no turning back the wheel of history. The popular culture itself offers us its *hemidernal* alternative precisely because a collective subject operates within it having sufficient creative ability to rearticulate signs, rites and symbols, religious beliefs and mythologies—sufficient creative ability to

---

2. Octavio Paz declares: "Any contact with the Mexican people, even fleeting, shows that, under the Western forms, the ancient beliefs and customs are still latent. These offscourings, still alive, are a testimonial to the vitality of the pre-Cortesian cultures" (Paz 1990:81).

revitalize them at the heart of a culture that continues along its course of modernization. Here is a mentality rooted in tradition, but not in tradition as the simple sedimentation of a past relived literally and in a way that indicts the present, a past incapable of projection toward the future. Here is a mentality rooted in tradition as a living tradition, that retrofeeds and updates the old, criticizing the present for its antihuman content and projecting itself toward a future through the mediation of the dreams and utopian energies of religious imagination.

## Coexistence of Science and Magic

In order to penetrate the collective mentality of the popular groups and classes in comprehensive fashion, we shall refer to the concepts of "collective thought" or "popular mentality" in a form analogous to the concept of "worldview" as used in the acceptation conferred upon it by the sociology of knowledge. We gather together here, in typological form, only the central tendencies of an articulation of the popular common sense, prescinding from the fact, which we grant, that in the framework of this popular mentality, different *models* of cultural and religious representations can be structured that approach or depart from this central type which we reconstruct heuristically for analytic purposes. The purpose of our reflection is to spark a novel interpretation of the Latin American popular religious phenomenon and of its sociocultural context; and so, inevitably, our typology will not escape the schematism of any new proposition that seeks to accentuate certain traits in order to distinguish them from others.

Having made this necessary methodological clarification, we now address the structural composition of the popular worldview, in which we shall distinguish at least three areas of interest. We shall explore the representation, in that worldview, of (1) the human being's relations with nature, (2) social relations, and (3) the logical articulations that characterize the popular mentality. Finally, we shall engage in a reflection on the hermeneutic problem posed by the logic of a popular mentality that differs from the Cartesian logic dominating the "common sense" of the enlightened Latin American intellectual community.

As for a reading of the human being's relations with nature, there is a set of aspects at hand on the basis of which it is possible to assert that, in the popular groups and classes, traits of a magical, mythic thought subsist. Folklore, especially peasant folklore, is filled with legends, refrains, fables, stories, and myths. But even in the culture prevailing among the popular groups of the great metropolises, we discern the enduring presence of magical and mythic traits, especially with regard not so much to a comprehensive worldview of natural phenomena—here, we observe the penetration of a more scientific rationality—as with regard to coping with certain events that disrupt daily life, events having their origin in the uncontrollable emergence of the natural: biological, physical, or geographical phenomena (see chap. 5).

The data and facts indicated in chapters 5 and 9 are merely a sampling, offered for the purpose of affording the reader an opportunity to appreciate that, within the semantic and semiological codes structuring the popular common sense, we find, not a clear, modern-enlightenment rationality, but a more magico-mythic reading of nature in combination with a more scientific reading. Just as recourse is had to God or to the traditional healer for the healing of a disease, so recourse is had to the physician and the hospital as well. But it is obvious that there is no contradiction here, given that, as Lévi-Strauss has shown apropos of the primitive mentality, magic is not opposed to science (Lévi-Strauss 1962). Indeed, the two approaches can be complementary and mutually consistent, as we observe in various manifestations of the popular cultures and subcultures.

In an investigation into popular religious beliefs carried out in Chimbote (a recently industrialized city on the coast of Peru), an inquiry was made of members of the popular cultures concerning the supposed cause of earthquakes. Earthquakes, for the populations living along the Pacific coast of America, constitute a traumatic, although frequent, experience. Thirty-seven percent alluded to God, or mysterious forces, as their cause, while 29% postulated a causality more in keeping with scientific explanations. Six percent cited a combination of causes, and 15% blamed the French nuclear experiments in the Pacific. As for the cause of diseases, the mythic mentality is represented by only 11% of the persons surveyed (Irarrázaval 1978).

The popular mentality has a much stronger proclivity toward miracles and the marvelous, in its need for a meaning that will take into account the less manageable aspects of natural and social surroundings. But like any other culture, the popular has a need for tools to *cope* with its surroundings. In its relation with nature—whether more directly, as in the case of the peasantry, or more through the mediation of technological and mass civilization, as in the case of the urban popular classes—the popular mentality surely produces a rationalization of the ideas representing this relation; but this process does not succeed in altogether suppressing certain significations of a religious type, although the tendency indicates that a type of causal explanation of a magical order is indeed disappearing, now being replaced by natural explanations more influenced by a scientific and technological culture. But in many of the symbolical "arrangements" within the semantic models of popular-world representation, this type of more "scientific" idea appears rather to correspond to rational complements of magic. Accordingly, such ideas do not suppress or threaten the persistence and reproduction of magic as a category of interpretation when it comes to natural phenomena.

The explanation that we have offered leads us to reconsider our disparagement of the "superstitions" and "magic" that we see at work in various popular manifestations. Still, we must get beyond the level of collective representation and its supposed rationality or "irrationality." After all, religion is not only theodicy, nor only a conceptual or doctrinal representation of the world; basically, in the popular world, religion is a practice, a ritual, a communication, a plastic and bodily expression bearing upon the transcendent, upon the sacred beings and powers and their wills. It is worth recalling here the general collective, *community* character attaching to practically all expressions of the various popular religions in Latin America. This community character is expressed in a variety of ways, depending on whether we find it in the base communities of a Catholicism of renewal, in a multitude of pilgrimages, in festivities of popular religion, or in the Pentecostal congregations and Afro-American cults. Nevertheless, even those practices that seem more individual—such as promises and votive offerings, or the rituals of healing sought by distressed individuals—contain a very characteristic collective meaning. Wherever popular religion is orientated toward magical rites of healing, it becomes a means to alleviate a distressing experience of the everyday (see chap. 8) and, in that sense, is a means of symbolical practice whose utility for the individual must be felt as immediate. Nevertheless, we are far from the classic schema of pragmatic magic, especially from that of the "witchcraft" type, which indeed manifests itself as an individual act: an evil deed solicited individually from the sorcerer, who in secret prepares a "fetish" for the client. On the contrary, the ritual acts that appear as "superstitious" and "magical" in the most common expressions of popular religion are actually "white magic"—magic "for" someone or something, rather than a black magic "against" someone or something, which, theoretically, at least, is condemned even by the *curanderos*, the *pai de santos*, and the shamans. The communitarian nature of the rituals of "religious magic" that we have analyzed is more available to our grasp when we interpret them as a collective response on the part of social classes and groups sharing a collective situation of incertitude and crisis—a situation provoked by social conditioners or by natural causes, but strongly affected by the social. A chance accident is a more serious catastrophe for a "poor one" than for a "powerful" or "wealthy" person; and although objectively it is an unexpected event for both, the material and social resources at the disposition of the wealthy person for overcoming the adversity are immensely greater. In this sense, the solicitation of "help," "healing," or a "favor" or "miracle" by a subject already steeped in (material, moral, or spiritual) misery concerns not only this subject as an individual, and his or her ills or misfortunes, but the collectivity as well, with its tensions and roadblocks. "The healing of each is transformed into the redemption of all" (Balandier 1982:348).

Belief in a higher god, present with regularity in nearly every pure or syncretic manifestation, contributes to the removal of the stereotypical component of superstitious magic in many of the ritual practices of the people. While popular syncretic Christianity's monotheism does not always appear in very sharp outline, given the breadth of signification accorded other figures of the pantheon (the Blessed Virgin, saints, and so on), the figure of God the Father and Creator remains central. The need for ready access to iconic objects and symbols or tangible rituals tied to concrete life situations or group situations, a need so characteristic of popular religion, does not foment magical manipulation, despite Weber (1969:412ff.). Belief in a provident God who "works miracles" (generally through the intercession of the Blessed Virgin, the saints, and/or the departed souls or certain spirits) is premised on an interiorization of the notion that the divinity is not a simple symbolical projection in function of one's immediate needs—a divinity that can be "manipulated coercively by magic"—but an omnipotent otherness with a wholly independent will, who is an object of supplication.

The fact that oftentimes those practical rules prevail in the framework of celebrations or liturgical expressions accompanied by a profound and manifest festive sense further contributes to the safeguarding of these practices from an esoteric, occultist, and alienating meaning. Bastide will say here, vis-à-vis the Afro-American cults, in which a heftier component of the superstitious and magical can be presumed to be present: "Thus, Afro-American religion presents itself to be studied by the ethnologist more as a religion of joy than as a religion of fear" (Bastide 1982:76).

An in-depth study of the religious worldview of the "singers to the divine and the human"—a type of popular intellectual among the Chilean peasantry at the beginning of the twentieth century—shows that the verse produced by the spontaneity of the popular poet, along with its opposition to the city on the basis of the "corruption and sin" of the latter, develops a beautiful image of God, the Blessed Virgin, Jesus, and the saints, as over against an official theology (Salinas 1991). A detailed analysis shows that Weber's comprehensive categories (the traditional-rational continuum) fall short here of grasping a far richer and more complex phenomenon.

In the face of the imposition of a theology and ascetical religious rationality which prioritize the patriarchal figure of God the Father, renouncing the affective virtues, love, and woman and demonizing secular concerns, arises a religious sensitivity and wisdom beautifully versified in quatrains and strophes. From the Passion of Christ—the dominion of Satan—in an ascending movement, it insists on the triumph of love over death, Mary's love and "tenderness," Christmas as the carnival of the poor, and the communion of the saints on the road to the fiesta of heaven, that bucolic, carnival utopia of popular agrarian redemption. The Church and its official, clerical, educated, city culture contrasts with popular Christianity and its peasant, oral, and rural folklore.

Popular religion and official religion rise up in confrontation. As Weber has suggested, in the historical development of religion, the evolution from a popular, magical religion to an official, priestly religion occurs primarily on the basis of a "rationalization" of the relationship of the human being with the divine (see pp. 6-7 above; Weber 1964:344-45).

It is worth noting, apropos of this production of popular religion, that it enables us to view this contraposition between official religion and popular religion in another light. Popular religion is seen as having a more inner-worldly direction, without, for all that, sacrificing a profound spiritual content. The supplication, sacrifice, and adoration of religion are a way of arriving at God, but it must be granted that festival, song, the burlesque laugh, and carnival are another way of approaching the Creator. So-called "magical" rituals are no longer manipulative coercion of the gods and "demons," but come to be, on the contrary, rites of profoundly emotive, expressive, plastic, and even sensual communication with the more loving face of God, by means of the tenderness of Mary, the one who protects the lowly. Finally, the urbanizing, modernizing "rationality" of official religion, which represses the body and wholesome pleasure and dominates the human being and nature, alienates persons from that communion of participation between men and women, between human beings and the goods of nature, and between the "heaven and earth" that finds its expression in popular faith. For these poets of the people, the face of God— a face familiar to the vast majority of urban poor—is merciful and good. This is the God who accompanies the natural cycles of life, the God who is the opposite of the idol that has unleashed the modern Prometheus of the rationality of a scientific technology.

### Religion and Representation of Society

It is a fact, investigated to the point of ennui, that in the metropolitan countries the processes of capitalistic industrialization and urbanization lead to the secularization of representations of society. Especially in terms of modernity, the very foundations of society are now explained and legitimated in altogether secular terms. The bourgeois ideology is secularizing: it posits the human being and reason at the center of its enterprise, and relegates God and religion to an altogether private, secondary plane. Neither does the ideology of the proletariat, socialism, have recourse to religious legitimations—although there exist, in this ideology's historical manifestations, traits assimilable to religious behavior, leading many sociologists to speak of an actual functional substitute for religion. For socialism, religion has been an ideology of domination par excellence, an ideology to be eliminated through the destruction of the social order that requires it for its reproduction. The emancipation of the workers is said to *require* an awareness of alienation and, accordingly, to require the suppression of all mystification, of the entire veil of religious ideology, by turning to human beings as the foundation of themselves and society.

As for the intervention of religion as a factor in the legitimation of dominant social relations, the idea of a divine providence continues to be widespread, reinforcing a secular fatalism among popular elements endowed with a lesser critical awareness. We find this not only among the peasantry but among urban subproletarian and marginalized sectors as well. In the Santiago poll to which we have referred, some 60% of those interviewed agree with the statement

"God has willed that there always be rich and poor"; only 27% disagree. Similarly, 53% are in complete agreement with the statement "Christ taught that we must not rebel against authority." Still, paradoxically, we observe that 83% believe that Jesus was a prophet who fought for the poor and was put to death for doing so. Of course, frequently the person being interviewed will not have formed an explicit opinion before the interview, and will simply give the first answer that comes to mind. But this kind of response, from the standpoint of the process of enunciation, is very meaningful, because it reproduces, unconsciously and unintentionally, what the person being interviewed has heard "people say" in the symbolical reference group—that is, what the individual has already internalized as part of the everyday, proper cognition of the reference group. These same interviewees, in the context of the Pinochet regime in Chile, which had fostered only contempt for those who defended the human rights repeatedly violated by that regime, responded in a proportion of 84% that the struggle for human rights is a worthy, noble task.

Both in the investigation carried out in Lima which we have mentioned (Kudo 1980) and in the investigations we ourselves made in Santiago de Chile, the aspiration for social and racial equality seems to be a value very proper to the popular culture. In Lima, more than 90% of those interviewed believe in the equality of human beings "before God." In Santiago, 95% of those interviewed asserted that the *mapuches* are the equals of the rest of Chileans. The assertion that God "wills the existence of rich and poor," or that "Christ has taught us not to rebel," does not always seem to function as the index of a mythic mentality sacralizing social relations of domination and social injustices.

In general terms, the data seem to coincide in the fact that never do more than one-fourth of those interviewed offer an explanation of social inequality based on postulates of a mythic and fatalistic kind directly or indirectly legitimated by way of religion. The data do present a hierarchized view of human beings that tends to consecrate the domination of some over others, possibly as the residue of a precapitalistic mentality on the lips of the rural immigrant recently proletarianized or subproletarianized in the urban periphery. One of the conclusions of the study made in Chimbote is very suggestive in this respect: "As for the mythic traits in the awareness of the popular classes, . . . these have considerable weight where the forces of nature are concerned, but they have little impact on an understanding of the historical situation" (Irarrázaval 1978:108).

For a large majority of the membership of the urban subordinate classes, their view of society manifests the influence of a social logic of a modern type, although these persons may be divided into three groups:

1. Those who read social relations in terms of the basic categories of the dominant ideology;
2. Those who see the capitalistic social relations that prevail, but only in their consequences, which they criticize without perceiving the structural causes;
3. Those who clearly perceive the relations of capitalistic domination and exploitation to which they are subjected, and who criticize these relations in a manner consistent with their perception of the same.

In these various views of the social, religion appears to fulfill different functions, offering different significations. In the first two representations of society, religion seems to have no active role, but only to act in parallel fashion with its subjects' readings of the social, assuming a function of symbolical adaptation to the situation of domination in which those sectors live. In the last case, and herein lies a novelty to which little attention has been called, a *class consciousness* and a *liberative popular religion* combine for mutual reinforcement.

Unlike the classic divorce between religion and class consciousness in the proletariat of the countries of central capitalism, in Latin America the progressive social and political awareness of a great proportion of the working masses does not seem to bring them into conflictive confrontation with their religious representations.

In various manifestations of popular religion, it is possible to observe what Domitila's familiar testimony posits for us: class awareness and social struggle do not eliminate the religious sense, but are founded on and nourished by it.

So, since my fight with Jehovah's Witnesses, I haven't joined any other religious group, even though I haven't lost faith in God. And that might be something that I really don't share with what I've read in the books on Marxism, where the existence of God is always denied. At least this is what it looked like to me, isn't that right? But to me it seems that denying the existence of God would be denying our own existence. [Viezzer 1977:68-69]

In certain circumstances, the popular mentality can even come to accept anticlerical attitudes, to the extent that it sees church apparatus as aloof from, and an enemy of, the longings and interests of the people.[3] In the north of Chile, in the genesis of the proletariat of the saltpeter industry, the anticlerical socialistic ideology has merged with the apogee of devotion to Our Lady of La Tirana. Dance and song to the Virgin, an expression of life's longings and popular song, are complemented by the workers' organizing and their struggle with exploitation by mine owners (Parker 1987). Today the same phenomenon continues to be observed among the Bolivian, Peruvian, and Chilean miners of Aymara or Quechua origin, even among many militant workers, all the way up to members of Marxist parties in various regions of Latin America who retain their religious beliefs. This may explain the persistence of certain expressions of popular religion in today's revolutionary Cuba. There the devotion to Saint Lazarus and Our Lady of Charity of Cobre is practiced by great numbers of persons (Pereira 1986). Everything would seem to indicate that popular religious practice grows in direct proportion to the waning of official religious practice. In Sandinista Nicaragua, the first leftist revolution in which Christians have actively participated, there existed in certain circles an enlightened Christianity of liberation that fostered and complemented the revolutionary commitment. But there was also an *aggiornamento* of traditional practices and rites—such as the massive devotions to Saint Dominic and to Mary Most Pure—not only among the groups that were against the Sandinistas but also among the popular masses that supported the government (Richard and Irarrázaval 1981).

## On Syncretic Thought

Frequently and repeatedly, we hear of "religious syncretism." The concept is used to refer to the complex phenomenon by which two religious systems enter into contact without the production of either an absolute synthesis or a mere juxtaposition of elements. Etymologically the word means "to act like a Cretan," and was used in the

---

3. Emile Pin called attention to the vacuums left by traditional church structure. In the popular mentality, other symbols and values can occupy those vacuums without persons' losing their faith. "The communists were able to replace, without encountering telling resistance, the evil 'imperialistic clergy' with a new clergy, who were 'good, and friends of the people'" (Pin 1963:45).

Hellenistic world to denote the inclusion of foreign gods in one's own pantheon. The acceptation that we follow here is that of Marzal, who uses it to refer to a religious system formed on the basis of the dialectical interaction of two systems in contact (Marzal 1986). The result of this dialectic will be neither the persistence nor the total disappearance of either original system but, rather, either their synthesis or a reinterpretation of one of the two. Marzal offers us the example of three types of reinterpretation: (1) the Christian rite is accepted and is given an indigenous meaning; (2) the indigenous rite is preserved and is given a Christian meaning; and (3) the Christian rite is accepted, but new meanings are added to its original meaning.

However, I propose to broaden the concept "syncretic" by imposing on it a kind of syncretism in my own turn—that is, by reinterpreting it—with a view to a more comprehensive understanding of what we have been observing and discussing apropos of the presence of the religious element in the Latin American popular mentality. I think that certain symbolical processes, certain beliefs and rites, certain representations and meaning structures—some of which we have mentioned—are open, in their complexity, to an understanding as manifestations of a thought structure that obeys neither the canons of traditional mythic thought nor those of modern, technological, scientific thought. I therefore propose to speak of a "syncretic thought" underlying not merely representations and rites but the whole complex of popular beliefs, thought, and opinions on the world, society, politics, culture, the family, life, and the cosmos.

The syncretism analyzed by Marzal is exclusively religious, and is thereby susceptible of a more precise analysis. When we speak here of "syncretic thinking," we refer not only to objectifications manifest in a content but also, on a deeper level, to the complex process operating within the popular collective mentality by which the syncretism in question is established. Although this kind of thought could be investigated in a manner analogous to that in which myths or scientific postulates and theories are studied (Godelier 1977), its study is more complex. We are dealing with a process of symbolical work of an "informal" nature, in terms of which the popular genius constructs or reconstructs systems or representations through the use of various residues, discarded material, and new contributions, all seemingly disparate, in such wise that, out of a composition of old and new works, new syntheses are produced. This symbolical production, of a *bricolage* or "tinkering" type, is rather far removed from the rational, formal, planned, systematic, and sometimes standardized production of representations and concepts which employ content from ideas previously criticized and refined and characterize intellectual and "cultured" thought.

The surprising thing here—and this is the basis of our proposal with regard to syncretic thought—is the frequency of the recurrence of paradoxes in popular discourse, representations bearing on religion and other aspects of popular discourse that are paradoxical in the intellectual's systematic, noncontradictory eyes. That is, characteristic of the expressions of the various popular religions of Latin America is the fact that they are the fruit of the confluence of two different planes on which the collective awareness represents the world and life: the properly religious plane, which is subject to the specificity of the religious field; and the plane of popular thought, which is subject to the popular forms of representation and linguistic expression. Our main interest, for now, is in this latter aspect.

Popular thought, on the foundation of which popular religion "shakes down" and takes shape in a nontransparent articulation, from the viewpoint of the content of its representations is plural, heterogenous, and syncretic, if we regard its relations and its processes of symbolical elaboration. The coexistence of magical and modern scientific rationalities is not only an expression of the religious field; it is the reflex of complex processes of symbolical interaction and sociologic influences with which the collective mentality of the popular masses is shot through and which in a certain measure constitute it in its various models expressive of subsystems of representational content.

No less decisive for the crystalization of cultural matrices such as the one that we call the "popular mentality," here characterized, for the case of the Latin American subordinate groups and classes, as "syncretic thought," is the passage of historical time. Indeed, in the history of the thought of the popular groups, especially of the vast majority of "mestizos," the fusion of traits of autochthonous native thought with Western thought must be understood apart from a strict conception of the races. It must be understood as the confluence, on the level of the deep structures that shape worldviews, of different cultures, each with its peculiar style of thinking. Therefore, if it is possible to analyze the articulating nucleus of indigenous thought, characterized by Kush as "seminal thought" (Kush 1976), in contradistinction to the rational and causalist thought of the West, then it is feasible to postulate, as does Kush, the persistence of certain basic traits of that style of non-Western thought in popular thought. Thus, the style of mentality characterizing the "mestizos," or persons of mixed ancestry[4]—not only those called *cabecitas negras* in Argentina, *cholos* in Peru and Bolivia, *ladinos* in Guatemala, and *rotos* in Chile but, also those persons who, while not racially mestizos, are that by cultural influence—would indeed in its profound structures, be a "syncretic thought."

## A Problem of Interpretation

In terms of what we have set forth, it is clear that it is no longer a question of attributing to the people any "inferior" mental conditions, no longer a matter of looking down on them from an ethnocentric, prejudiced, pedestal. It also seems arbitrary to link popular religion in its manifold manifestations to psychic or mental structures that would be "deviant" from what official culture defines as psychological "normality." At bottom, as Lanternari asserts, what is attributed as specific to popular religion is actually the property of all religious behavior (Lanternari 1982:138).

It is perfectly reasonable to think that, with the advance of civilization, religious thought, in general, has been the object of some degree of rationalization on the part of even the most faithfully practicing and most committed members of the respective churches. It is claimed that this process alienates religion from the materiality of the world—that it spiritualizes religion, but at the price of alienating it from the human body, the corporeal, and the sensible, from the production, reproduction, and exchange of that materiality. By contrast, the religion of the dispossessed masses maintains tangible, bodily semiological coordinates. In the relation between temporal well-being and salvation, for example, it is surely evident that, for the popular mentality, human well-being is conceived integrally. In the popular holistic view, the health of the body is intimately bound up with the health of the soul (salvation). Indeed, in popular thought, the view of the human being is itself integral. Such a conception is foreign to the Greco-Roman philosophy underlying the dualism of the

---

4. We reject the racist connotation of the concept of "mestizo," whose customary reference is too closely bound up with a biologistic conception ("mix of bloods"). On the contrary, we assert the category of "mestizo" in its relation, on the level of culture, with the fusion of cultural elements and traits of two different ethnic currents. Unlike our concept of "syncretism," which refers to the level of mentality and collective thought, the corresponding concept of "mestizo" extends more broadly, to the various levels of culture.

classic Christian anthropology of the West, which separates body from soul with a heavy hand, assigning to the latter dimension priority over the former. The spiritualistic abstraction of dominant Western Christianity, in our case, is alien to the greater number of historical experiences of those religions for which "religious salvation has been historically joined to concepts of physical well-being" (Turner 1988:115). The Semitic conception, expressed in the anthropology of the Old Testament (Dussel 1969), is closer to our popular conception of the well-being of the body than is the Christian view of Western scholasticism.

This same unitary mentality, coming down through the centuries in an unbroken line, characterizes religion and magic. Indeed, the distinction between magic and religion made its appearance in high European culture only in a particular era, around the seventeenth century, along with the distinction between science and magic (Ginzburg 1977). We may likewise assert, in light of the scientific knowledge of physics, chemistry, biology, psychology, and parapsychology, that the extraordinary phenomena characterizing "black magic" and "witchcraft" have another, extramagical explanation in the vast majority of cases, and that the interpretations more frequently assigned these practices by theology and inquisitorial demonology constitute mere "errors of interpretation" (Kloppenburg 1977). That is, they owe their origin to frameworks of a theoretical interpretation built by the theologian—including that of the "witch" herself—that would reconstruct reality under the potent influence of certain cultural categories of their era. Just as the Inquisition was so persistent in its theories of the "pact with the devil," so also the very persons accused of sorcery, falling into a trance state, ended by believing themselves so perverse as indeed to have entered into a plot with Satan, flown through the sky at night, and celebrated frightful banquets with incubi and succubi.

But none of this offers an adequate explanation of the fact of a cultural difference, not necessarily tied to psychic attributes but certainly originating in structures of reasoning and thought that are different from those of the enlightened, intellectual, "educated and scientific" dominant culture. Popular culture, which is so much more symbolical, dramatic, and sapiential than it is intellectual, with all of its "popular wisdom," represents a "different logic." It is by no means an antilogic or a primitive state of the faculty of reasoning (and in this sense it is not prelogic, to borrow the expression used by Lévy-Bruhl 1977), but represents the use of reason under another system, one at once much more empirical and symbolical, and much more sapiential and dialectical, than Cartesian and positivistic.

Latin American philosophy, especially the Argentinian school, in recent years, has embarked upon a systematic reflection on Latin American being and culture. Rodolfo Kush, one of the most outstanding of these Americanists, proposes a reflection on the "geoculture" of the American person as having its origin in the ontological category *estar*—specific, immediate being—rather than in the classic Western metaphysical category *ser*, the generalized being underlying all else (Kush 1976). His contribution is very important for an understanding of the Western indigenous thought of our autochthonous populations, although it suffers from a reflection on its interaction with Latin American modernity. Carlos Cullen has proposed a definition of our Latin American culture in terms of its "baroque" character (Cullen 1981). J. C. Scannone speaks of the "sapiential logos" in Latin American popular culture and religion (Scannone 1978a, 1978b). Enrique Dussel, in another context, speaks of a "material *poiesis*" and a "symbolical *poiesis*" in culture, and describes what he calls the "revolutionary popular culture" in Latin America (Dussel 1984). These are all hermeneutical efforts to think out a *hemidernal*, non-Western American worldview that is shot through semantically with Western cultural categories and influences, that harvests pre-Columbian ancestral traditions, and that insists on being thought out in categories of its own still in gestation, still the object of search (and therefore indebted to categorical structures that come from Western tradition). That worldview, in its "vital synthesis," in its religious syncretism and cultural hybridization, has never been entirely Western and yet from the moment of the *Conquista* has ceased to be entirely indigenous.

All of these specifically philosophical and theological efforts actually constitute a great challenge for the sociological conceptualization that means to be "scientific" and not philosophical or sapiential. But while giving systematicness and method their due, we must acknowledge that sociology is more than a "science" in the positivistic sense of the natural sciences: it is a "human science" as well and, as such, must include concepts that broaden its field to include areas not altogether open to "explanation" in a functional or structuralist sense. Sociology's field is comprehensively hermeneutical as well. Popular religion, such as it presents itself nowadays among the subordinate classes of our large Latin American cities, represents a special field of observation, inasmuch as, experimentation being impossible in the social sciences, such a phenomenon at least has the virtue of showing the emergence of popular "mentality types" subjected to exogenous influences, changes, and strong pressures flowing from the fact of being situated between the traditional culture and the modern culture of city, science, and market.

Evans-Pritchard, in a well-known work on primitive religions (Evans-Pritchard 1971), poses the basic problem of the major confusions that arise in any attempt to understand a culture different from that of the observer.

A first error is to base one's stand on evolutionist notions, when there is actually no basis for maintaining these notions. We have seen how the persistence and internal transformations of religious beliefs and practices among the urban popular classes in Latin America give the lie to the developmentalistic theses that—whether in their modernizing/secularizing or Marxist/scientistic variants—postulated the inevitable decline of religion in the urbanized popular mentality. But the second error cited by Evans-Pritchard is the one that seems to us to be more relevant here. We refer to the attempt by the classic anthropologists (Taylor, Frazer, Müller, Marett, Durkheim, Crawley, Averbury, Lévy-Bruhl) to interpret the religion of primitive persons without field work, which meant a speculation based not on the actual primitive mentality in its real context, but on attributions emerging solely from introspection. Nowadays this phase of social science is a thing of the past, but not the subsequent defect originating therein: the problem of *translation*.

When the social scientist is faced with a set of beliefs and practices that, prima facie, appear irrational, what procedure ought to be followed? Are these beliefs and practices actually irrational, or are they merely alternative forms of rationality? These are the questions Lukes asks as he analyzes the theories of Leach, Beattie, Taylor, Frazer, Evans-Pritchard, and Winch on the "rationality" of a primitive magical thought (Lukes 1985). The central idea is that the concepts of a given culture can be seriously interpreted only in the context of those groups' way of life. Not that all rationality is necessarily contextual. There is also a rationality of universal validity. Lukes calls contextual rationality "criteria *1* rational," and the universally valid rationality "criteria *2* rational." Any given belief ought to be evaluated on both criteria of rationality, the contextual and the universal. In all cases, the criteria of contextual rationality are enlightening, and we have seen this in the foregoing chapter, in our interpretation of magical religious components in the light of the conditions and lifestyles of the popular groups. But this does not render the criteria of universal rationality superfluous. Indeed, it is the question of the rationality prevailing in popular culture, in the syncretic thought of the popular mentality and consequently in its religious expressions, that has led us to develop the problem *in extenso* in this chapter.

What to Western thought is supernatural is utterly natural for primitive thought and for popular thought. If there is really a belief in a magical causality for death, then the nonnatural, in the semantic context of the thought style in question, will be a death that would not be provoked by witchcraft. Neither, obviously, are our concepts theirs, nor, even if their signifiers were to be the same as ours, would they have the same significates as ours. In linguistic expression as well, certain obstacles blur a diaphanous, direct translation.

Standing opposite "cultured" thought, whose vehicle is a conceptual, abstract language that creates its denotations through a vast lexical network and an inflated rhetoric characteristic of any "lettered" culture—a rhetoric rigorous in its semiotic "honing" of reality to the measure of normativeness and repression—popular syncretic thought is expressed by images and symbols, by means of an oral expression utilizing a laconic rhetoric of few words but great expressivity and charged with its own popular-lexicon connotations (massive, sensual, coarse, witty, dramatic, playful), along with a network of gestures constituting its significative support as authentically as do its words.

One may not ask of popular beliefs and rites that which an erudite system of official theology accomplishes through abstraction from and rationalization of sensible, daily experience and systematically registered and codified collective experiences. Here is a problem not only of different kinds of mentality but, besides, of distinct types of processing in the act of reasoning, a processing heavily influenced by a differential approach to the means of symbolical production. Official, educated religious production generally possesses accumulated symbolical capital and superior material and formative resources that are institutionalized and that have a broader communicational extension. The popular religious symbolical system reproduces its beliefs and rituals through an intensive use of the natural techniques of human communications (not the artificial mechanical, electronic, modern techniques), especially means of oral and aural communication, means of direct interaction—semiologies whose expressivity of body, gesture, and vision is far more within reach of any devotee, however lowly and illiterate he or she may be. The "technology" of the production of the priestly class, the initiate group, is characterized by the constant establishment of proceedings and habits accessible only to a reduced and select number of initiates. Thereby, religious "knowledge" officially consecrated as such, as guarantee of access to sacred power, is maintained and reproduced in jealous alienation from the "lay" masses, who, when all is said and done, are seen as simple "consumers" of the goods of salvation. Here, seen from the viewpoint of the system of symbolical production maintained by official religion, Weber's theory, as redeveloped by Bourdieu (1971), is correct. That same theory is in error, however, when it generalizes its conception of the religious field as a simple "market" of salvation goods. It fails to understand that the "consumers" of those goods are actors as well—in their fashion—and that, as collective actors, they too are "producers" of their own goods of symbolical consumption. But their production is specifically of "popular" goods (goods of use). That is, they produce goods that are conceived by the collective mentality as goods that identify the collective "us," and thereby these goods semantically delimit a boundary beyond which official "religious goods" (goods of exchange), while indeed acknowledged as such, are marked by the seal of official production, that is, by the ecclesial sacerdotal group or by the religious expressions of the other social classes that form no part of the semantic universe of the popular "us." We are dealing with a religious discourse and practice of the people standing in contradistinction to cultivated "knowledge." We are dealing with a core component of the *other*, *distinct* popular wisdom, which cannot always be expressed in the canons of rationalistic, Western logic.

What makes interpretation more problematic, in our situation as Latin American scholars and/or impassioned admirers of this popular reality, is the fact that, unlike the primitive cultures, the popular cultures are among us. We interact on a daily basis with subjects who live, think, and believe in a different way from ourselves, although we share the same public spaces: streets, stairways, buses, offices, schools, markets, sidewalks, industries, squares, and so on. Here the otherness of the popular culture is blurred by a thousand intersections between our culture and theirs. It is quite a difficult thing to objectify and analyze "from the outside" something that, to a certain extent, we, too, carry within.

### A Hemidernal Popular Style: The "Different Logic"

In her profound study on the mentality of the Bolivian miners of Oruro, June Nash comes to the conclusion that the technique of the syncretization of Western and indigenous elements in the style of the Spaniards seems strange to the Bolivians' way of thinking. "It refers to a way of thinking that accepts only one, singular, hierarchized, and defined system of ideas. Native thought is able to maintain coexisting, seemingly contradictory worldviews" (Nash 1979:122). Identifications between concepts and figures in Western thought and syncretic thought are only superficial, and when one has the opportunity to come to know the popular mentality more in depth, one realizes that these nominally identical concepts and figures do not actually coincide.

In religion, as a connotative language, as the symbolic medium par excellence, we observe more clearly how this "syncretic thought" operates. But it operates at all other levels of life as well, and certainly has an influence on the various popular conceptions of the world. At work are linguistico-semantic and semiological structures, and their processes of elaboration and reproduction, that are immune from direct and mechanical conditioning by the material conditions of life and that, ultimately, are bound up with productive practices and class positions only via the field of collective practices. The creation of new meanings, as we know, occurs within frameworks imposed on them by linguistic, semantic, and comprehensive cultural codes already in force in a given group at a given historical time. Thus, every form of personal thought is socially conditioned by cultural language and codes, and every form of collective thought will be conditioned by the determinate prevailing social languages and great cultural codes. Hence the feasibility of utilizing a concept very important in the history of art and speaking of various "styles" (Hauser 1969) of thought, which obey certain macrosocial conditionings straddling the frontiers of each microsocial situation. Not that there is a universal popular thought for the entire Latin American continent. But there are analogous thought processes, corresponding to structural and historical situations that are analogous as well, which do engender a determinate style, a particular type of mentality.

This explains how it comes about that, within certain "models" of representation of society and religious life, there coexist views, at times even magical views, endowed with a critical class consciousness. It can happen that more ethical and liberative religion will replace the magic; but it can also come to coexist with it. One visits the doctor and the healer for the healing of infirmities, indistinctly and simultaneously. There is no irrationality and inconsistency here, as a cold, analytical, enlightened mentality might observe. The articulation of elements at work is not entirely modern; but neither is it antimodern. The combination is *syncretic* and, in the Latin American context, *hemidernal*. We think it possible to approach this syncretic thought, at least in part, through a fairly simple analytical schema, in which the religious representation of the world in question will give us our interpretative key.

A universe of representations, the product of the complex process of symbolical production, is objectified in heterogeneous codifications generally projected for the following purposes:

1. For the purpose of confronting the human being's natural world. Included here are all of the processes of the physical and biological life of nature, as well as the representations of the human being's relations with that life, along with these human beings' mediations, through which they strive to manage and transform it to their own benefit (tools and technological science).

2. For the purpose of confronting and symbolically reconstructing the social world, which is partially constituted in its own content by the ensemble of representations that significatively weave social relations. Included here are representations concerning society, social groups and classes, and basic fundamental (economic, political, cultural, etc.) social relations.

3. Finally, for the purpose of confronting the questions that have always been the thorn in the side of human existence: those bearing on the meaning of life, on personal and collective destiny, on the origin and destiny of the universe and history, and, last, on the origin and meaning of evil, pain, death, and the mysterious and marvelous.

These processes of symbolical production, all relating to different spheres of reality, operate within the various mentalities. But when it comes to what is typical of the popular mentality, given the tendency of that mentality to weave a vital synthesis[5] rather than to engage in the analytical dissection proper to Western science, these processes are not present in an exclusive manner, and intersections frequently occur, in such wise that the end results tend to appear as

---

5. The Final Document of the Third General Conference of the Latin American Episcopate, held at Puebla, declares, referring to popular piety: "The Catholic wisdom of the common people is capable of fashioning a vital synthesis. It creatively combines the divine and the human" (Puebla Final Document, no. 448).

"disparate" to the eyes of an enlightened, more analytical and critical mentality. For example, let us take disease. In certain popular groups, there coexist an interpretation in terms of religious magic, obeying a causalistic explanation but of a metaphysical order, and a scientific explanation, which is causalistic but naturalistic. In this case are we not dealing with a peculiar kind of semantic selection and combination of concepts in terms of which popular common sense tends to "discriminate" in a completely different way the same reality that "scientists" tend to discriminate under their exclusively analytical, rationalistic codifications?

Proletarians who maintain a critical view of society and even become active in Marxist parties preserve their traditional beliefs and are devotees of the Virgin and the saints. Homemakers explain their children's illnesses by "evils" that need to be healed by blessing, but are quite aware that, at the proper moment, they must apply to the doctor and to the saint for the healing of their infirmities. There does not seem to be, in the popular mentality, the crisp distinction between the sacred and the profane of which Durkheim tells (Durkheim 1979:53ff.). Between the sacred and the profane is compenetration, and the maximal manifestation of the sacred may be in filling to overflowing and in "fulfilling" the profane, which is pregnant with sacred meanings in its own turn. There is no confusion, however, but only an overlapping. And the overlapping or intermingling occurs on the strength of logical associations that are not only of a rational kind but also in terms of affective symbols. In this sense, syncretic thought, in its own logic, does not obey the principle of identity—is not obliged to abstain from contradiction—and obeys a sort of law of participation, in virtue of which "representations . . . objects, beings, phenomena can be, in a manner incomprehensible to us, at once themselves and something distinct from themselves" (Lévy-Bruhl, quoted in Cuvillier 1971:68).

As a synthesis, we can say that, with the popular mentalities, in the warp and woof of collective representations there is customarily an interpenetration of the spheres of reality: the natural, the social, and existential meaning.

Religion, in this case, can give meaning to existence and even intervene in representations of nature and society. Indeed, magical conceptions of nature and religious legitimations of the social do subsist and coexist, even in the presence of processes of—relative—"secularization" that tend to rationalize thought. The religious, ultimately, given its relative autonomy, retains its validity on the level of the popular sense of existence. Through faith, a Latin American people gives meaning to its life, its work, its marriage and family, its suffering and death. The people do not obtain meaning from the school, the media, secularistic ideologies, or even leftist parties. But we have seen how different their religious expressions can be, and how varied the meanings and senses of these expressions.

Max Scheler has distinguished various forms of knowledge (see Merton 1972:468-69), organic developments occurring over long lapses of time: *Weltanschauungen* that can be listed according to their respective degrees of superficiality. Scheler distinguishes seven forms of knowledge: 1. myth and legend; 2. knowledge implicit in the natural popular language; 3. religious knowledge (ranging from a vague emotional intuition to the dogma of a church); 4. mystical knowledge; 5. metaphysical philosophical knowledge; 6. positive knowledge of the sciences (formal, natural, and cultural); 7. technological knowledge. Scheler's classification has been criticized for failing to offer enough evidence for its establishment or to define what it understands by "superficiality." But it is sufficiently illustrative for our purposes to situate what we have here called "syncretic thought" in the Latin American popular mentality as a style of thought proper to the forms of cognition of the natural popular language.

This schema of classification spares us a slip into the evolutionist trap at the basis of arguments such as the one to the effect that popular thought in Latin America is only a manifestation of a transitional thought, a prelogical, premodern thought trapped by its peculiar position in social development and structures, caught between the mythic thought of the native American cultures and the rational and scientific technological thought of the official cultures.

Syncretic thought is not a transitional aberration—a less evolved or inferior stage destined to disappear with progress. Syncretic thought is a *different* form of thought, with ties of kinship to mythic, religious, and scientific cognitions, but essentially distinct in the interplay of its logical and symbolical rules. Latin American popular syncretic thought is modern, and yet its relationship with modernity, one of criticism and attraction, is ambiguous. On the one hand, it is premodern, being rooted in an entire history and popular tradition, but it is not "just one more hindrance from the past." Syncretic thought obeys a "different logic": it is a *hemidernal* thought, coexisting with modernity, profiting from modernity, and at the same time rejecting and criticizing modernity.

Syncretic thought is a style of thinking characterizing the popular mentality in the framework of a peripheral modernity, on an under-developed continent with the characteristics, trajectories, and social, religious, and cultural histories proper to Latin America. It is a thought housed in a different type of vital synthesis, a thinking lodged be-tween the indigenous synthesis and the Hispano-Lusitanian synthe-sis, between the Eastern synthesis and the synthesis proper to the West, between the aboriginal cultures and the transnational culture of a capitalism functioning under the hegemony of North America.

It is arresting to note the syntony of popular thought, which we have barely sketched, with neurobiology's new discoveries with re-spect to the right hemisphere of the brain. It would be interesting to explore Latin American popular culture along the lines of investiga-tion broached by biologists today, and to contextualize those investi-gations in the framework of that culture. For the moment, let it suf-fice to register some immediately evident analogies.

Popular syncretic thinking, unlike the rationalistic, analytical thinking of the West, would seem to have its neurophysiological base in the intensive use of the "other hemisphere" of the brain, the right hemisphere.[6] Indeed, according to recent discoveries made in the course of research into the brain, it is now established that a cerebral asymmetry, or hemispheric predominance, prevails. The dominant traits of the left hemisphere are linearity and succession of sequences; thus, there are good reasons for designating it the quantitative, vi-sion side of the brain, and thus for associating it with analytical, in-tellectual, formal, and written language. In the right hemisphere, by contrast, the simultaneous, the global, and the synthetic predomi-nate, so that the right hemisphere of the brain comes to be desig-nated as the qualitative, acoustic side and is associated with gestaltic, creative, artistico-symbolical, emotive, and oral language. We may assert, then—by way of hypothesis—that, in popular syncretic thought (and consequently in its religious expressions), the predominant space is the acoustic, associated with the right hemisphere, as, for example, with the Inuit Eskimo culture studied by Trotter. We might conceive the acoustic space as a sphere whose center is everywhere and cir-cumference is nowhere. It is the "acoustic" kind of understanding, or "simultaneous understanding," that endows the right hemisphere with the power of "facial recognition." The numerous facial traits that iden-

---

6. We speak of a neurophysiological base in the cerebral structure precisely as a natural seat of the sociocultural production of mentality, and in no way as a determining biological factor of thought such as a reductionistic view would be tempted to impose. See Trotter, (1976: pp. 218ff.) cited in MacLuhan 1982:67.

tify to me a person with whom, for example, I may be speaking cannot be recognized as a figure or shape by the left hemisphere of my brain, since that hemisphere is associated to visual space, and visual space, as Euclidian geometry presents it, has its basic characteristics in linearity, connectibility, homogeneity, and stability.

Theorist of modern communications Marshall MacLuhan (1982: 67ff.) adduces new arguments in favor of our analogy. According to MacLuhan, the right hemisphere predominates in third-world societies, where oral and aural language still predominate. In the countries of the First World, on the other hand, societies tend to be visual (left hemisphere), although the emergence of an acoustical sense is beginning to be observed in consequence of the electronic technological revolution. Eastern culture makes use primarily of the abilities of the right hemisphere. By contrast, Western capitalism has persisted in its program of destruction of the environment and alienation of the human being in consequence of its predominantly linear conception of communication processes. Still, the ultimate Western technologies are electronic and simultaneous, and are governed by the right hemisphere: they are "Eastern" in their nature and effects. But Western dominant culture continues to be linear and visual. Our theory would set this Western cultural pattern over against the syncretic thought of the Latin American popular cultures and religions.

Surely there would be much more to say. But the important thing is to go ahead with theoretical and empirical investigations into this style of thought that we have denominated syncretic. Our interpretation has barely begun to penetrate the logical, semiological, and sociological characteristics of that style of thought. We are still dealing with a rough portrait, perhaps still only an outline, of this "different," *hemidern* thought proper to the popular mentality of our people, or of a goodly part thereof. Its study has only just begun. Anthropology now knows a considerable amount about the religion of our forebears; we still have a great deal to learn about our contemporaries.

Despite the enormous gap in our knowledge here, we can conclude, in the hope of encouraging further studies, that Lévy-Bruhl's theory on the "prelogical" thought of the primitives is open to reinterpretation. The thought in question is not irrational or antecedent to logic, but is a style of thought that moves within a "mystical" reality, in the sense of a *gestalt* of "synthetic" reality. Our hypothesis is that the thought of the primitives would correspond to the predominant use of the acoustic space proper to the right hemisphere of the brain. Hence the fittingness of speaking of a "different logic" present in the popular cultures and religions and structuring those cultures and religions. Beyond all doubt, this logic is an alternative to the Western rationality dominant in the culture of transnational capitalism. It is a logic of life, emotivity, simultaneity, symbol, and the sensible, standing over against the logic of reason, form, linearity, the successive, and the depersonalized.

# Chapter 11

# On the Horizon for the Twenty-First Century: Popular Christianity and Latin American Cultural Identity

Whereas the "originality of the Latin American person" or the "essence of the American" previously tended to be seen in the mirror of Western philosophy (Zea 1987), a new Latin American consciousness—in a theology, sociology, and philosophy now specifically Latin American—entails today, for the first time, the beginnings of an original thought that goes in quest of the ancestral wisdom of our indigenous cultures and means to harvest the contemporary wisdom of our popular cultures. This thought is still only in its infancy, is yet hesitating, and unsure of itself. But it is not, for all that, less valiant and impassioned. A breach with the myths of the Latin American way of being, derived from a Western modernity reproduced for, and adapted to, our dependent situation, has been effected in recent decades at the cost of enormous sacrifices.[1]

## Doubtful Quest

The utopias of emancipation embraced by Latin Americans in the 1960s shattered on the crude reality of the repression of the National Security regimes in the 1970s. And the situation of the 1980s through-

---

1. As Gabriel García Márquez asserted, upon receiving the Nobel Prize for Literature, on the "monstrous reality" that the European perceives in America "no paper reality, but one that lives with us and determines each instant of our countless daily deaths, and that sustains an insatiable spring of creation, full of haplessness and beauty . . . All of us creatures of that outrageous reality have had to leave something to the imagination, since the greatest challenge for us

out the region, in the presence of acute economic crisis and instability, prolonged violence in Central America, Colombia, Peru, and other countries, drug traffic and corruption, and the foreign debt that suffocates weak and dependent economies even more, conjoined with the new international capitalistic configuration and the crisis of socialism in the countries of the East, has contributed remarkably and powerfully to the spread of skepticism and disenchantment in the 1990s. We are assisting at the rise of an intellectual fad: postmodernism, an ideology that is spreading from the countries of "postindustrial capitalism." But the ideology of skepticism has its connatural soil in a Latin America that has lived the harsh experience of oppression, an experience in which Creole frustration plies a painful course and generates a new reality freighted with perplexity. Disenchantment is growing among the popular masses with regard to the promises of secular salvation spouted by the continent's political class, traditional or revolutionary.

Perplexity, translating into a collective incertitude concerning the fate of Latin America and the world, imposes the need to rethink this emerging cultural reality and to reinvent hope on different foundations. The "unshakable hope" of the 1960s, placed in development and freedom and expressed in the concrete liberation projects of the 1970s, has evaporated. Now we have a continent comparatively less developed, more dependent on world trade, and beset with more conflicts than could have been imagined: more poverty and social oppression, an exorbitant foreign debt, economic crisis and inflation, violence and the drug traffic.

It must be acknowledged, however, that recent decades have also left us a wise lesson.[2] That lesson resides fundamentally in the growth of an awareness that it will be impossible to emerge from the impasse in which we find ourselves without implementing a series of conditions. Among these conditions: human rights must win respect; economic, political, and social participation by the masses, especially women, youth, and ethnic minorities, must grow; totalitarian ideological positions will have to be abandoned; and finally, routes to democracy, dialogue, and peace must be sought. There is also a widening awareness of the need to preserve the earth from destruction, the

---

has been the insufficiency of conventional resources for making our life believable . . . The interpretation of our reality through alien schemata only contributes to making us more and more unknown, less and less free, more and more solitary" (García Márquez 1982: 4-5).

2. On the challenges to Latin America in the near future, see Ottone (1991), Arroyo (1991).

need to attempt to solve acute socioeconomic problems through courageous transformations to a just and equitable structure, and the need to confront the challenge of integration into the new international order in the framework of a new realism and of an effort at Latin American integration.

### Growing Globalization and Growing Cultural Diversity

Against the background of today's accelerating globalization, a rethinking of the cultural identity of our continent from a point of departure in Christianity not only is not superfluous but is actually necessary. An indispensable condition for this new conceptualization will be to accept an increasing pluralization of cultures and go on from there. This, in turn, will entail a critique of the false universalisms of the theories of modernization currently in vogue (Archer 1990).

Here let us recall, once more, that the tendency toward a homogenization of cultural processes of modernization collides with a counterprocess tending to heterogenization in the underdeveloped societies. As we have come to appreciate in other chapters, the historical development and structural heterogenization characteristic of the modernizing process of Latin American capitalism give rise to a plurality of cultural and religious expressions. In peripheral modernity, the religious field fragments and diversifies; the same occurs in the cultural field.

Contemporary cultural mutations—even in the countries of the developed North, which had manifested a considerable tendency to the homogenization imposed by the hegemony of opposed modes of production, here a capitalistic, there a socialistic—also indicate fissures in the cultural monolith. Consumer propaganda, as a necessary mechanism for the reproduction of the markets of transnational capitalism, tends to impose itself in all corners of the planet, homogenizing in a mercantile language not only bodies of knowledge but manners and styles of doing and thinking (García Canclini 1982). Paradoxically, however, the dialectic of this homogenizing process, structural in its roots, has its own limits and appears to have "bottomed out." The cultural field is exploding with new contradictions. This occasions certain reconceptualizations of the capitalistic phenomenon, culture, and modernity, such as that proposed, from a variety of perspectives, by authors such as Daniel Bell (1979), Peter Berger (1990:245-65), or Jürgen Habermas (1975).

Modern society speaks a common language. But at the same time, monolithic, homogeneous cultures no longer characterize the majorities of the various peoples, nations, and ethnic groups. New movements are demanding the "right to be different." Groups jostling for space in function of their ethnic or national identity, their gender and age, their religious or philosophical persuasions, are springing up everywhere we look.

The explosions of ethnic nationalism in Eastern Europe, the Balkans, the former Soviet Union, and Central Asia, the separatist movements in Canada, Spain, Belgium, and Yugoslavia, the racial struggles in South Africa, Liberia, Ethiopia, Sri Lanka, the Philippines, and India, the struggles of religious nationalism in Ireland, the Middle East, and the Persian Gulf, to mention only a few cases, are clear indicators that ought to move us to do some reflecting. In this new context, our Latin American thought, while continuing to regard itself in the universalistic categories provided it by the West, will henceforward be able to read the particularism of its tradition, identity, and historical destiny only in comparative terms, and not exclusively in terms of a comparison with Western Europe. Now our Latin American thought will have to regard its identity and history in the framework of a worldwide culture: it will have to consider the whole diversity of the world's cultural situations; it will have to acknowledge itself frankly as part of the Third World; it will have to compare its cultural expressions with those of the other peoples of the South, in the framework of their contradictory relations with the North; it will have to strike a dialogue with the wisdom of the civilizations and seek to solve problems posed today on a planetary scale, as Roger Garaudy has on more than one occasion suggested (Garaudy 1979). In order to advance in this new and different view, Latin American thought will be required to shake off its provincialism and its inferiority complex vis-à-vis Europeans and North Americans. Only by means of this purging or refinement of thought, which must be translated into theoretical and epistemological innovation, will our Latin American thought be able to rouse its cultural heritage to life— that admirable, age-old pre-Columbian legacy (closer to Asia and the Pacific than to Europe and the Mediterranean), the Hispano-Lusitanian legacy (whose Mozarabic roots must be frankly acknowledged), and the Afro-American (with deep roots in sub-Saharan Africa). But especially, Latin American thought will have to acknowledge its roots in the original, multiform, and plural *mestiza* culture, and thereby detect the sources of inspiration that will permit it to reconstruct an identity of its own. Simultaneously, the reconstruction of this identity will prefigure an alternative horizon of emergence from this crisis provoked by the transition of civilization confronting the world at the dawn of the twenty-first century.

Now, if we observe the cultural panorama of Latin America, we shall see that it is multiple. It is surely more diverse today than it was in the eighteenth and nineteenth centuries, despite the fact that the universal culture transmitted by the mass media of communication seeks to homogenize, from out of its own transnationalizing rationality, what constitutes for it an economic, and potentially cultural, "world market."

Today the Latin American cultural mosaic seems to have been pulverized. Not only do we distinguish a dominant culture, an imperfect copy of the North Atlantic culture, but that dominant culture itself has become diversified, without mentioning the multiplication of expressions of emerging indigenous and popular cultures—subjugated millenary cultures that are slowly waking from their lethargy; cultures of poor and oppressed classes that are partially shaking off the cultural alienation in which they were living by solving their basic problems of subsistence. The cultural range of the continent has become kaleidoscopic. A blaze of colours is today enlivening the cultural panorama of brown America. Beneath this cultural dynamism are processes leading to structural heterogeneity that make it possible. Its main impetus, however, comes from the characteristics of the cultural producer and his or her mentality: the Latin American popular subject. There is an inexhaustible vitality at the heart of his or her culture that resists domination.

### Christianity as Root of Cultural Identity

In the light of what we have set forth above, we may legitimately state that, at the meaning-core of Latin American popular culture—notwithstanding all of the breadth and diversity of its manifestations—it is possible to discern the dynamism of the Christian faith, not in exclusive form, but nevertheless in decisive form (Gomes de Souza, 1987, 1989).

Thus, against this panorama of sociocultural transformations and the enormous challenges of the contemporary world, the question of Christianity recovers new meaning. It is the old question that so concerned classic sociology: the force and contribution of religion in the shaping of society and culture. This time, however, the challenge arises once more in its Latin American setting.

From the outset, let us observe that the form of the question itself reveals the proper conceptual framework of its formulation. The necessary epistemological conditions for our question are given within a conceptual and cultural universe proper to and characteristic of modernity. The self-reflexive question of religion—which theology posits in its terms, apropos of faith and revelation—arises in Western Europe with modernity and the secularization of thought. If we pose this question today, in the here and now of our continent, it is precisely because, to a large extent, our thought is the child of modernity. But there is more. If we pose this question today, here and now, it is also because our thought is an attempt to approach abstractly a real phenomenon whose movement, of course, evinces a relative process of secularization in the various ambits of the social task. The theoretical route to be taken in the search for a response to our problem here requires the input of our initial thesis: that religion, especially Christianity in Latin America, is still a factor of relevance in the cultural fabric, *despite our peculiar processes of "secularization."*

The statement that we have constructed calls for certain decisive explanations. Indeed, we think it impossible to make progress in sociological responses to the problem without a theoretical and epistemological breach with the most widespread theories on popular religion in Latin America. The first explanation we must here propose has to do precisely with the need to question conceptions—outmoded, in our judgment—concerning the relation between culture and religion in Latin America. The second is a corollary of the first, and deepens the sociological critique of the conceptions in question, in the light of more up-to-date knowledge.

In the first place, we think that it will be possible to establish our proposition only when at least two interpretations, fairly widespread today among theoreticians of culture and religion in Latin America, have been given the lie. The first states that our continent, although with its own variations, is slowly but inexorably undergoing the same secularization process that modernity imposed both on countries of central capitalism and on those of a now failed "real socialism." The response, as we have said, is not in the classic theory of secularization, but in the process of its critique. Peripheral "secularization" is relative. Any concept of peripheral "secularization" must come under a critical razor and, in light of real historical processes, be reformulated in depth.

The second interpretation postulates that the basis of Latin American culture is constituted by the "Catholic substrate." This assertion is based on three premises:

1. That religion constitutes no more and no less than the essence

of culture—every culture, and so, of course, Latin American culture;

2. That Catholicism has been, is now, and always will be the religion of the broad majority on our continent, a proposition that is expressed in other terms when it is said that Latin America is a "Catholic continent";

3. That Christianity bestows a spiritual unity—in its capacity as substrate of faith—that justifies speaking of "one" culture, in self-identity, despite the great diversity of the manifold threats that lurk for Latin American culture.

This thesis is very widespread among theologians and scientists of culture with ties to church circles, especially to the contemporary Catholic field. As one of its exponents acknowledges, this thesis "needs to be demonstrated, of course, in all of its details, a demonstration which, as of this date, has been offered only partially with the rigor required by science" (Morandé 1984:140).

## A Secularizing Modernization and the Revitalization of the Religious

As we have stated, there is not, in modern society, a linear, progressive process of secularization. The cultural dialectic of society, which is subject to the communication and information revolution, determines ebbs and flows in the tide of significations and symbolisms. In the religious field, this dialectic of *secularization / sacralization* is actually fostered by the culture industry. In other words, a sort of "resacralization" of certain spaces of functionality is occurring—a phenomenon introduced by technological scientific rationality itself. The most advanced products of technological science are actually used and represented by the vast majority of the public with an attitude analogous to that with which it regards sacred objects of a magical character. The user of a television set or a computer actually knows very little about complex microelectronic engineering or about the "chips" and semiconductors that make it possible to use these instruments to fill his or her hours of work or leisure, and is little interested in the same. But it is a fact that these "instruments" acquire a symbolical value that exceeds their exchange value, and constitute far more than a functional apparatus. Furthermore, they contain a hefty dose of mystery—banalized, but not, for all that, absent—analogous, in a lesser degree, to the mystery with which the "savage" listens to a radio for the first time and believes there is a "little person in there" speaking to him or her. Television is the tribe's new "sorcerer," dissolving in the routine of the everyday the mystery that once upon a time manifested itself so powerfully in rites—in moments of collective effervescence—to piece together once more psychic elements threatened with disintegration by anesthetizing the disruptive tensions. Only, television fails to satisfy the societal requisites once accomplished by the wizard's rites, and widens the breach between the unsatisfied needs of the collective subject and any symbolical and real opportunities for their satisfaction.

Modern electronic technology has revolutionized—nothing less, these past fifteen years—the entire reproductive machinery of the collective imagination by placing technology at the service of the regeneration of old fantasies and myths. We refer to the fantasies and myths emanating from the ancestral queries and fears that disturb the human being, which technology itself fails to calm but, rather, feeds—all of these fantasies and myths being reiterated, on the basis of the archetypes, throughout the history of humanity.[3] Besides the films and videos that reproduce the old fairy tales, we have animated cartoons that recycle old themes, modern science-fiction films (animated or not), and video games that present once more the antique legends and myths of ancestral oral tradition. We also have the new myths of the "westerns," or films of intrigue, action and adventure, police or war films, terror and suspense—all feeding anew the ancient thrusts of the collective consciousness. Underlying, in all of this modern dramatization, are the old themes that make up the structuring nuclei of traditional mythology: the quest for happiness, the eternal struggle of good and evil, the existence of uncontrollable supernatural powers and the need to dominate them (dominate them at least symbolically, by vicarious means), threats to the existence and regulation of society, want and its solutions, life and death as the dialectic of the human event, and, finally, the mystery living deep within the face-to-face relationship: love, eroticism, fertility, the polarity of the daily and the extraordinary in the ebb and flow of life.

Surely, the worldwide spread of the "televiewer culture," with its videos and "canned" programs and the accompanying exponential leap over film's potential as regenerator of mythic representations, for one

---

3. "The great mythological themes continue to repeat themselves in the obscure depths of the psyche . . . It seems that a myth itself, as well as the symbols it brings into play, never quite disappear from the present world of the psyche; it only changes its aspect and disguises its operation" (Mircea Eliade quoted in Cox 1973:280).

thing, and of the personal computer, with its electronic games and corresponding "computer culture," in which software replaces the creative capacity, for another, has revolutionized the world of communications these last twenty years. But it has done so at the price of remythologizing by way of "canned products," generating a communicational circuit whose redundancy finally impoverishes, and activates the self-limitation of precisely the expansive capacity of communication which that technology is intended to enhance.

And so we are in the presence of processes of "desecularization" that, in virtue of their internal contradictions—functionality and mythologization—bear the seed of authentic collective processes of spiritual search, so that religious replacements are generated for the modern "technology myth" that tends to self-exhaust. If, in this "secularization," the false gods of the "beyond" have died, to be replaced by a "polytheism of values," as Weber prophesied they would (Weber 1958), then everywhere we look there emerge cults to the new false gods of the "here." Goods enchant, and fetishism is no longer merely that of merchandise—a fetishism analyzed at length by Marx—but becomes a fetishism of technological science itself. The culture industry has assigned itself the task of reviving the fantasies of ritual symbolism, of magic and mystery, in a word, of the mythic backdrop of humanity now functionalized in terms of the logic of exchange.[4] But the human mentality, in this modern ambient, smothers and rebels, and directs its gaze once more toward the old god, in a ceaseless spiritual quest.

In no way are we suggesting that, according to our definition, religion is "at the base" of the constitution of culture. Religion is a form of manifestation of the symbolical and semiotic tissue of culture, but it

---

4. Marx himself, in the second half of the past century, prophesied a "spellbinding" potential that he discerned in modern means of social communication. In a letter to Kugelmann, Marx declared: "Up until the present, it was believed that the formation of the Christian myths under the Roman Empire would not have been possible without the mediation of the fact that printing had not yet been invented. Nothing could be further from the truth. The daily press and the telegraph . . . fabricate in a single day more myths (and the flock of bourgeois accepts and spreads them) than those produced of old in a century" (Letter of Karl Marx to Kugelmann, July 27, 1871). Bastide, in turn, asserts this same position: "The cinema has caused this propagation or fabrication of myths to grow greater still. Such propagation and fabrication are all the more effective for the fact that they largely escape the word, to submerge us, by means of images, in a concrete universe transformed into a meaning. These archetypal, unprecedented myths continue to possess the function of bestowing a meaning on our destiny or explaining the world to us; nevertheless, as a new destiny is now being inscribed in a history, . . . they take on new characteristics" (Bastide 1973:271-72).

is no longer possible to approach the subject of culture by returning to the idealism of the nineteenth-century German Romantics. Culture has no "essence," or even "spirit." Partisans of the contrary run the risk of reifying anew a social reality, transforming it into a transcendent entity. Culture, we have said, is historical, the social product of historical collectivities, a fabric of human subjects, and not an entelechy. Hence the great danger of the expression "cultural substrate," with its equivocal geological analogy.

The problem does not reside in the fact that this analogy inverts the Marxist theory of the conditioning of the superstructure by the material base. The actual problem resides in the geological metaphor's basis in a concealed essentialist, static, and "fixist" conception of culture, which forgets, precisely, the producing subject of culture—furthermore, hiding not only conflict and the dialectic that this conflict produces and that enwraps it, but also the historico-social conditioners of all culture as human enterprise and not as an omnipresent supra- or infra-reality determinative of the human being.

Those theories of secularization are both false, then, that either indissolubly associate progress and a loss of the sense of God or identify religion as the authentic essence of culture.

Modernization is not only an unfolding of the logos: it is also a new form of ritual and mythology. True, the "independentization" of the economic functions of the temple in tributary societies generates a "secularized market." But we must not forget that the capitalistic market now functions on the basis of its own sacrificial rite as well, with its own victims immolated to the new gods of trade, a ritual performed by the new priests of the temple of trade and legitimated by the new "sages" and "prophets" of trade (of that corrected perfection of the market in what we know as contemporary neoliberalism) and of the society of consumption.

The current crises of Western "modern" society reveal that this new sacralization of trade, now of a "secular" trade, carries within itself the limit of its own horizon, since it has no possible escape from its own golden calves and shatters on the ultimate unsatisfaction of vital human needs, including the deepest longings of the human being of today.

Dominant modernization entails a destructive sacrificial process. In wresting sacrifice from its traditional societal framework, it strips it of its vital meaning. In traditional society, sacrifice was performed for the purpose of ensuring the reproduction of life, in order to placate and conjure away threats against life (sickness, drought, pestilence, war, and so on). The immolation of propitiatory "victims" was performed in order to placate the menaces of chaos and to reestablish the significative (and real) *nomos*. Victims were selected from among human beings in limited number as the condition, in solidarity, of the reproduction and subsistence of the collectivity. Contemporary sacrifice is addressed to the modern Baals, and more life is won only for a small minority, at the price of the oppression, misery, repression, torture, and death of millions of human beings[5] as well as the merciless destruction of natural resources and the ecological balances of life. Now it is the collectivity that is immolated, and the immolation is performed no longer in order to guarantee the life of that collectivity, but to produce the asymetrical structure that guarantees the life of those who have the power to keep on sacrificing. The new immolation is the destruction of the foundational solidarity of the collectivity. Within modern culture, there lurks the destruction not only of "traditional" culture but, quite simply, of culture's very capacity for survival. Principally, then, modern culture opens the way for the resurgence of the religious. After all, it is in its sense of the religious that the collectivity rediscovers its foundational solidarity and is capable of rebuilding itself as a collectivity that will overcome (really or ritually) the imponderables and arbitrary elements that threaten its very subsistence as a collectivity. True, the search for the restoral of the foundational bond of the collectivity finds other pathways as well; but the route of the religious is always available, and is what the overwhelming majority of third-world peoples are using.

On the other hand, the ideologies that have proposed to defeat the alienating condition of capitalism not only as an abstract entity but also in its historical versions have bequeathed us an inconclusive program. In its course, which is not ascending but dialectical, with ebbs and flows, we have observed how, in one form of application of modern rationality—in orthodox Marxism-Leninism in Eastern Europe—the religion once so militantly combated is now beginning to reappear as a dominant factor in the culture of those peoples. Integralists rejoice, but a danger lurks: what we have is a religious resurgence of variable sign, whose disintegrating potential, when one fantasizes and bows to blind chauvinisms, is enormous and therefore calls for attentive observation. As for the developed, sophisticated, technetronized capitalism of Western Europe and North America, we hear of

---

5. Conservative sources estimate that, by 1990, the number of persons detained and "disappeared" in Latin America had climbed to ninety thousand.

"new religious movements" in those countries, constituting a phenomenon worthy of attention and, in the case of certain "new sects," profound concern.

### Popular Christianity: Novelty in the Face of Fatigued Modern Reason

We are witnessing the crisis of the ideologies—not the end of all ideology, and still less the end of history, *pace* Francis Fukuyama (Fukuyama 1989). Socialism's collapse is not necessarily capitalism's triumph; and even if it were, that would be no guarantee that history had been consummated in the tiresome paradise described by Fukuyama's simplistic reading of Hegel (Gallardo 1990). What is certain is that the crisis of the totalitarian ideologies, the introduction of pragmatism, and the ethic of freedom understood as the right to indifferentism are the reflection of a crisis of civilization.

The revolution of productive forces, which began with the industrial revolution, replacing manual labor with machinery, is now being manifested in the replacement of work with robotization and automatization, including the replacement of thought with artificial intelligence. These variations can be promising: after all, along with revolutionizing the bases of future social life, they can certainly swell the human being's capacities—on condition, of course, that they occasion profound changes in current social structures, changes that would signify a mutation of our civilization (Schaff 1987) and potentially would make way for a civilization based on cooperation and solidarity (John Paul II 1981). Nevertheless, the future is not guaranteed.

True, the Cold War is over, and a new era of peace among nations is under way. Conflicts tend to be circumscribed and regionalized, but they do not disappear, as the Persian Gulf War agonizingly demonstrated. There is a greater awareness of the limitations of human progress. But the future continues to be irremediably uncertain. Few of the threats of self-destruction deriving from poor management of nuclear energy, from microbiology, or from an impoverished ecological conception of development have been entirely eliminated. The future today is more uncertain than ever for the poor countries of the Third World (Latin America included), cast adrift, or rather, abandoned to their fate, by a First World now focusing on the Second (which is in the process of being absorbed by the First) and planning a future of relations and interchanges calculated to install a stable, lasting common life.

In the last analysis, the contemporary crisis is the crisis of a style of thought that has constituted the core of the dominant Western European culture since the Renaissance—a core that was extended to the rest of the world with the expansion of mercantile, then manufacturing, industrial, and financial, and now transnational and technotronic, capitalism. This same logic—with a different content—underlies as well the historical ascent that incarnated the alternative model of society, socialism.

The crisis is not provoked by the materiality of scientific and technological advances, with their obvious benefits, nor by the sound autonomy of thought of the old myths and superstitions. It is a crisis because of the manner in which the dominant modern mentality unfolds in its relation with nature—in the relation of human beings with one another, with things, and with the transcendent. It is the crisis of instrumental rationality carried to its ultimate expression, that is, to its definitive fatigue. In the dialectical course of the advance of reason, the latter—contradicting Hegelian evolutionism—has not progressively unfolded as self-realization, but has found itself trapped by the immanence of its own logic and is now turning toward other expressions and dimensions of human existence. Here is that rationality whose basis is the "ethos of accumulation," present in contemporary phenomena as important as consumerism, exploitation, authoritarianism, imperialism, as well as in phenomena as unlike these as corruption and drug addiction. Here we see a series of expressions of the logic that has preyed on human beings and on an enhanced nature since Hobbes and Machiavelli, Ricardo, Smith, Franklin, Engels, and Stalin. It is a sacrilegious, perverse conception, however nonreligious it may seem, in view of the fact that it sets up reason as a god of the intellect in order to legitimate actions orientated toward ends without any consideration of the value of the means, ultimately leading to the unscrupulous self-destruction of persons and their cultural and natural surroundings. It is modern human beings who are in crisis, since their relation with themselves and their ecosystem is in crisis. Human beings are splitting, have sundered, their original harmony.

As Erich Fromm expressed it more than three decades ago, modern human beings have let themselves be absorbed by the construction of the new industrial mechanism.

> [Man's] energies in another time had been devoted to the search for God and salvation. Now they were directed to a dominion over nature, and an ever loftier condition of material welfare. He left

off using production as a means for better living and, on the contrary, hypostatized it into an end in itself, an end to which life was subordinated. In the process of an ever more minute division of labor, an ever more complete mechanization of work, and ever larger social agglomerations, man transformed himself into a part of the machinery, instead of being its master. He felt himself to be a piece of merchandise, an investment. His finality was reduced to having success—that is, to selling himself on the market in the most profitable manner possible. His value as a person is rooted in his "salability," not in his human qualities of love and reason, nor in his artistic talents. [Fromm 1971:294]

That universe of values and categories that maintained an entire age of Promethean dreams, the basis of the conservative, liberal, and developmentalist utopias as well as of the historical socialisms, has collapsed. We are witnessing the collapse of the ordered and coherent framework of comprehension of the cosmos and of history as a rising, progressive, and unilinear course. "We must also abandon the notion, still so widespread after twenty-five years, that we have at last found the idea of the good society, of authentic development—that our sciences of the human being and nature were almost complete, that we had attained genuine consciousness," states E. Morin (1990).

The tragedy of the current ideologies is that they leave the terrain wide open for quests to be conducted in enormous irresponsibility, skepticism, license, and hedonism. But they also open up a by no means inconsiderable space for spiritual quests that could open the way for a reencounter with the human being, as a human being genuinely free and liberated. In the framework of this crisis, modern human beings seek some symbolic purchase or "handle" that would give them new meaning for their lives and reorientate their efforts. Here the religious proposal acquires validity and force, and this explains the resurgence, even in societies that yesterday were quite secularized, of new movements and expressions of faith. After all, the offer of religious meaning is not solely or exclusively ideational and rational; it attains the deepest fibers of the symbolical and ritual, bodily and mystical, dimension of the integral needs and demands of the human being.

The Christian faith, across the gamut of its manifestations among the Latin American people, in all of its plurality of languages and sapiential cognitions, in its pathos and syncretic mentality structure, offers alternatives of meaning in the framework of a conjuncture of cultural transition. To be sure, the strengthening of religious expressions in Latin America and the world can bring with it a component of ambiguity. The pluralization of the religious field on our continent— once monopolized by the Catholicism of a colonial, oligarchical view and attitude—with the expansion of sects, Eastern-style cults, fundamentalisms and integralisms, and, finally, various superstitious, even satanic, practices, which seem to revive the embers of magic in the popular mentality, can be fraught with new alienations. But it is equally certain that, as we have demonstrated, the popular mentality, in its option for life, preserves a dose of rebellion deep down—a sane, sound way of resisting the sudden attacks of a dominant culture that, at every step, threatens the integrity of its culture and human existence itself.

It is no longer possible to assert that the religion of the people is everything the enlightened elite once criticized in any manifestation of symbolic ritual. Neither is the romantic utopianism any longer acceptable of those who lauded all that comes from the people because it comes from the people. We have stated that the cultural-religious reality of the Latin American people is multiple and heterogeneous. Does that mean that there is nothing common there? Are we dealing with the scattered parts of a jigsaw puzzle that can never be reconstructed? Is this reality irremediably segmented and atomized? Those who answer in the affirmative are those whose theoretical framework depends on the premise of a unity lost and the project of a unity to be rebuilt. In order to escape this sort of reductionist, dangerously unitarian focus, one must recognize diversity—not as a chaotic juxtaposition of elements, however, but as a reality articulated in complexity. We think that only typologically will it be possible to apprehend this multiform, plural reality in terms of a comprehensive framework that would go beyond the segmenting tendency, proper to the Cartesian categories, of classic epistemology and empirical sociology. In the trajectory of Latin American capitalism, in the light of our historical, descriptive-explanatory, interpretative sketch of the evolution of the religious phenomenon within the popular cultures, we may venture the following framework of comprehension.

We maintain that, at the base of the syncretic religious mentality of the Latin American structure, in the structuring code of that mentality's multiform plurality, lies a sort of vitalistic anthropology, alternative to the Promethean anthropology of Western modernity. It is a chthonic, maternal anthropology, derived from the great telluric intuitions of the pre-Columbian cultures, as over against a dualistic, pantocratic, patriarchal anthropology derived from the Western Greco-Roman worldview. We see an ecological, holistic anthropology over against an anthropology that separates the subject from the object and divides the human being up according to function.[6] Underlying this, is a *hemidernal* project of the integral human being. It is a question no longer of primitive human beings immersed in nature (without having yet developed their cultural rationality), nor of Western, modern human beings suffocating in their instrumental, privatistic rationality. It is a question of the "Latin" human being, neither pre- nor postmodern.

We have found a hemidernal anthropology, not antagonistic but cooperative and, under many aspects, alternative to Western modernity. We have found a different human conception, multiple and holistic, the human being who harmonizes, from amidst an ancestral wisdom, feeling and reasoning, thinking and acting, seeking and hoping, rejoicing and mourning. Ultimately, what we have found is the anthropology of a different praxis, one centered on the fertility of love-solidarity. That is, we find a love that exists for its own sake, love in the sense of a popular category of basic solidarity, fecundating reality with new life and gladness and not with that rationalistic, ascetical praxis of an "efficacious" love understood as normativeness of self-disciplined commitment to a particular cause (as in the ethics of bourgeois asceticism or proletarian militancy). At the core of this integral conception of the Latin American human being of the people, Christian faith fulfills an irreplaceable function in the conveying of a transcendent dimension. God the Father, the God of life, the God who by his intermediaries (the Virgin, the saints, the departed souls) bestows health and sustenance on the body and the soul (simultaneously, not dualistically), the God whose favorite persons are the lowly and the despised, the God who accompanies all of the stages and circumstances of life (birth, puberty, marriage, crisis, death), with their anguishes and their joys. Here is a God who walks with the human being in the latter's quest for a sound, gladsome, radiant well-being, a well-being in the spirit of carnival—an individual and collective welfare, from which the category of accumulation and worldly "success" is radically absent.

We have found an autochthonous utopian conception, which, in different ages, the various peoples and ethnic groups have manifested in the Andean utopias, in the Tupiguaraní "Land without Ills," in the "Black Republic" of Palmares, in the movement of the Canudos and

---

6. The anthropology latent in the Latin American popular culture is substantially similar to the new, holistic metaphysics and anthropology now transcending the anthropology and metaphysics that are offspring of technological scientific development since the Renaissance. See Berman (1981).

the Contestados, in the Mapuche native republic, but a conception reflected, as well, in an alternative way of understanding human beings in themselves and in their world, in popular medicine, in popular craft, in dance, song, fiesta, and the inversion of the world affected by these—in a word, in the various forms of popular self-management in current societies (Irarrázaval, 1990b). We have no moralistic God here, let alone a divinity rigid, stoic, blaming, and punishing. Ultimately, the God praised by the popular mentality is a God of liberation—not in enlightened terms, of course, but in the categories of popular wisdom. We find a God honored not in rationalistic terms, but in terms of that "other" rationality of Latin popular otherness.

Over and against a universalized bourgeois selfishness maintained under the form of a utilitarian secular ethics, a selfishness detached from rational natural law and succeeding and replacing religion and philosophy, a laicist, "scientistic" selfishness (Habermas 1975:102), arises this anthropology—a vital synthesis of popular wisdom, faith, and philosophy—that reinvents the utopian content of the traditions and resumes ideational constructions that justify a more balanced and harmonious relationship in the relations of persons among themselves and with nature.

Here, at the heart of the Christian religion of the vast majority of Latin Americans, from out of their popular, community wisdom, a new paradigm emerges—the paradigm of a new, autochthonous utopia, in terms of which the encounter with the other—in the connatural solidarity of the poor, in the practice of a daily ritual of gift and reciprocation—is the presage of a *new culture of solidarity*. Christianity, thus understood as a cultural factor, may well be the novel horizon for the construction of a new Latin American civilization for the twenty-first century. Christianity bids fair to constitute the dynamizing horizon—and not the "fixist" substrate—of the project of a non-Western civilizing transformation that must needs be enfleshed in historical projects incorporating the best of the libertarian and socialistic utopias, developing in a profound democratic sense, weaving a culture and economy of solidarity—thus avoiding, on one side, the totalitarian culture that throttles liberty and, on the other, the exploitative temptation of a deregulated market that assaults equity.

The condition for the historical viability of this emerging paradigm is related to the complex solution that will have to be found for a harmonious articulation between an inevitable technological scientific progress and this "different" rationality, in the framework of the building of a new society—which must, in its own turn, be part of a comprehensive transformation in the international order. The contemporary crisis generates conditions for reflecting on this alternative for our continent without succumbing to the dangers of particularism or regionalism. There are urgent tasks, however, and Latin America demands to be integrated today into the world market under favorable conditions. In order to do this without Latin America's selling out its cultural and religious identity, policies will have to be projected that move from an awareness of the merely possible, at the level of thought, to conditions of real possibility investing concrete projects. This is the challenge facing those who will be charged with giving pragmatic formulation to these policies and programs, in order to render the ideals that we have cited historically viable and possible.

But Christianity is not only a cultural expression. It is a comprehensive phenomenon. It is faith in the "God of the Christians" (Muñoz 1988). And it is praxis: ritual, real, effective, symbolical, affective, and efficacious praxis in the love whose chief characteristic is solidarity. Thus we may say that Christianity is both a root and a horizon of the new Latin American culture—not the sole root or sole horizon, but surely a powerful and undeniable one. Deep within a dying culture, cultural Christianity—understood abstractively and ahistorically—is dying with it. And at the heart of the culture being born of this crisis, popular Christianity, understood as vital synthesis, is a dynamizing germ of new relations to be struck by human beings among themselves, with nature, and with the transcendent.

# Bibliography

Acosta, José de (1954), *Obras del Padre José de Acosta*, BAE, Madrid.

Adorno, Theodor, et al. (1973), *La disputa del positivismo en la sociología alemana*, Grijalbo, Barcelona.

Alcalá, Alfonso (coord.) (1984), *Historia general de la Iglesia en América Latina. México*, Vol. V. CEHILA, Sígueme/Paulinas, Salamanca.

Alliende, Joaquin (1979), "Religiosidad popular en Puebla. La madurez de una reflexión," in *Puebla: religiosidad popular*, Colección Puebla, 14.1, CELAM, Bogota, pp. 7-45.

Altimir, Oscar (1981), "La pobreza en América Latina: un examen de conceptos y datos," *Revista de la CEPAL*, 13, pp. 67-95.

Alvear, Enrique, et. al. (1983), *La Iglesia de los Pobres en América Latina: Antología*, PEC, Santiago, Chile.

Amin, Samir (1973), *Le développement inégal. Essai sur les formes du capitalisme périphérique*, Minuit, Paris.

Ansión, Juan (1990), "Sendero Luminoso: la política como religión," *Cristianismo y Sociedad*, XXVIII/4, 106, pp. 115-129.

Arboleda, Carlos (1983), "Factores religiosos de la religiosidad colombiana," *Cuestiones Teológicas*, 10, 26, pp. 36-49.

Arboleda, José Rafael (1986), *La historia y la antropología del negro en Colombia*, Pontificia Universidad Javeriana, Bogota, Colombia.

Archer, Margaret (1990), "Unidad y diversidad. Crítica del falso universalismo en las teorías de la modernidad," XII Congreso Mundial de Sociología in Madrid, *El País*, Temas de Nuestra Época, 138, July 5, pp. 3-4.

Arias, Maximino (1977), "Religiosidad popular en América Latina," in *Iglesia y religiosidad popular en América Latina*, CELAM, Bogota, Colombia, pp. 17-37.

Arroyo, Gonzalo (1991), "Desafíos presentes y futuros para América Latina," *Tópicos '90*, No. 3, pp. 13-30.

Azzi, Rolando (1983), *"A instituiçao eclesiástica durante a primeira época colonial,"* in *História da Igreja no Brasil*, Paulinas/Vozes, Petrópolis, Brazil, pp. 151-242.

Balandier, Georges (1982), "Los movimientos de innovación religiosa en el África negra," in Henri-Charles Puech (dir.), *Movimientos religiosos derivados de la aculturación*, Siglo XXI, Madrid, pp. 312-351.

Barrett, David (ed.) (1982), *World Christian Encyclopedia*, Oxford University Press, London/Nairobi.

Bastián, Jean Pierre (1986), "Religión popular protestante y comportamiento político en América Central," *Cristianismo y Sociedad*, 88, pp. 41-56.

Bastián, Jean Pierre (1990), *Historia del protestantismo en América Latina*, CUPSA, Mexico.

Bastide, Roger (1973), *El prójimo y el extraño*, Amorrortu, Buenos Aires.

Bastide, Roger (1974), "Contribución a una sociología de las religiones en América Latina," *Contacto*, 11, pp. 12-27.

Bastide, Roger (1982), "Los cultos afroamericanos," in Henri-Charles Puech (dir.), *Movimientos religiosos derivados de la aculturación*, Siglo XXI, Madrid, pp. 51-79.

Baum, Gregory (1983), "Sociología de la religión (1973-1983)," *Concilium*, 190, pp. 466-476.

Beaud, Michel (1981), *Histoire du capitalisme de 1500 à nos jours*, Seuil, Paris.

Bell, Daniel (1979), *The Cultural Contradictions of Capitalism*, Heinemann, London.

Benedict, Ruth (1952), "Magic," *Encyclopaedia of the Social Sciences*, X, Macmillan, New York, pp. 39-44.

Benkö, Antonius (1975), "Pesquisa aspectos psico-sociais da religiosidade no Estado na Guanabara," *Sintese*, 2/3, pp. 49-103.

Bentué, Antonio (1972), *Religión y marginalidad social*, Doctoral thesis at the University of Strasbourg.

Bentué, Antonio (1975), "Función y significado de un tipo de religiosidad popular al interior de una subcultura," in *Religiosidad y Fe en América Latina*, Mundo, Santiago, Chile, pp. 61-76.

Beozzo, José Oscar (1990), "Evangelização e V Centenário," en *Revista Eclesiástica Brasilera*, 50, No. 199, pp. 556-617.

Berger, Peter (1969), *El dosel sagrado*, Amorrortu, Buenos Aires.

Berger, Peter (1990), "El capitalismo como fenómeno," *Estudios Públicos*, 38, pp. 245-265.

Berger, Peter; Berger, Brigitte; Kellner, Hansfried (1973), *The Homeless Mind: Modernization and Consciousness*, Random House, New York.

Berman, Morris (1981), *The Reenchantment of the World*, Cornell University Press, Ithaca.

Betancourt, Silvia (1988), "La industrialización latinoamericana: dependencia, deformación estructural y crisis," *Economia y Desarrollo*, 103, No. 2, pp. 63-75.

Bingemer, María Clara (1990), "A seduçao do sagrado," *Atualidade em debate*, Caderno 1, Centro Joao XXIII, Rio de Janeiro, pp. 37-54.

Boff, Leonardo (1981), *Igreja, carisma e poder*, Vozes, Petrópolis, Brazil. In English, *Church: Charism and Power*, New York, Crossroad, 1986.

Borrat, Héctor (1982), *El caminar actual de la Iglesia en el Brasil*, Pro Mundi Vita, Brussels.

Boulard, Fernand; Remy, Jean (1968), *Practique religieuse urbaine et régions culturelles*, Les Editions Ouvrières, Paris.

Bourdieu, Pierre (1966), "Condition de classe et position de classe," *Archivo Europeo Sociológico*, VII, pp. 210-223.

Bourdieu, Pierre (1971), "Genèse et structure du champ religieux," *Revue Française de Sociologie*, XII, pp. 295-334.

Brown, Diana; Vilas, María Helena; Negrao, Lísias; Birman, Patricia; Seiblitz, Zelia (1985), *Umbanda e política*, Marco Zero, Río de Janeiro, Brasil.

Bruneau, Thomas (1980), "The Catholic Church and Development in Latin America: The Role of the Basic Christian Communities," in *World Development*, 8, pp. 535-544.

Brunner, José Joaquín (1985), *Notas sobre cultura popular, industria cultural y modernidad*, FLASCO, Santiago, Chile.

Buitelaar, Rudolf (1989), "El debate sobre el futuro de la industrialización en América Latina, o cómo subir la senda escarpada hacia crecimiento y equidad," *Pensamiento Iberoamericano*, 16, pp. 265-271.

Büntig, Aldo (1969), "El catolicismo popular en la Argentina," *Mensaje Iberoamericano*, 43, pp. 8-13.

Büntig, Aldo (1970), *¿Magia, religión o cristianismo?* Bonum, Buenos Aires.

Büntig, Aldo (1973a), *Religión—enajenación en una sociedad dependiente*, Guadalupe, Buenos Aires.

Büntig, Aldo (1973b), "Dimensiones del catolicismo popular latinoamericano y su inserción en el proceso de liberación. Diagnóstico y reflexiones pastorales," in *Fe cristiana y cambio social en América Latina*, Sígueme, Salamanca, pp. 129-150.

Burga, Manuel (1990), "Utopia y emergencia andina," *Allpanchis*, XXII, 35-36, pp. 579-598.

Business International (1990), *Global Forecasting*, Service Latin America, Regional Overview, First Quarter.

Cáceres, Jorge; Opazo, Andrés; Pochet, Rosa Maria; Sierra, Oscar R. (1983), *Iglesia, política y profecia*, Educa, Costa Rica.

Caravias, José Luis (1978), *Religiosidad campesina y liberación*, Indoamerican Press-Service, Bogotá, Colombia.

Cardenal, Rodolfo (coord.) (1985), *Historia general de la Iglesia en América Latina. América Central*, VI, CEHILA, Sígueme, Salamanca.

Carrión, Luis (1986), paper presented in the seminar "¿Qué espera el FSLN de los cristianos, y qué esperan éstos del FSLN en la revolución nicaragüense?" *Cuadernos*, DEI, 4, pp. 31-41.

*Cartas de relación de la conquista de América*, Nueva España, Mexico (no date).

Carutti, Eugenio; Martínez, Carlos (1974), "Culto popular en la Argentina: Eva Perón," *Nuevo Mundo*, IV, 7-8, pp. 148-169.

Cassirer, Ernst (1964), "La función del mito en la vida social del hombre," in I.L. Horowitz (sel.), *Historia y elementos de la sociología del conocimiento*, EUDEBA, Buenos Aires, 1964, II, pp. 24-35.

Castells, Manuel (1978), *La cuestión urbana*, Siglo XXI, México.

Castillo, Fernando (1986), *Iglesia liberadora y política*, ECO, Santiago, Chile.

CELAM (1977), *Iglesia y religiosidad popular en América Latina*, Bogota.

CEPAL (1983), *La urbanización, el crecimiento urbano y la concentración en el proceso de asentamiento en América Latina: Una visión general*, Consejo Económico y Social, United Nations.

CEPAL (1990), *Transformación productiva con equidad*, CEPAL, Santiago, Chile.

CEPAL (1992), *Balance preliminar de la economia de América Latina y el Caribe*, CEPAL, Santiago, Chile.

CEPAL/ONUDI (1985), *Industrialización y desarrollo tecnológico 1985*, CEPAL/ONUDI, División Conjunta de Industria y Tecnologia, Informe No. 1, Santiago, Chile.

Champion, Françoise (1989), "Les sociologues de la post-modernité religieuse et la nébuleuse mystique-ésotérique," *Archives des Sciences Sociales des Religions*, 67-1, pp. 155-169.

CISOR (1970), *Religiosidad popular en Venezuela*, Estudio preliminar, Centro de Investigaciones en Ciencias Sociales, Caracas.

Cockcroft, James (1983), "Inmiseration, Not Marginalization: The Case of Mexico," *Latin American Perspectives*, X, 37-38, No. 2-3, pp. 86-107.

Codina, Victor; Irarrázaval, Diego (1987), *Sacramentos de iniciación*, Paulinas, Madrid.

Colón, Cristóbal (n.d.), "Carta del Almirante Cristóbal Colón escrita al Escribano de Ración de los señores Reyes Católicos" (Segunda Carta, 15 de febrero de 1493), in *Cartas de relación de la conquista de América* (n.d.), Nueva España, Mexico.

Comblin, José (1968), "Momentos socio-religiosos de la Iglesia en Brasil," *Mensaje Iberoamericano*, 30, pp. 10-13.

Comblin, José (1972), "Critica de la teología de la secularización," in *Fe y secularización en América Latina*, CELAM/IPLA, Bogota, pp. 35-50.

Conferencia Regional sobre la Pobreza en América Latina y el Caribe (1991), "Declaración de Quito," *Comercio Exterior*, 41, 5, May, pp. 463-466.

Correa, Enrique (1986), "Cristianismo de izquierda e Iglesia popular," *Nueva Sociedad*, 82, pp. 102-109.

Cortés, Hernán (n.d.), "Carta enviada a la Reina Doña Juana y al Emperador Carlos V" (Primera Carta, 10 de julio de 1519), in *Cartas de relación de la conquista de América* (n.d.), Nueva España, México.

Costa-Filho (1990), "Planificación y futuro: una relación mai vista," *Pensamiento Iberoamericano*, 18, pp. 295-302.

Cox, Harvey (1965), *The Secular City: Urbanization and Secularization in Theological Perspective*, Macmillan, New York.

Cox, Harvey (1973), *The Seduction of the Spirit: The Use and Misuse of People's Religion,* Simon and Schuster, New York.

Cox, Harvey (1984), *Religion in the Secular City: Towards a Postmodern Theology*, Simon and Schuster, New York.

Cullen, Carlos (1981), "El ethos barroco. Ensayo de deffinición de la cultura latinoamericana a través de un concepto sapiencial," in *Racionalidad técnica y cultura latinoamericana. Ponecia y comunicaciones*, Tercer Seminario Internacional Interdisciplinar de Intercambio Cultural Alemán-Latinoamericano, Santiago, Chile, July, pp. 10-36.

Cuvillier, Armand (1971), *Sociología de la cultura*, El Ateneo, Buenos Aires.

Damen, Franz (1986), "Los Pentecostales: algunos rasgos," *Fe y Pueblo*, III, 14, pp. 31-49.

Davis, Kingsley; Casis, Ana (1957), "Urbanization in Latin America," in Hatt, P., and Reiss, A. (eds.), *Cities and Society: The Revised Reader in Urban Sociology*, The Free Press, New York, pp. 141-156.

Debesse, Paul (1991), *Mártires Latinoamericanos de hoy*, Paulinas, Santiago, Chile.

De Carvalho Azevedo, Marcelo (1983), "Evangélisation des sociétés sécularisées en Amérique Latine," *Foi et développement*, 105, Paris.

Deelen, G. (1980), *La Iglesia al encuentro del pueblo en América Latina: las comunidades de base en Brasil*, Informes Pro Mundi Vita, 81, Brussels.

DEI (Departamento Ecuménico de Investigaciones) (1980), "Centroamérica: cristianismo y revolución," *Cuadernos* 4, DEI, Costa Rica.

Delooz, Pierre (1988), "¿Fin de la religión popular en Occidente?" *Estudios*, Pro Mundi Vita, 6, Brussels.

Depestre, René (1982), "Participaçao africana nas culturas de América Latina e do Caribe," *Vozes*, 7, pp. 505-516.

De Roux, Rodolfo (coord.) (1981), *Historia general de la Iglesia en América Latina. Colombia y Venezuela*, VII, CEHILA, Sígueme, Salamanca.

De Roux, Rodolfo (1983), *Una iglesia en estado de alerta. Funciones sociales y funcionamiento del catolicismo colombiano: 1930-1980*, Servicio Colombiano de Comunicación Social, Bogota, Colombia.

DESAL (1969), *La marginalidad en América Latina: un ensayo de diagnóstico*, Herder, Barcelona.

Dewart, Leslie (1963), *Christianity and Revolution: The Lesson of Cuba*, Herder and Herder, New York.

Di Filippo, Armando (1982), "Distribución del ingreso, necesidades básicas, pobreza," *Pensamiento Iberoamericano*, 2, pp. 199-208.

Durkheim, Emile (1974), *Reglas del método sociológico*, La Pléyade, Buenos Aires.

Durkheim, Emile (1979), *Les formes élémentaires de la vie religieuse*, PUF, Paris.

Dussel, Enrique (1969), *El humanismo semita*, EUDEBA, Buenos Aires.

Dussel, Enrique (1972), *Historia de la Iglesia en América Latina. Coloniaje y liberación 1492/1972*, Nova Terra, Barcelona.

Dussel, Enrique (1980), "La chiesa latinoamericana da Medellín a Puebla (1968/1979)," in *Chiesa e Rivoluzioni nell'America Latina*, Paperbacks/ Saggi, 42, Newton Compton Editori, Rome, pp. 93-128.

Dussel, Enrique (1982), "Racismo, América Latina negra e teologia de liberataçao," *Vozes*, 7, pp. 485-504.

Dussel, Enrique (1983), *Historia general de la Iglesia en América Latina. Introducción general*, I/1, CEHILA, Sígueme, Salamanca.

Dussel, Enrique (1984), "Cultura latinoamericana y filosofía de la liberación," *Concordia*, 6, pp. 10-47.

Dussel, Enrique (1986), "Popular Religion as Oppression and Liberation: Hypotheses on its Past and its Present in Latin America," *Concilium* 186, pp. 82-96.

Duvignaud, Jean (1974), *Fêtes et civilization*, Weber, Geneva.

Duviols, Pierre (1976), "Religionese y represión en los Andes en los siglos XVI y XVII," in R. Jaulin (ed.), *El etnocidio a través de las Américas*, Siglo XXI, Mexico, pp. 84-94.

Eisler, Riane (1987), *The Chalice and the Blade*, Harper and Row, New York.

Eliade, Mircea (1957), *Mythes, rêves et mystères*, Gallimard, Paris.

Eliade, Mircea (1975), *Traité d'histoire des religions*, Payot, Paris.

Evans-Pritchard, E. E. (1971), *La religion des primitifs*, Payot, Paris.

Ezcurra, Ana María (1982), *La ofensiva neoconservadora*, IEPALA, Madrid.

Fajnzylber, Fernando (1989), "Industrialización en América Latina: De la 'caja negra' al 'casillero vocaio,'" *Cuadernos de la CEPAL*, 60, 1989.

Fals Borda, Orlando (1961), "La transformacón de América Latina y sus implicancias sociales y económicas," *La Nueva Economía*, I, 2, pp. 17-18.

Faria, Vilmar (1983), "Desenvolvimento, urganizaçao e mudanças na estrutura do emprego: A experiencia brasileira dos ultmos trinta anos," *Seminario sobre cambios recientes en las estructuras y estratificación sociales en América Latina. Análisis comparativo de paises y perspectivas regionales en los '80*, Santiago, Chile, September 12-15, 1983, CEPAL, Santiago, Chile.

Farrel, Gerardo (1976), *Iglesia y pueblo en Argentina: 1860-1974*, Patria Grande, Buenos Aires.

Farrel, Gerardo; Lumerman, Juan (1979), *Religiosidad popular y fe*, Patria Grande, Buenos Aires.

Fenn, Richard (1978), *Towards a Theory of Secularization*, SSSR, Monograph Series, Storrs, Connecticut.

FERES-AL (1969), *Religiosidade popular na America Latina. Projeto da pesquisa*, FERES-AL, Rio de Janeiro, Brasil.

Frazer, James George (1969), "Magic and religion," in N. Birnbaum and G. Lenzer (eds.), *Sociology and Religion: A Book of Readings*, Prentice Hall, New York, pp. 31-39.

Frías, Patricio (1977), *Cesantía y estrategias de supervivencia*, FLACSO, Santiago, Chile.

Frisque, Jean, et al. (1964), *Bilan du monde. Encyclopédie catholique du monde chrétien*, Eglise Vivante-FERES, Casterman, Pontigny.

Fromm, Erich (1971), *Psicoanálisis de la sociedad contemporánea*, Fondo de Cultura Económica, México. (First English edition, 1955).

Fukuyama, Francis (1989), "The End of History?" *The National Interest*, Summer.

Gabaja, Regina (1972), "Religión y secularización entre campesinos y obreros," *Revista Mexicana de Sociologia*, XXXIV, 2, pp. 193-244.

Galilea, Segundo (1977), *Pastoral popular y urbana en América Latina*, CLAR, Bogota, Colombia.

Gallardo, Helio (1990), "Francis Fukuyama y el triunfo del capitalismo burgués," *Pasos*, 27, pp. 28-41.

Garaudy, Roger (1979), *Comment l'homme devint humain*, J.A., Brussels.

García Canclini, Néstor (1982), *Las culturas populares en el capitalismo*, Nueva Imagen, Mexico.

García Márquez, Gabriel (1982), *La soledad de América Latina*, 1982 Nobel Conference, Stockholm.

Garcia-Ahumada, Enrique (1981), *Antropologia para personal apostólico*, ONAC, Santiago, Chile.

Garcia-Ahumada, Enrique, (1991), "La primera evangelización de América," *Mensaje*, 396, pp. 8-13.

Gatto, Franciso (1990), "Cambio tecnológico neofordista y reorganización producitiva," in Alburquerque, F., et al., *Revolución tecnológica y reorganización productiva*, ILPES/IEU-PUC, GEL, Santiago, Chile.

Germani, Gino (1969), *Politica y sociedad en una época de transición*, Paidós, Buenos Aires.

Gibson, Magnolia (1989), "Recientes teodicéias inspiradas na tradiçao oriental: Conservadorismo e ou mudança social," *Religiao e sociedade*, 83, 6, pp. 659-674.

Giménez, Gilberto (1978), *Cultura popular y religión en el Análuac*, Centro de Estudios Ecuménicos, Mexico.

Ginzburg, C. (1977), "Stregoneria, magia e superstizione in Europa fra Medio Evo ed etá moderna," *Ricerche di storia sociale e Religiosa*, pp. 128ss.

Godelier, Maurice (1977), *Horizon, trajets marxistes en anthropologie*, II, Maspero, Paris.

Godelier, Maurice (1978), "La part idéelle du réel," *L'Homme*, XVII, 3-4, pp. 155-188.

Gogolok, O. E. (1986), "Pastoral Aspects of Popular Religion in Brazil," *Concilium*, 186, pp. 105-112.

Gomes de Souza, Luis Alberto (1982), *Classes populares e Igreja nos caninhos da história*, VOZES, Petrópolis, Brazil.

Gomes de Souza, Luis Alberto (1986), "Secularizaçao em declinio e potencialidade transformadora do sagrado," *Revista Eclesiástica Brasilera*, 46, pp. 384-395.

Gomes de Souza, Luis Alberto (1987), "A utopia nao estará surgindo no meio de nos?" *Presença*, 10, pp. 70-82.

Gomes de Souza, Luis Alberto (1989), "O novo e a novidade no 'Mundo das creenças,'" in *Sinais dos tempos. Igrejas e seitas no Brasil*, ISER, pp. 43-51.

Gomes de Souza, Luis Alberto (1990), "Elementos éticos emergentes en las prácticas de los movimientos sociales," *Páginas*, 104, pp. 17-28.

Gómez Moreira, Aparecido (1987), "La JOC en México (1959-1985)," *Christus*, LII, 603/604, pp. 51-60.

González, José (1985), "El huanca y la cruz: Migración y transformación de la mitologia andina en las barriadas de Lima," *América Indigena*, XLV, 4, pp. 747-785.

González, José Luis (1987), *La religión popular en el Perú*, Instituto de Pastoral Andina, Cuzco.

Gramsci, Antonio (1954), *Letteratura e vita nazionale*, Turin.

Gramsci, Antonio (1972), *Introducción a la filosofía de la praxis*, Península, Barcelona.

Grebe, María Ester; Rajs, Dana; Segura, José (1971), "Enfermedades populares chilenas. Estudio Antropológico de cuatro casos," *Cuadernos de la Realidad Nacional*, 9, pp. 207-238.

Guarda, Gabriel (1973), *Los laicos en la cristianización de América*, Nueva Universidad, Santiago, Chile.

Gunder Frank, André (1978), *Dependent Accumulation and Underdevelopment*, Macmillan Press, London.

Gutiérrez, Gustavo (1983), *La fuerza histórica de los pobres*, CEP, Lima. In English, *The Power of the Poor in History*, Orbis Books, Maryknoll, New York.

Habermas, Jürgen (1975), *Problemas de legitimación en el capitalismo rardío*, Amorrortu, Buenos Aires.

Hauser, Arnold (1969), *Introducción a la historia del arte*, Guadarrama, Madrid.

Hernández, Guillermo (1990), *De los chibchas a la Colonia y a la República*, Paraninfo, Colombia.

Herskovits, Melville J. (1937), "African Gods and Catholic Saints in New World Religious Belief," *American Anthropologist*, XXXIX, pp. 635-643.

Hill, Martin (1973), *A Sociology of Religion*, Heinnman, London.

Hollenweger, Walter (1976), *El pentecostalismo, historia y doctrina*, La Aurora, Buenos Aires.

Hoornaert, Eduardo (1991), *O cristianismo moreno do Brasil*, Vozes, Petrópolis, Brazil.

Hoornaert, Eduardo; Azzi, R.; Van der Grijp, F.; Brod, B. (1983), *História geral da Igreja na America latina. História de Igreja no Brasil*, II/1, Paulinas/Vozes, Petrópolis, Brazil.

Houghton Pérez, Teresa (1979), "Características de la religiosidad popular," *Análisis*, 29, pp. 63-75.

Houtart, François (1977), "Religion et champ politique: cadre théorique pour l'étude des sociétés cápitalistes péripheriques," *Social Compass*, XXIV, 2-3, pp. 265-272.

Houtart, François (1979), "Religion et lutte des classes en Amérique Latine," *Social Compass*, XXVI, 2-3, pp. 115-236.

Houtart, François (1989), *Religión y modos de producción precapitalistas*, Iepala, Madrid.

Houtart, François; Pin, Emile (1965), *L'Eglise à l'heure de l'Amérique Latine*, Casterman, Tournai.

Hugon, Philippe (1980), "Dualisme sectoriel ou soumission des formes de production au capital, peut on dépasser le débat?" *Revue Tiers Monde*, XXI, pp. 237-244.

Hurbon, Laennec (1972), *Dieu dans le Vudu Haitien*, Payot, Paris.

Hurbon, Laennec (1987), "Nuevos movimientos religiosos en el Caribe," *Cristianismo y Sociedad*, XXV/3, 93, pp. 37-63.

ICODES (1970), *Aspectos de la religiosidad popular en Colombia*, Instituto Colombiano de Desarrollo Social, Bogota, Colombia.

IEPALA (1982), *Las relaciones entre cristianismo y revolución*, Encuentro sobre las Relaciones entre Cristianismo y Revolución, Madrid (December 5-12, 1981) IEPALA, Madrid.

"Iglesia y clase obrera en América Latina," *Revista Mexicana de Sociologia*, XLIX, 3, 1987.

ILPES (1986), *Coloquio internacional sobre nuevas orientaciones para la planificación en economías de mercado*, ILPES, Santiago, Chile.

Instituto Histórico Centroamericano (1979), "Fe cristiana y revolución sandinista en Nicaragua," in *Apuntes para el estudio de la realidad nacional*, 3, Managua.

Irarrázaval, Diego (1978), *Religión del pobre y liberación en Climbote*, CEP, Lima.

Irarrázaval, Diego (1981), "Nicaragua, una sorprendente religiosidad," in *Religión y política en América Central*, DEI, Costa Rica.

Irarrázaval, Diego (1990a), "500 años vistos por la fe de los indígenas," *Pastoral Popular*, 199, pp. 38-41.

Irarrázaval, Diego (1990b), "Utopia autóctona, progreso moderno, Reinado de Dios," *Tópicos*, 90, 1, Santiago, Chile, pp. 183-208.

Isambert, François (1974), "Les ouvrières et l'église catholique," *Revue Française de Sociologie*, XV, pp. 529-551.

Isambert, François (1976a), "Religion (sécularisation)," in *Encyclopaedia Universalis*, XIV, pp. 573-589.

Isambert, François (1976b), "La sécularisation interne du christianisme,"

*Revue Française de Sociologie*, XVII, pp. 573-589.

Isambert, François-André (1982), *Le sens du sacré, fête et religion populaire*, Minuit, Paris.

Jaulin, R. (ed.) (1976), *El etnocidio a través de las Américas*, Siglo XXI, México.

Jiménez, Gilberto (1978), *Cultura popular y religión en el Anáhuac*, Centro de Estudios Ecuménicos, Mexico.

Johansson, Cristián (1990), "Religiosidad Popular entre Medellín y Puebla: Antecedentes y desarrollo," *Anales de la Facultad de Teología*, XLI, Pontificia Universidad Católica de Chile, Santiago, Chile.

Johansson, Cristián; Pérez, I. (1987), "Bibliografía sobre religiosidad popular," *Teología y vida*, XXXVIII, 1-2, pp. 105-173.

John Paul II (1981), *Encyclical Laborem Exercens*, Rome.

Kanbur, Ravi (1990), "Pobreza y desarrollo: El informe sobre el desarrollo humano y el informe sobre el desarrollo mundial, 1990," *Pensamiento Iberoamericano*, 18, pp. 203-221.

Kerkhofs, I. (1989), "Panorama des valeurs en Europe: Permanence et adaptation," in Colloquium: L'Ethique dans le débat public, Bruxelles, January, 1989.

Klaiber, Jeffrey (coord.) (1987), *Historia general de la Iglesia en América Latina. Perú, Bolivia y Ecuador*, VIII, CEHILA, Sígueme, Salamanca.

Kloppenburg, Boaventura (1977), "La irrealidad de la magia o brujeria," *Medellín*, III, 9, pp. 55-73.

Kloppenburg, Boaventura (1978), "Movimientos religiosos autónomos en América Latina," *Medellín*, IV, 15-16, pp. 456-473.

Kloppenburg, Boaventura (1980), "Los afro-brasileños y la umbanda," *Medellín*, VI, 24, pp. 517-530.

Konetzke, Richard (1971), *América Latina. La época colonial*, Siglo XXI, Mexico.

Kowarick, Lucio (1975), *Capitalismo e marginalidade na America Latina*, Paz e Terra, Rio de Janeiro.

Krausz, Ernest (1971), "Religion and secularization: A matter of definitions," *Social Compass*, XVIII, 2, pp. 203-212.

Kudo, Tokihiro (1980), *Práctica religiosa y proyecto histórico II*, CEP, Lima.

Kuhn, Thomas (1971), *La estructura de las revoluciones cientificas*, Fondo de Cultura Económica, Mexico.

Kush, Rodolfo (1970), *El pensamiento indigena y popular en América*, Hachette, Buenos Aires.

Kush, Rodolfo (1976), *Geocultura del hombre americano*, García Cambiero, Buenos Aires.

Labbens, Jean (1978), *Sociologie de la pauvreté*, Gallimard, Paris.

Lacalle, Luis Alberto (1990), "Religiones y nuevo gobierno," *Carta*, OBSUR, April.

Lafaye, Jacques (1973), *Quetzalcóatl y Guadalupe. La formación de la conciencia nacional en México*, Fondo de Cultura Económica, Mexico.

Lagos, Humberto (1983), *La función de las minorías religiosas, el caso del protestantismo chileno en el período 1973-1981 del gobierno militar*, Doctoral dissertation in sociology, Catholic University of Louvain, Louvain, Belgium.

Lagos, Humberto (1988), *Crisis de la esperanza. Religión y autoritarismo en*

*Chile*, PRESOR-LAR, Santiago, Chile.

Lagos, Humberto; Chacón, Arturo (1986), *Religión y proyecto político autoritario*, PRESOR-LAR, Santiago, Chile.

Lalive, Ch.; Zylberberg, J. (1973), "Desarrollo desigual, conciencia de clase y religión," *Cuadernos de la Realidad Nacional*, 17, pp. 105-151.

Lalive d'Epinay, Christian (1968), *El refugio de las masas*, Ed. del Pacifico, Pacífico, Santiago, Chile.

Lalive d'Epinay, Christian (1975), *Religion, dynamique sociale et dépendance*, Mouton, Paris.

Landim, Lailah (org.) (1989), *Sinais dos tempos. Igrejas e seitas no Brasil*, ISER, Rio de Janeiro.

Lanternari, Vittorio (1965), *Movimientos religiosos de libertad y salvación de los pueblos oprimidos*, Seix Barral, Barcelona.

Lanternari, Vittorio (1982), "La religion populaire. Perspective historique et anthropologique," *Archives de Sciences Sociales des Religions*, 53/1, pp. 121-143.

Las Casas, Bartolomé de (1942), *Del único modo de atraer a todos los pueblos a la verdadera religión*, Fondo de Cultura Económica, Mexico.

Las Casas, Bartolomé de (1972), *Brevísima relación de la destrucción de las Indias*, Nascimento, Santiago, Chile.

Lazarte, Rolando (1990), "Detrás de las paredes: El hombre en la sociología," *Cristianismo y Sociedad*, XXVIII/2, 104, pp. 79-91.

Lejarza, Fidel de (1949), "Religiosidad y celo misionero de Hernán Cortes," *Anuario de Estudios Americanos*, Madrid, 1/341.

Lévi-Strauss, Claude (1962), *La pensée sauvage*, Plon, Paris.

Lévy-Bruhl, Lucien (1977), "L'âme primitive," *Archives de Sciences Sociales des Religions*, 43/1, pp. 19-22.

Lewis, Oscar (1961), *Antropología de la Pobreza*, Fondo de Cultura Económica, Mexico.

Lewis, Oscar (1969), *La vida. Una familia puertorriqueña en la cultura de la pobreza—San Juan y Nueva York*, J. Moritz, Mexico.

Lewis, Oscar (1988), "La cultura de la pobreza," in Mario Bessols et al. (comp.), *Antología de sociología urbana*, UNAM, Mexico, pp. 240-251.

Lewis, Oscar (1990), *La vida*, Joaquin Moritz, Mexico.

Linz, Juan (1980), "Religion and Politics in Spain: From Conflict to Consensus above Cleavage," *Social Compass*, XXVII, 2/3, pp. 255-277.

Lomnitz, Larissa (1975), *Cómo sobreviven los marginados*, Siglo XXI, México.

López, Baltasar (1972), "Rasgos del catolicismo popular mexicano," *Servir*, VIII, 41-42, pp. 523-536.

Lozano, Javier (1979), "Cultura y religiosidad popular. Pespectivas desde Puebla," in *Puebla: Religiosidad, popular*, Colección Puebla, 14.2, CELAM, Bogota, Colombia, pp. 51-78.

Luckmann, Thomas (1973), *La religión invisible*, Sígueme, Salamanca.

Lukes, S. (1985), "Some Problems about Rationality," in R. Bocock and K. Thompson (ed.), *Religion and Ideology*, Manchester University Press, Manchester, pp. 100-109.

MacLuhan, Marshall (1982), "Los hemisferios y los medios masivos," in Jean Duvignaud (comp.), *Sociología del conocimiento*, Fondo de Cultura Económica, Mexico, pp. 67-80.

Maduro, Otto (1982), *Religion and Social Conflict*, Orbis Books, Maryknoll, N.Y.

Maduro, Otto (1987), "La démocratie chrétienne et l'option de liberation des oprimés dans le catholicisme latinoaméricaine," *Concilium*, 213, pp. 111-125.

Maffesoli, Michel (1990), "El desarrollo de la vida cotidiana en el mundo moderno," Address given in the Facultad de Sociologia, Universidad Academia de Humanismo Cristiano, Santiago, Chile, November.

Magendzo, Abraham (ed.) (1991), *¿Superando la racionalidad instrumental?* PIIE, Santiago, Chile.

Magnet, Alberto (1953), *Nuestros vecinos justicialistas*, Pacífico, Santiago, Chile.

Maldonado, Luis (1975), *Religiosidad popular*, Cristiandad, Madrid.

Mallimaci, Fortunato (1988), *El catolicismo integral en la Argentina (1930-1946)*, Biblos, Buenos Aires.

Mannheim, Karl (1954), *Ideology and Utopia: An introduction to the Sociology of Knowledge*, Harcourt Brace, New York.

Mariátegui, José Carlos (1979), "El factor religioso," in *Siete ensayos de interpretación de la realidad peruana*, ERA, Mexico, pp. 146-174.

Marins, José; Trevisan, Tolide; Chanona, Carolee (1978), *Praxis de los padres de América Latina. Documentos de las Conferencias Episcopales de Medellín a Puebla (1968-1978)*, Paulinas, Bogota, Colombia.

Martin, David (1969), *The Religious and the Secular*, London.

Martin, David (1978), *A General Theory of Secularization*, Basil Blackwell, Oxford.

Martín, Gustavo (1986), "Magia, religión y poder: Los cultos afroamericanos", *Nueva Sociedad*, 82, pp. 157-170.

Martín Baró, Ignacio (1987), "El latino indolente. Carácter ideológico del fatalismo latinoamericano," in M. Montero (coord.), *Psicología política latinoamericana*, Panado, Venezuela.

Martinez, Abelino (1989), *Las sectas en Nicaragua, oferta y demanda de salvación*, DEI, Costa Rica.

Martínez, E.; Luengo, E.; García O.L. (1979), "Religiosidad popular urbana," *Christus*, 44, 522, pp. 25-38.

Martínez, Javier; Tironi, Eugenio; Weinstein, Eugenia (1990), *Personas y escenarios en la violencia colectiva*, SUR, Santiago, Chile.

Marx, Karl and Engels, F. (1979), "Contribución a la crítica de la filosofía del derecho de Hegel," in *Sobre la religión*, H. Assmann, R. Mate (eds.), Sígueme, Salamanca. (Original edition, Paris, 1844.)

Marx, Karl; Engels, Friedrich (1972), *L'Ideologie allemande*, Ed. Sociales, Paris.

Marzal, Juan F. (1967), *Cambio social en América Latina. Crítica de algunas interpretaciones dominantes en las ciencias sociales*, Solar/Hachette, Buenos Aires.

Marzal, Juan F. (1979), *Dependencia e independencia. Las alternativas de la sociología latinoamericana en el siglo XX*, Centro de Investigaciones Sociológicas, Madrid.

Marzal, Manuel (1970), "La religiosidad de la cultura de la pobreza," *Catequesis Latinoamericana*, 2, 7, pp. 305-381, and 8, pp. 494-512.

Marzal, Manuel (1977), *Estudios sobre religión campesina*, PUC, Lima.

Marzal, Manuel (1986), "Análisis etnológico del sincretismo iberoamericano," *Cristianismo y Sociedad*, XXIV, 88, pp. 27-40.

Marzal, Manuel (1988), *La transformación religiosa peruana*, Pontificia Universidad Católica del Perú, Lima.

Marzal, Manuel (1990), "Catolicismo y pluralismo en el Perú contemporáneo," *Cristianismo y Sociedad*, 106, pp. 9-21.

Maslow, Abraham (1963), *Motivación y personalidad*, Sagitario, Barcelona.

Maturana, Humberto; Varela, Francisco (1980), *Autopoiesis and Cognition: The Realization of the Living*, Riedel, Boston.

Mauss, Marcel (1980), *Sociologie et anthropologie*, PUF, Paris.

Max-Neef, Manfred; Elizalde, Antonio; Hopenhayn, Martin (1986), "Desarrollo a escala humana. Una opción para el futuro," *Development Dialogue* (special issue), CEPAUR/Dag Hammarskjöld Foundation, Upsala, Sweden.

Medellín, Fernando (1985), "Religiones populares contra la emancipación," *América Indígena*, XLV, 4, pp. 625-646.

Medina, José Toribio (1956), *Historia del Tribunal de la Inquisició de Lima*, Fondo Histórico y Bibliográfico J. T. Medina, Santiago, Chile, 2 vols.

Mendoza, Andrés (1979), *La Iglesia en México*, Informes Pro Mundi Vita, 15, Brussels.

Merton, Robert (1972), "La sociología del conocimiento" in *Teoria y estructuras sociales*, Fondo de Cultura Económica, Mexico, pp. 437-522.

Mesters, Carlos (1975), *Una iglesia que nace del pueblo*, Documento 17-18, MIEC-JECI, Lima.

Methol Ferré, Alberto (1977), "Marco histórico de la religiosidad popular," in *Iglesia y religiosidad popular en América Latina*, Secretariado General CELAM, Bogota, Colombia, pp. 45-75.

Meyer, Jean (1975), *La christiade. L'église, l'état et le peuple dans la révolution méxicaine, 1926-1929*, Payot, Paris.

Meyer, Jean (1989), *Historia de los cristianos en América Latina*, Siglos XIX y XX, Vuelta, Mexico.

Michelat, Guy; Simon, Michel (1978), "Catholiques déclarés et irréligieux communisants: Vision du monde et perception du champ politique," *Archives de Sciences Sociales des Religions,* 35, pp. 57-111.

Michelat, Guy; Simon, Michel (1982), "Une état du catholicisme en France," *Archives des Sciences Sociales des Religions*, 53/2, pp. 193-204.

Míguez Bonino, José (1974), "La piedad popular en América Latina," *Concilium*, 96, pp. 440-447.

Mires, Fernando (1988), *La rebelión permanente*, Siglo XXI, Mexico.

Monast, Jacques (1969), *On les croyait chrétiens. Les aymaras*, CERF, Paris.

Morandé, Pedro (1984), *Cultura y modernización en América Latina*, Cuadernos del Instituto de Sociología, Pontificia Universidad Católica de Chile, Santiago, Chile.

Morandé, Pedro (1986), "Religiosidad popular como contracultura de la Ilustración," *Nexo*, 7, pp. 54-60.

Moreno, Jaime (ed.), (1975), *Religiosidad y fe en América Latina*, Mundo, Santiago, Chile.

Morin, Edgar (1990), "L'homme domine-t-il sa planète?," *Le Nouvel Observateur*, Collection Dossiers, 2.

Morren, Lucien (1989), "Science, technologie et valeurs spirituelles," *Nouvelle Revue Théologique*, III/1, pp. 83-96.

Muñoz, Ronaldo (1983), *La Iglesia en el pueblo. Hacia una eclesiología latinoamericana*, CEP, Lima.

Muñoz, Ronaldo (1988), *El Dios de los cristianos*, Paulinas, Santiago, Chile.

Muratorio, Blanca (1982), *Etnicidad, evangelización y protesta en el Ecuador*, CIESE, Quito.

Nash, June (1979), *We Eat the Mines and the Mines Eat Us*, Columbia University Press, New York.

Navarro, Julio, et al. (1975), "Devoción a la 'animitá' de la Estación Central," in *Religiosidad y fe en América Latina*, 2, Mundo, Santiago, Chile, pp. 189-193.

Nesti, Arnaldo (1980), "Religion et classe ouvrière dans les sociétés industrielles (une hypothèse de recherche)," *Social Compass*, XXVI 2/3, pp. 169-190.

Niebuhr, Richard (1954), *The Social Sources of Denominationalism*, World Publishing, New York.

Opazo, Andrés (1987), *Costa Rica: La Iglesia Católica y el orden social*, DEI, San José, Costa Rica.

Ottone, Ernesto (1991), *¿Un futuro democrático para América del Sur?* FLACSO, Serie Contribuciones, 73, Santiago, Chile.

Pannet, Robert (1974), *Le catholicisme populaire: 30 ans après—la France, pays de mission?*, Centurion, Paris.

Parker, Cristián, (1986a), *Religión y clases subalternas urbanas en una sociedad dependiente: un estudio de caso en Chile*, CSRS, Catholic University of Louvain, Louvain, Belgium.

Parker, Cristián, (1986b), *Iglesia y pueblo en América Latina*, Documento de Trabajo, 2, CERC, Santiago, Chile.

Parker, Cristián, (1986c), "Popular Religion and Protest against Oppression: The Chilean Example", *Concilium*, XXII, 186, pp. 28-35.

Parker, Cristián, (1987), "Anticlericalismo y religión popular en la génesis del movimiento obrero en Chile 1900-1920," *Revista Mexicana de Sociología*, XLIX, 3, pp. 185-204.

Parker, Cristián, (1989), "Cultura e identidad popular en Chile," in *Teología de la liberación y realidad chilena*, Centro Ecuménico Diego de Medellín, Santiago, Chile.

Parker, Cristián, (1990), "El aporte de la Iglesia a la sociedad chilena bajo el régimen militar," *Cuadernos Hispanoamericanos*, 482-83, Madrid, pp. 31-48.

Parker, Cristián, (1991a), "Modernización y cambio en el sistema de necesidades: el nuevo fetichismo de la mercancía tecnotrónica," *Tópicos 90*, 2, pp. 151-158.

Parker, Cristián, (1991b), "Christianity and Popular Movements in the Twentieth Century," K. Aman and C. Parker (eds.), *Popular Culture in Chile*, Westview Press, Boulder-San Francisco-Oxford, pp. 41-68.

Parker, Cristián, (1992a), "Mentalidad popular y religión en América Latina," in H. Vidal, *Hermenéuticas de lo Popular*, Institute for Study of Ideologies and Literature, Minneapolis, Minnesota, pp. 73-126.

Parker, Cristián, (1992b), "Perspective critique de la sociologie de la religion en Amerique Latine," in F. Houtart et al., *Rupture Sociales et Religión*, Editions L'Harmattan, Paris, pp. 35-52.

Parker, C.; Barra, W.; Recuero, M.A.; Sahli, P. (1982), *Rasgos de cultura popular en poblaciones de Pudahuel*, Vicaria Zona Oeste, Archdiocese of Santiago, Chile.

Paviani, Aldo (1985), "La urbanización en América Latina. El proceso de constitución de periferias en las áreas metropolitanas," *Revista Interamericana de Planificación*, SIAP, XIS, 73, pp. 74-95.

Paz, Octavio (1973), "Prefacio" to Jacques Lafaye, *Quetzalcóatl y Guadalupe. La formación de la conciencia nacional en México*, Fondo de Cultura Económica, Mexico.

Paz, Octavio (1990), *El laberinto de la soledad*, Fondo de Cultura Económica, Buenos Aires.

Pearce, David (1990), "Población, pobreza y medio ambiente," *Pensamiento Iberoamericano*, 18, pp. 223-258.

Perani, Claudio (1981), "Comunidades eclesiales de base e movimento popular," *Cuadernos do CEAS*, 75, pp. 25-33.

Pereira, Cristóbal (1986), "Religiosidad pervive en Cuba revolucionaria," *Puebla*, 8, 35, pp. 13-15.

Pereira de Queiroz, María Isaura (1968), *Réforme et révolution dans les sociétés traditionelles*, Anthropos, Paris.

Pike, Fredrick (1970), "South America's Multifaceted Catholicism: Glimpses of Twentieth-Century Argentina, Chile, and Peru," in H. Landsberger (ed.), *The Church and Social Change in Latin America*, University of Notre Dame, Notre Dame, Indiana, pp. 39-53.

Pike, Fredrick (1977), "La Iglesia en Latinoamérica de la independencia a nuestros días," in *Nueva historia de la Iglesia, V, La iglesia en el mundo moderno (1848 a Vaticano II)*, Cristiandad, Madrid.

Pin, Emile (1963), *Elementos para una sociología del catolicismo latino-americano*, FERES, Freiburg.

Piña, Carlos (1981), *Sector informal. Estrategias ocupacionales y orientaciones ideológicas*, Monografía 20, Orr/PREALC, Santiago, Chile.

Pinto, Aníbal (1973), *Inflación: Raíces estructurales*, Fondo de Cultura Económica, Mexico.

Pinto, Aníbal (1985), "Reto y metropolización: Razones e implicaciones," *Pensamiento Iberoamericano*, 7, pp. 23-30.

Pinto, Aníbal; Di Filippo, Armando (1978), "Desarrollo y pobreza en América Latina; un enfoque histórico estructural," *Estudios Sociales*, 18, pp. 11-27.

Plath, Oreste (1981), *Folklore médico chileno*, Nascimento, Santiago, Chile.

Poblete, Renato (1970), "Aspectos sociológicos de la religiosidad popular," *Mensaje*, 51, pp. 10, 11 and 14.

Poblete, Renato (1975), "¿Secularización en América Latina?" in *Religiosidad y fe en América Latina*, Mundo, Santiago, Chile, pp. 33-49.

"Politique et religion en Amérique Latine," *Social Compass*, XX (special issue), 1979.

Pollak-Eltz, Angelina (1974), "El catolicismo popular en Venezuela," *Mensaje Iberoamericano*, 99, pp. 8-11.

Portelli, Hugues (1974), *Gramsci et la question religieuse*, Anthropos, Paris.

Prandi, Carlo (1976), "Religion et classes subalternes en Italie. Trente années de recherches italiennes," *Archives des Sciences Sociales des Religions*, 42, pp. 93-139.

PREALC (1986), *Cambio y polarización ocupacional en Centroamérica*, PREALC, San José, Costa Rica.

PREALC (1988), *Deuda social, ¿Qué es, cuánto es y cómo se paga?* PREALC, Santiago, Chile.

PREALC (1990), *El sector informal. Más allá de la regulación*, PREALC, Santiago, Chile.

Prezia, Benedito; Hoornaert, Eduardo (1989), *Esta terra tinha dono*, CEHILA POPULAR-CIMI, FTD, São Paulo.

Prien, Hans Jürgen (1985), *La historia del cristianismo en América Latina*, Sígueme, Salamanca.

Programa Ecuménico de Estudios del Cristianismo (1983), *La Iglesia de los pobres en América Latina: Antología*, ECO-SEPADE, Santiago, Chile.

Puebla Final Document, Conferencia General del Episcopado Latino-americano (1979), *La evangelización en el presente y en el futuro de América Latina (Documento de Puebla)*, Conferencia Episcopal de Chile, Santiago, Chile. In English, found in John Eagleson and Philip Scharper, eds., *Puebla and Beyond: Documentation and Commentary*, Maryknoll, New York, Orbis Books, 1979.

Puech, Henri Ch. (dir.) (1982), *Movimientos religiosos derivados de la aculturación*, Siglo XXI, Madrid.

Quijano, Aníbal (1972), "La constitución del 'mundo' en la marginalidad urbana," EURE, III, 5, pp. 90-106.

Razeto, Luis, et al. (1983), *Organizaciones económicas populares*, Programa de Economía del Trabajo, Academia de Humanismo Cristiano, Santiago, Chile.

Read, Margaret (1966), *Culture, Health, and Disease*, Tavistock, London.

Remy, Jean; Voyé, Lilian (1976), *La ciudad y la urbanización*, Instituto de Estudios de Administración Local, Madrid.

Ribeiro de Oliveira, Pedro (1972), "Le catholicisme populaire en Amérique Latine," *Social Compass*, XIX, 4, pp. 567-584.

Ribeiro de Oliveira, Pedro (1979), "Catholicisme populaire et hégémonie bourgeoise au Brésil," *Archives des Sciences Sociales des Religions*, 47/1, pp. 53-79.

Ribeiro de Oliveira, Pedro (1985a), "Comentarios a la visita de Juan Pablo II," *Jornal do Brasil*, April 13.

Ribeiro de Oliveira, Pedro (1985b), *Religiao e dominaçao de classe. Gênese estructura e funçao do catolicismo romanizado no Brasil*, Vozes, Petrópolis, Brazil.

Ricard, Robert (1947), *La conquista espiritual de México*, Jus, Mexico.

Ricci, F. (1977), *Gramsci dans le texte*, Eds. Sociales, Paris.

Richard, Pablo (1976), *Cristianos por el socialismo*, Sígueme, Salamanca.

Richard, Pablo (1980), "Religiosité populaire en Amérique Latine, histoire de l'interpretation," *Amérique Latine*, 4, pp. 41-45.

Richard, Pablo; Irarrázaval, Diego (1981), *Religión y política en América Central. Hacia una nueva interpretación de la religiosidad popular*, DEI, Costa Rica.

Richard, Pablo; Meléndez, Guillermo (eds.) (1982), *La Iglesia de los pobres en América Latina Central*, DEI, Costa Rica.

Rodrigues Brandão, Carlos (1987), "Creencias e identidad: campo religioso y cambio cultural," *Cristianismo y Sociedad*, XXV/3, 93, pp. 65-106.

Rodrigues Brandão, Carlos (1988), "El banquete de los brujos," in Gutiérrez E. Manuel (comp.), *Mito y ritual en América*, Alhambra, Madrid, pp. 397-446.

Rodríguez, Daniel (1981), "Discusiones en torno al concepto de estrategias de supervivencia," *Demografía y Economía*, XV, 2 (46).

Rolim, Francisco Cartaxo (1979), "Pentecôtisme et société au Brésil," *Social Compass*, XXVI, 2-3, pp. 345-372.

Rolim, Francisco Cartaxo (1980), *Religiao e classes populares*, Vozes, Petrópolis, Brazil.

Rolim, Francisco Cartaxo (1989), "A face conservadora do pentecostalismo," *Religiao e Sociedade*, 83, 6, pp. 645-658.

Rosenthal, Gert (1991), "Balance preliminar de la economia de América Latina y el Caribe, 1990," *Comercio Exterior*, 41, 3, pp. 281-303.

Rueda, Marco Vinicio (1982), *La fiesta religiosa campesina, (Andes ecuatorianos)*, EDUC, Quito.

Ruiz-Tagle, Jaime; Urmenteta, Roberto (1984), *Los trabajadores del Programa de Empleo Mínimo*, PET, Academia de Humanismo Cristiano, Santiago, Chile.

Rutherford, John (1971), "The Church," in *Mexican Society during the Revolution: A Literary Approach*, Clarendon Press, Oxford, pp. 279-292.

Saint Martin, Monique de (1984), "Quelque questions à propos du penetecôtisme au Brésil," *Actes de la Recherche en Sciences Sociales*, 52/53, pp. 111-114.

Salas, Alberto M. (1986), *Tres cronistas de Indias*, Fonda de Cultura Económica, Mexico.

Salinas, Maximiliano (1980), *Clotario Blest, profeta de Dios contra el capitalismo*, Rehue, Santiago, Chile.

Salinas, Maximiliano (1984), "Cristianismo popular en Chile: 1880-1920," *Nueva Historia*, 12, Santiago, Chile.

Salinas, Maximiliano (1987), *Historia del pueblo de Dios en Chile*, CEHILA/Rehue, Santiago, Chile.

Salinas, Maximiliano (1991), *Canto a lo divino y espiritualidad del oprimido en Chile*, Universidad Pontificia de Salamanca, Impr. Soc. La Unión, Santiago, Chile.

Salvat, Pablo (1991), "Hacia una nueva racionalidad. La tarea de construir un paradigma basado en los derechos humanos," in Abraham Magendzo, *¿Superando la racionalidad instrumenta?* PIIE, Santiago, Chile, pp. 119-147.

Samandú, Luis Eduardo (1989a), "El universo religioso popular en Centroamerica," *Estudios centroamericanos*, 51, pp. 81-95.

Samandú, Luis Eduardo (1989b), "Estudios de lo religioso popular en Guatemala, Nicarague y Costa Rica (inventarización preliminar)," *Estudios centroamericanos*, 51, pp. 151-155.

Sánchez, José (1990), "Los carismáticos y la política en una parroquia popular de Lima," *Cristianismo y Sociedad*, XXVIII, 106, pp. 23-42.

Santo Domingo Final Document, Fourth Conferencia General de Episcopado Latinoamericano (1992), *Nueva Evangelización, Promoción humana, Cultura Cristiana, Jesucristo ayer, hoy y siempre (Documento de Santo Domingo)*, Episcopal Conference of Chile, Santiago, Chile. In English, found in Alfred Hennelly, *Santo Domingo and Beyond*, Maryknoll, New York, Orbis Books, 1993.

Santore, Salvador (1981), "Los muertos se quedan con nostros. El velorio del angelito," *Liturgia*, 46, pp. 97-104.

Scannone, Juan Carlos (1978a), "Religion, lenguaje y sabiduría de los pueblos," *Stromata*, 34, pp. 27-42.

Scannone, Juan Carlos (1978b), "La racionalidad científico-tecnológica y la racionalidad sapiencial de la cultura latinoamericana," in *Racionalidad técnica y cultura latinoamericana. Ponencia y comunicaciones*, Tercer Seminario Internacional Interdisciplinar de Intercambio Cultural Alemán-Latinoamericanao (July), Santiago, Chile, pp. 461-467.

Scannone, Juan Carlos (ed.) (1984), *Sabiduria popular, símbolo y filosofía. Diálogo internacional en torno a una interpretación latinoamericana*, Guadalupe, Buenos Aires.

Scannone, Juan Carlos (1985), "Enfoques teológico-pastorales latinoamericanos de la religiosidad popular," *La Antigua*, 26, pp. 55-67.

Schaden, Egon (1982), "El mesianismo en América del Sur," in H. Ch. Puech (dir.), *Movimientos religiosos derivados de la aculturación*, Siglo XXI, Madrid, pp. 80-151.

Schaff, Adam (1973), *Langage et connaissance*, Anthropos, Paris.

Schaff, Adam (1987), "La crisis de la civilización industrial," *Leviatán*, 29/30, pp. 115-126.

Schmitt, J.C. (1986), "Religion populaire et culture folklorique," *Annates*, E.S.C., XXXI, pp. 941-953.

SEDOC (1979), *Una Iglesia que nace del pueblo*, Sígueme, Salamanca.

Seiblitz, Zelia (1985), "Umbanda e potencial contestador da religao," *Simposio sobre religión popular*, 45o Congreso Internacional de Americanistas, Bogota, July 1-7.

Silva Gotay, Samuel (1983), *El pensamiento cristiano revolucionario en América Latina y El Caribe. Implicaciones de la teología de la liberación la sociología de la religión*, Sigueme/Cordillera San Juan, Puerto Rico.

Silva Herzog, Jesús (1964), *Breve historia de la Revolutión Mexicana*, Fondo de Cultura Económica, Mexico.

Smith, Brian (1982), *The Church and Politics in Chile*, Princeton: Princeton University Press.

*Social Compass*, XX, April (special issue), 1973.

Soneira, Jorge Abelardo; Lumerman, Juan Pedro (1986), *Iglesia y nación*, Guadalupe, Buenos Aires.

Sosa, Antonio; Sosa, María Elena; Hernández, Mercedes (1973), "El culto a María Lionza: ¿Una religión venezolana?" SIC, XXCVI, 354, pp. 158-160.

Sosa, José (1989), "Desarrollo económico y concentración urbana en América Latina," *Comercio Exterior*, 39, 9, pp. 743-750.

Stanford Central America Action Network (1983), "The Church and Liberation," in *Revolution in Central America*, Westview Press, Boulder, Colorado, pp. 344-378.

Süess, Paulo (1979), *O catolicismo popular no Brasil*, Loyola, São Paulo, Brazil.

Süess, Paulo (1990), "A multiplicidade das vozes na conquista espiritual das Americas," Report presented to *Al Seminario Internacional 500 Años del Cristianismo en América Latina*, July 18-21, Santiago, Chile.

Tennekes, H. (1985), *El movimiento pentecostal en la sociedad chilena*, CIREN, Iquique, Chile.

*Teologia y Vida* (1987), XXVIII, 1-2, pp. 105-173.

Titiev, Misha (1979), "A Fresh Approach to the Problem of Magic and Religion," in William A. Lessa and Evon Z. Vogt (eds.), *Reader in Comparative Religion*, Harper and Row, New York.

Todorov, Tzvetan (1982), *La conquête de l'Amerique. La question de l'autre*, Seuil, Paris.

Touraine, Alain (1977), "La marginalidad urbana," *Revista Mexicana de Sociología*, XXXIX, pp. 1105-1142.

Triana, Humberto (1987), *Evangelización y sociedades negras en América Latina*, Pro Mundi Vita, Brussels.

Troeltsch, Ernst (1950), *The Social Teachings of the Christian Churches*, George Allen & Unwin, London.

Trotter, Robert (1976), "The Other Hemisphere," *New Science*, 109.

Turner, Bryan (1988), *La religión y la teoria social*, Fondo de Cultura Económica, Mexico. In English, *Religion and Social Theory*, Heineman, London, 1983.

United Nations (1990), *Demographic Yearbook*, Department of Social and Economic Affairs, Washington.

United Nations Development Programme (1994), *La Dimensión Política del Desarrollo Humano, Avance para la Cumbre Hemisférica de Miami de diciembre 1994*, PNUD, Santiago, Chile.

Uribe, Juan (1974), *La Virgen de Andacollo y el Niño Dios de Sotaqui*, (n.p.), Santiago, Chile.

Urmeneta, Roberto (1988), *Les nouveaux composants du "secteur informel urbain": Le cas du capitalisme autoritaire au Chili*, Doctoral dissertation in sociology, Catholic University of Louvain, Louvain, Belgium.

Valderrey, José (1985), "Las sectas en Centroamérica," *Pro Mundi Vita*, 100, Brussels.

Vallier, Iván (1971), "Las elites religiosas en América Latina: Catolicismo, liderazgo y cambio social," in S. M. Lipset and A. Solari, *Elites y desarrollo en América Latina*, Paidós, Buenos Aires, pp. 150-189.

Van Kessel, Juan (1977), *El desierto canta a María. Bailes chinos de los santuarios del Norte Grande*, photocopy, Santiago, Chile.

Van Kessel, Juan (1988), *Lucero del desierto*, Free University of Amsterdam/CIREN, Iquique, Chile.

Vargas Ugarte, Rubén (1956), *Historia del culto de Maráa en iberoamérica y de sus imágenes y santuarios más celebrados*, Talleres Gráficos Jura, Madrid, 2 vols.

Vásquez de Acuña, Isidoro (1956), *Costuníbres religiosas de Chiloé y su raigambre hispana*, Centro de Estudios Antropológicos, Universidad de Chile, Santiago, Chile.

Vatican, Secretary of State (1975), *Annuarium Statisticum Ecclesiae*, Vatican City.

Vatican, Secretary of State (1988), *Annuarium Statisticum Ecclesiae*, Vatican City.

Veckemans, Roger (1969), *La prerrevolución latinoamericana*, DESAL/Troquel, Buenos Aires.

Vega-Centeno, Imelda (1985), *Aprismo popular: Mito, cultura e historia*, Tarea, Lima.

Vega-Centeno, Imelda (1986), *Ideologia y cultura en el aprismo popular*, Tarea/Fundación F. Ebert, Lima.

Vega-Centeno, Imelda (1991), *Aprismo popular: Cultura religión y política*, CIESPA, Tarea, Lima.

Velásquez, Primo Feliciano (trans.) (1981), "Nican Mopohua: Las apariciones de la Virgen de Guadalupe," Ed. Facsimilar, Antonio Valeriano, *Estudios Indigenas*, VIII, 2, March, pp. 177-215.

Verbeek, Yves (1976), *Histoire de l'esclavage des origines à nos jours*, II, Famot, Geneva.

Vicuña Cifuentes, Julio (1947), *Mitos y supersticiones*, Nascimento, Santiago, Chile.

Vidales, Raúl; Kudo, Tokihiro (1975), *Práctica religiosa y proyecto histórico*, CEP, Lima.

Viezzer, Moema (1977), *Si me permiten hablar . . . Testimonio de Domitila. Una mujer de las minas de Bolivia*, Siglo XXI, Mexico.

Vrijhof, Pieter; Waardenburg, Jacques (eds.) (1979), *Official and Popular Religions: Analysis of a Theme for Religious Studies*, Mouton, La Haya.

Wackenheim, Charles (1973), *La quiebra de la religión según Karl Marx*, Península, Barcelona.

Weber, Max (1958), *The Protestant Ethic and the Spirit of Capitalism*, Charles Scribner's Sons, New York.

Weber, Max (1964), *Economia y Sociedad*, Fondo de Cultura Economica, Mexico (*Economía y Sociedad*, 1922).

Weber, Max (1969), "Gods, Magicians and Priests," in Roland Robertson (ed.), *Sociology of Religion*, Penguin, Middlesex, pp. 407-418.

Wilkie, James (ed.) (1980), *Statistical Abstract of Latin America*, 20, University of California Press, Los Angeles, California.

Willems, Emil (1969), "Religious Pluralism and Class Structure: Brazil and Chile," in R. Robertson (ed.), *Sociology of Religion*, Penguin, Middlesex, pp. 165-217.

Williams, Peter W. (1980), *Popular Religion in America*, Prentice-Hall, New Jersey.

Wilson, Bryan (1966), *Religion in Secular Society: A Sociological Comment*, Penguin, London.

Wolf, Eric (1979), "The Virgin of Guadalupe: A Mexican National Symbol," in William A. Lessa and Evon Z. Vogt (eds.), *Reader in Comparative Religion*, Harper and Row, New York, pp. 226-230.

World Bank (1990a), *Informe sobre el desarrollo humano. La pobreza*, World Bank, Washington.

World Bank (1990b), *Social Indicators of Development: 1990*, Johns Hopkins University Press, Washington.

World Bank (1992), *Informe sobre desarrollo y medio ambiente*, World Bank, Washington.

Zea, Leopoldo (1987), *Filosofía de la historia americana*, Fondo de Cultura Economica, Mexico.

Zenteno, Arnaldo (1972), "Religiosidad y evangelización en una colonia proletaria," *Servir*, VII, 38, pp. 191-212.

Zenteno, Arnaldo (1979), "Del Dios verdugo al Padre Liberador," *Christus*, 44, 519, pp. 19-24.

Zubillaga, Carlos; Cayota, Mario (1988), *Cristianos y cambio social en el Uruguay de la modernización (1896-1919)*, CLAEH/Banda Oriental, Montevideo.

Zuluaga, Francisco (1985), "Magia, relión, superstición: Tipología de las religiones," *La Antigua* 26, pp. 27-38.

Zuluaga, Francisco (n.d.), *Religiosidad popular en Colombia*, Pontificia Universidad Javeriana, Colección Profesores, 7, Bogota, Colombia.

# Index

Adventists, 147, 157, 170
Afro-American syncretic cults
    growth in, 57, 92, 148-54, 155, 188;
    politics and, 153-54, 177-79, 182,
    185; religious practices in, 156,
    201, 225, 226-27; scholarly studies
    of, 20, 138; symbolical efficacy of,
    194
Afterlife, 102, 112, 195, 198-99
Alienation
    fatalism and, 203, 205; moderniza-
    tion and, 115, 245; official religion
    and, 228, 234; peasant, 121;
    Pentecostal, 145-46; pluralism
    and, 261; rituals countering, 110-
    11, 204, 210, 212, 226, 257;
    socialism and, 228; theories on,
    191-94
All Saints' Day, 102, 184
Amulets, 104, 105
*Animitas*, 195-99, 202, 213
Anthropology
    classical, 235, 237; reconcep-
    tualizing, 220, 245, 261-62,
    263
Anticlericalism
    in Argentina, 176; democratization
    and, 184; Mexican Revolution and,
    171-73, 188; in Peru, 174, 179, 188;
    popular mentality and, 231;
    secularization and, 168, 180
APRA. *See* Peru
Aprismo, 174, 175, 179-80, 183
Argentina
    *animita* beliefs in, 196; Catholic
    social reform in, 126, 127;
    Peronism in, 165, 174, 175-77, 179,
    188, 189; philosophical studies in,
    236; secularization in, 58, 63
Aristide, Jean Bertrand, 185
Atheism
    growth in, 57, 158; proletarianiza-

tion and, 129; secularization and,
    56, 212
Aymara, 87, 99, 122, 231
Aztecs, 5, 14, 99
Azzi, Rolando, 9-10
Baptism
    Christianization and, 8, 12, 95;
    festive aspects of, 100-101, 107;
    prevalence of, 94-97; protective
    aspects of, 104-5; voodoo and, 149
Base church communities, 135, 136,
    145-46, 207-8, 225
Bastide, Roger, 64, 152, 226-27
Berger, Peter, 41, 68, 70, 249
Biology and popular thought, 244-45
Birth rates, 94-95
Blacks, 8, 11. *See also* Afro-American
    syncretic cults; Slaves
Bolivia, 239-40
Bourdieu, Pierre, 239
Brazil
    African religious elements in, 149-
    50, 152-54, 177-79, 188; base
    communities in, 207-8; Catholic
    social reform in, 125-26; democra-
    tization in, 178, 183; messianism
    in, 124, 164, 168-70, 188, 214;
    native uprisings in, 11;
    Pentecostalism in, 142-46, 188;
    politics and religion in, 165, 173-
    74, 177-79; secularization in, 58,
    63; spiritism in, 158, 170; urban-
    ization in, 169-70
Brown, Diana, 152
Buddhism, 158, 159
Büntig, Aldo, 64, 65, 177
Burga, Manuel, 7
Caggiano, Cardinal, 175-76
Calles, Plutarco, 172, 173, 188, 214
Câmara, Hélder, 130, 134
Candomblé, 150-51, 152
Canudos, 169, 262